The Law of Correspondence

The Law of Correspondence

قانون التناسب

Akram Almajid

الأستاذ أكرم الماجد

Translated by

Mukhtar H. Ali

SAGE PRESS

Title: The Law of Correspondence
(previously published as The Principles of Correspondences)
Author: Akram Almajid
Translator: Mukhtar H. Ali

Cover Illustration: Shah Jahan Mosque, Thatta, Sindh, Pakistan.

ISBN 978-0-9837517-6-2

This book is printed on acid-free paper and produced in a sustainable manner.

بسم الله الرحمن الرحيم

Contents

Translator's Introduction

The present work is a translation of select chapters from Professor Akram Almajid's work, *Manāzil al-sā'irīn: bāb al-firāsa*, which examines the science of *firāsa* (clairvoyance), often translated as physiognomy. As a preliminary to the main subject, he treats the law of correspondence as an independent study, foregrounding the philosophical foundations of Islamic spirituality in general, and the science of *firāsa* in particular. *Firāsa* is discussed in *Manāzil al-sā'irīn* (Stations of the Wayfarers) of Abū Ismāʿīl ʿAbdallāh al-Anṣārī al-Harawī (1006-1089 CE), also known as Khwāja ʿAbdallāh Anṣārī. ʿAbdallāh Anṣārī was an illustrious scholar, Sufi master and devoted Ḥanbalī traditionist in Herat. His lineage traces back to the venerable companion of the Prophet, Abū Ayyūb al-Anṣārī (d. 52/672). Anṣārī trained in the traditional religious disciplines and was also a prolific writer and literary savant, composing masterful prose and poetry in both Persian and Arabic. ʿAbd al-Raḥmān Jamī's (d. 898/1492) *Nafaḥāt al-uns* and ʿAṭṭār's (d. 618/1221) *Tadhkirat al-awliyā'* both contain detailed information on his life and works. More recently, A. G. Ravan Farhadi's has written a biography, *ʿAbdullah Anṣārī of Herāt*, and Nahid Angha produced a study with annotated English translation of Anṣārī's earlier Persian work, *Sad maydan*, in which he describes, as the title suggests, one hundred spiritual stations. Written some twenty years later, the *Manāzil al-sā'irīn* is a more mature and detailed analysis of the stations, having established itself as the consummate manual of spiritual wayfaring. The term "spiritual wayfaring" refers to one who traverses a spiritual path to God, as *sulūk* in Arabic means spiritual progression, method, behavior, comportment, demeanor, wayfaring, conduct, or manners employed on the Sufi path.

As one of the most authoritative works in Sufism, *Manāzil al-sā'irīn* is a sourcebook for spiritual practice, describing the stations of the soul as the wayfarer moves towards divine proximity and ultimately, the station of divine unity (*tawḥīd*). Several commentaries have been written on it, two of the most popular are by followers of Ibn al-ʿArabī (d. 638/1240), ʿAfīf al-Dīn al-Tilmisānī (d. 690/1291) and ʿAbd al-Razzāq al-Kāshānī (d. 731/1330). As for the reason for composing such a work, Anṣārī states in the introduction, "A group of Sufis from Herat and elsewhere were eager to know about the stations of the wayfarers on [the path] to God. Their request that I should to explain that knowledge which could serve as a lamppost on the spiritual path was long overdue ... So I wrote this book in chapters and doors... and arranged these waystations into one hundred stations (*maqāmāt*), and divided the book into ten sections."[1]

Anṣārī divides the stations into ten categories beginning with the Preliminaries (*bidāyāt*), followed by the Doors (*abwāb*), Interactions (*muʿāmālāt*), Morals (*akhlāq*), Roots (*uṣūl*), Valleys (*awdiya*), States (*aḥwāl*), Saintly Attributes (*walāyāt*), Realities (*ḥaqāʾiq*) and Ends (*nihāyāt*). The stations were further divided into three degrees, pertaining to the laypeople, the elect and the foremost of the elect. Anṣārī writes that every aspect of nearness is a station (*manzil*) and when one becomes established therein, it is called a rank (*maqām*). Kāshānī comments, "A state (*ḥāl*) is that which enters upon the heart purely as a bestowal, without exertion or bringing it upon oneself, such as sorrow, fear, expansion, contraction, or tasting. It disappears when the attributes of the soul become manifest, whether or not it is followed by a similar state later. When it becomes permanent and thus a disposition (*malaka*), then it is called a station (*maqām*)"[2]

Anṣārī notes in the introduction, "The servant may be transported from one state to a higher one, though a remnant of the previous state may remain in him whereby he would oversee the previous state and rectify it."[3] He also remarks that the wayfarer need not necessarily follow the prescribed order of the text, since each individual differs with respect to capacity, preparedness, and determination.

Firāsā in the Sufi Tradition

Anṣārī places *firāsa* as the sixty-fifth station in the section of the Valleys. He writes, "Most spiritual wayfaring takes place in the Valleys and the greatest effort is exerted here. It is the stage where the role of the intellect is ever present, the influence of Satan persists, and acquisition of excellences remains. This being the case, the wayfarer is vulnerable to destructive influences and fears, as well as doubts arising from the intrusion of the intellectual powers. Satan's deception is heavily at work, creating perils and advancing delusional claims made by the imagination. Were it not for divine assistance and guidance, most of the wayfarers would perish here due to the great number of

1 ʿAbdallāh Anṣārī, *Manāzil al-Sāʾirīn*, ed. M. Bīdārfar (Qum, 1993), 13.
2 ʿAbd al-Razzāq al-Kāshānī, *Sharḥ manāzil al-sāʾirīn*, ed. M. Bīdārfar (Qum, 1993), 21.
3 Kāshānī, *Sharḥ manāzil al-sāʾirīn*, 15.

pitfalls. But God guides with His light whomsoever He wills and, 'Whomever God guides, none can misguide him' (39:37)".[4]

The valleys are characterized by dependence on the acquisition of excellences, rather than divine bestowal. In these stations, the wayfarer is preoccupied with effort, struggle and acquisition, and divine bestowal has not overtaken his efforts. Gradually, divine bestowal and human effort are in equal proportions until divine bestowal overtakes acquisition, as in the case where tranquility (*ṭuma'nīna*) overtakes aspiration (*himma*).[5] Those stations that are called "states" (*ḥāl*) are from sheer bestowal.

Lexically, *firāsa*, (with the *kasra* on the *fā'*) is to examine (*naẓr*), ascertain (*tathabbut*) or observe a thing (*baṣar*). *Tafarrus* means to discern (*tawassum*) as in, "He discerned (*tafarrasa*) a promising sign of virtue in him."[6]

Technically, it is to gain insight (*isti'nās*) of a hidden principle (*ḥukm al-ghayb*) without rational proof and empirical study.[7] It is also defined as determining inward qualities from outer traits, or a type of natural knowledge through which people's characters are known through observing their outward states, such as color, shape and limbs. Or, it is determining people's character, strengths, gifts, and behavior by looking at the shape of their limbs.

There are two types of *firāsa*, the general and the specific. The former is to generally examine, ascertain, scrutinize and gain insight of the creatures. One can have *firāsa* of humans, animals, plants, inanimate objects, nations, trades and professions, walking, handwriting, homologues, and others in this vast discipline, which will be explained forthcoming. The latter is to examine, gain insight and discern only the human being. There are two branches of this type: the divine, enlightened insight (*al-firāsa al-ilāhiyya al-nūriyya*), [sanctioned] by the *sharī'a*, and philosophical, acquired insight (*al-firāsa al-ḥikmiyya, al-iktisābiyya*).[8]

Since *firāsa* is the awareness of hidden principles without prior reflection or experience, hidden realities behind the veils of material existence are revealed by observing outward characteristics. The Prophet mentioned this in his statement, "Be wary of the believer's *firāsa* for he sees with the light

4 Kāshānī, *Sharḥ manāzil al-sā'irīn*, 320.

5 Mukhtar Ali, "The Doctrine of Love in Khwāja 'Abd Allāh al-Anṣārī's *Manāzil al-sā'irīn* with a Critical Paraphrase of 'Abd al-Razzāq Kāshānī's Commentary." *Journal of Sufi Studies* 5, no. 2 (2016): 146.

6 Ibn Manẓūr, *Lisān al-'Arab*, 10:221.

7 Kashanī, *Sharḥ manāzil al-sā'irīn*, 343.

8 Akram Almajid, *Manāzil al-sā'irīn: bāb al-firāsa*, ed. H. Azrakī (Qum, 2008), 35. I have used this edition for the translation of the book.

of God."[9] The Sufis consider it a spiritual power or divine gift, or as Anṣarī writes, a station following that of excellence (*iḥsān*), knowledge (*ʿilm*), wisdom (*ḥikma*) and insight (*baṣīra*). Some may possess this gift through a certain kind of spiritual inheritance or by performing austerities and spiritual disciplines.

Tilmisānī writes in his commentary of the *Manāzil al-sāʾirīn*, "What I gather from experience is that the Sufi's *firāsā* distinguishes between those who are worthy to stand before God and those who are not. They recognize those who have receptivity and strive for the sake of God, and whether or not they have arrived at the Presence of Union (*ḥaḍrat al-jamʿ*). This is the *firāsa* of the gnostics.

The *firāsa* of the people of austerities (*riyāḍa*) is acquired through hunger, seclusion and purifying the inward, but without having arrived before God's presence. Their *firāsa* relates to the unveiling of forms and hidden matters specific to creation. They only convey things about creation because they are veiled from God. As for the Sufis, their sole preoccupation is the gnosis of God, so they impart [knowledge] concerning God."[10]

Muḥyī-l-Dīn Ibn al-ʿArabī, one of the most revered and influential figures of Sufism, defines *firāsa* in the following:

> *Firāsa* through faith is a divine light which God gives to the person of faith in the eye of his insight just like the light which belongs to the eye of sight. When a person has this perspicacity, its mark is like the light of the sun through which sensory objects appear to sight. When the light of the sun is unveiled, sight differentiates among the sensory objects.
>
> The reason that the light of *firāsa* is attributed to the name Allah, which is the name which brings together the properties of all the names, is that this light unveils both the praiseworthy and the blameworthy, both the movements of felicity pertaining to the next abode and the movements of wretchedness. Some of the people of clairvoyance have reached a point where, upon seeing a person's footprint in the ground—though the person himself is not present—they are able to say that he is a felicitous person or a wretched person. This is similar to what is done by a tracker who follows footprints. The man of spiritual insight says, for example, "The owner of this footprint was white and blind in one eye." Then he describes his character, as if he sees him,

9 Muttaqī al-Hindī, *Kanz al-ʿummāl* (Beirut, 1997), 11:88, no. 30730.

10 ʿAfīf al-Dīn Tilmisānī, *Sharḥ Manāzil al-sāʾirīn*, ed. M. Bīdārfar (Qum, 1992), 347.

> including various accidental matters connected to his character. He sees all this without seeing the person himself.[11]

Professor Almajid writes, "One endowed with *firāsa* hits the mark at the very first instance and does not resort to interpretation, supposition and calculation. He neither experiences neglect nor forgetfulness, rather it is God's judgement spoken on the tongue of the servant, unlike analytical *firāsa* that relies on knowledge and study, which at best, is speculative. The hadith states, 'Knowledge is not extensive learning but a light that God casts in the heart of whomever He wishes to guide.' Things are seen through this light, so let not the singularity of manifestation and deduction deceive you. 'Can they be compared to those who have clear proof from their Lord, recited by a witness from Him' (11:17)?"[12]

The Subject of *Firāsa*

Professor Almajid then discusses the subject and value of *firāsa* which is summarized in the following sections: Since *firasa* is awareness of the inward aspects and realities of things, its subject focuses on creation in general, with respect to perceiving its mysteries and hidden aspects, and the human being in particular, with respect to perceiving his inward aspect. Thus, there are two essential aspects of *firāsa*: the awareness of mysteries concerning the entities, and the awareness of mysteries concerning the human being

As for the first: Since the clairvoyant (*mutafarris*) gains awareness of the inward aspects and subtleties of the entities, fathoming the secrets of their creation and the manifestation of their origination, he sees the inward signs of God in addition to the outward signs, as God says, "We will show them our signs in the horizons and in themselves until it becomes clear that He is the Truth. Does it not suffice your Lord that He is a witness to all things" (40:53)? He can perceive the mystery of the correspondence between the signs on the horizons and the souls to correlate the two books and the two replicas, the share of each sign and manifestation of the theophanies of the Beautific and Majestic Names. Thus, every sign that he ponders with spiritual taste (*dhawq*), he makes it his remembrance and a ladder for the soul's ascension

11 Ibn al-ʿArabī, *Futūḥāt al-Makkiyya*, 2:232 (II 235.35), trans. Chittick, *The Sufi Path of Knowledge*, 304, with emendations.

12 Akram Almajid, *al-Khalq al-jadīd*, trans. M. Ali, *The New Creation* (London, 2018), 140.

and perfection ("read and ascend!"). The light of *firāsa* continues to illuminate the darkness and tear the veils to reveal, not God, but the mysteries of creation. The soul expands with knowledge and action, taking what it has perceived and grasped as a character trait (*khulq*) and divine quality (*takhalluq*).

The *mutafarris* alternates between the governances of the names, as in, "God has ninety-names, whoever assumes them enters paradise," at times, he assumes the inward and the outward with respect to mastery (*itqān*), so he remembers the name the Wise (*al-ḥakīm*), "Know that God is Mighty, Wise" (2:209); or through the subtleties of things and remembers the name the Aware (*al-khabīr*), "God is Subtle, Aware" (22:63); or through aspect of effusion insofar as God effuses to another reality, so he remembers the name the Originator, "He is God, the Creator, the Originator" (59:24); or from the perspective of being present, "God is a Witness to all things" (22:18); or from the aspect of safeguarding what he witnesses through the name the Protector (*al-ḥafīẓ*), "As for those who take protectors other than Him, God is watching them" (42:6). Thus, the *mutafarris* endowed with faith is always in remembrance and wayfaring. The knowledge of the names supports and protects him in his wayfaring, so he does not transgress God's limits and succumb to Satanic whispering, "He who is blinded from the remembrance of the Merciful, We appoint him a devil who becomes his companion" (43:36).

As for the second: *Firāsa* reveals vices and virtues for the *mutafarris*, their illness and cure, and promotes benefit so that one attracts the good and strengthens it, for the wicked cause ruin in the same way that vinegar ruins honey. They desolate the soul and remove intimacy and make life unbearable and torment it in this life before the hereafter. Having noted these two points, the reader can ascertain the importance of this noble discipline.

The Virtue of *Firāsa*

The knowledge of *firāsa* has certain virtues not possessed by any other type of knowledge. The fact that it reveals the secrets and subtleties of existence, it increases the clairvoyant in knowledge and action every time he sees, hears, smells, tastes or touches one of God's signs. The one who sees with the light of *firāsa* can read the signs in the book of existence and the soul. He is able to explain and interpret them, engage with them and measure himself accordingly, in the same way that he reads the written book and takes it as his

Imam and leader, as the Prophet said, "Hold fast to the Qur'ān and take it as your Imam and leader."[13]

Secondly, it suffices as a virtue that *firāsa* reveals the mystery and inward aspect of a person's virtues and vices, so he strives to remove the latter and adorn himself with the former. Thus, he evolves into a rational human from an animalistic human, as Imam ʿAlī describes, "His form is that of a human but his heart is that of an animal. He does not knows guidance so that he enters it nor the door of blindnes so that he shuts it. He is the dead among the living."[14]

Thirdly, through *firāsa* one can identify the appropriate invocation of the divine names and attributes, chapters, verses and supplications, making it a program, focal point and framework to govern the human kingdom. For, invocations for the soul are like medicines for the body. It can only be rectified by what is suitable and appropriate for its existence, the expansiveness or narrowness of its station and state, so that it reaches the furthest degree of perfection, fluctuating between the governance of the divine names and their Mothers which govern those invocations and actions.[15]

Fourthly, through the light of *firāsa* one comes to know his potential and receptivity for the type of knowledge and work that he is suitable for, as He says, "He gave everything its form then guided it" (20:50), and as the Prophet said, "Everyone is facilitated in that for which he has been created." Knowing a particular person and the suitable type of knowledge and work helps them to take advantage of opportunities and use their lifetime effectively. Likewise, *firāsa* helps one to distinguish between good and evil, and benefit and harm.

Finally, *firāsa* has been mentioned in the Qur'ān, "There are signs in that for the discerning" (15:75), and the hadith, "Be wary of the believer's *firāsa* for he sees with the light of God." Imam ʿAlī says, "Man is hidden under his tongue,"[16] and "The tongue of the intelligent is behind his heart and the heart of the fool is behind his tongue,"[17] and "Whatever one hides appears in slips of the tongue and expressions of the face."[18]

---

13 Hindī, *Kanz al-ʿummāl*, no. 4029.

14 ʿAlī b. Abī Ṭālib, *Nahj al-balāgha*, sermon 86, 181.

15 The divine names can be divided into those that have complete, universal scope and those that do not, even if they are inclusive of most things. Qayṣarī writes, "The first category of the attributes are the Mothers, called the Seven Leaders (*al-aʾimmat al-sabʿa*). They are: Life, Knowledge, Will, Power, Hearing, Sight, and Speech." Dāwūd al-Qayṣarī, *Sharḥ fuṣūṣ al-ḥikam*, ed. Ḥ. Āmulī (Qum, 2002), 73.

16 ʿAlī b. Abī Ṭālib, *Nahj al-balāgha* (Beirut, 1993), 715.

17 *Nahj al-balāgha*, 635.

18 *Nahj al-balāgha*, 631.

As Above, So Below

The law of correspondence is founded on the idea that Being is a singular reality that manifests on various planes of existence. Each plane is a part of a unified and interconnected whole as the famous Hermetic axiom states, "As above, so below; as below, so above." Since multiplicity originates from singularity, every entity bears the imprint of its source. The law of correspondence also holds that the human being is the convergence between this ultimate singularity and the multiplicity of existence, the synthesis of spirit and body that embraces every spiritual and material realm. In other words, the human being is an essence that possess multiple degrees. The body is the lower degree of the soul, and the soul is the totality of the body. The body is the corporealization of the spirit, the manifestation of its perfections and powers in the visible world. Neither body nor spirit is disassociated from the other as the spirit is the inward reality and the body is its outward form. Each has its harmonious and conflicting aspects, pleasures and pains, safeguards and perils, so there is a correspondence between the inward and the outward.

Qualities and states of the soul appear in the outward aspect of the body, mirroring the inward aspects of the spirit. Thus, one who exercises analytical *firāsa* judges the inward through the outward, whereas the inward is revealed to the divine clairvoyant as he sees realities directly. Every quality or state in a person has a specific effect on the body, which becomes evident, particularly on the face when a person becomes angry, happy or worried.

These correspondences represent realities and energies that animate the human being. They correlate to the human frame in some aspects and the imagination, intellect, spirit and other inward faculties in other aspecs. When the ancients observed phenomenon and meditated on the true nature of the human being, they systematized various branches of knowledge on the basis of these correspondences. Ancient medical wisdom, for example, observed that the human body subsists organically in nature insofar as natural forces apply to the creatures and man equally. The origin of disease is nature, as is the origin of cure, each caused by certain affinities and aversions man has with his environment.

As the pursuit of truth and reality is intrinsic to human nature, it is a universal aim for mankind, not just the spiritual adept. Thus, to know reality one must know the self, as Socrates declared, "Know thyself!" When the seeker of truth aspires for self-knowledge he gains a deeper understanding of reality. Through contemplations that enliven the intellect and burnish the tablet of the heart, one gains self-knowledge. The awakened intellect then begins to perceive reality as it truly is, free of delusion, impervious to the wiles of the lower self or the shadows of the ephemeral world. Gradual awareness of truth illuminates the path, orienting one to read the signs in existence, the eternal divine communications and their counterparts in the realms of the soul. In this respect, understanding reality is equivalent to unveiling the mysteries in creation through *firāsa* and finding meaning amidst material life.

Knowledge of the soul is more sublime than knowledge of the phenomenal world, and true knowledge is a divine light cast into the soul that actualizes its innate potential, as expressed by the greatest saint, Imam ʿAlī b. Abī Ṭālib, "Knowledge is not in the heavens so that it may descend upon you, nor in the depths of the earth that it may be excavated, rather it is fashioned in your very hearts. So, embody the character traits of the spiritual and it will manifest itself to you."[19] With an understanding of the correspondences between the soul and outward existence one begins to appreciate the universal divine order and the wise purpose of creation. Thereafter, one witnesses divine manifestations and assumes the divine character, finding the face of God in everything, as the Qurʾān states, "Wherever you turn, there is the face of God" (2:115). And in the words of the Greek sage Plotinus, "When there enters into it a glow from the divine, the soul gathers strength, awakens, spreads true wings and, however distracted by its proximate environment, speeds its buoyant way to something greater to its memory; its very nature bears it upwards lifted by the Giver of that love."[20]

The Present Work

The aim of this book is to describe human nature within the fabric of existence, to elucidate man's relationship with the Creator in the midst of His creation and delineate his spiritual curriculum in view of his subtle yet intimate bond with nature. Indeed, man is the child of nature and spirit, he is the fruit of the tree of Being and its quintessence. Thus, true religion is none other than the Way, the eternal Truth, and the divine paradigm that enjoins man to live in harmony within nature and his fellow man. It is to observe the sublime and the subtle, to live with the intellect's counsel and the heart's assent. However, since faculties and powers are a great many, it is only through

19 Muḥammad Bāqir al-Majlisī, *Biḥār al-anwār li-durar akhbār al-aʾimmat al-aṭhār* (Beirut, 1983), 66:316.

20 Plotinus. *The Six Enneads*, trans. S. MacKenna (Chicago, 1952), 333.

wise governance of the soul that one discovers the true nature of reality and thus brings contrary forces to a state of equilibrium. The ancient Chinese Daoist philosophers were well aware of this principle, as the mystic Guanzi states, "When that which occupies the center is a perfectly regulated heart, the myriad of beings obtain fair measure."[21]

The present work examines the human being from each plane of existence, body, soul, heart and spirit, which is inclusive of the powers of anger, desire, imagination, thought, memory and reflection. It investigates the composition of man in his mineral, vegetal, animal and angelic aspects, their interrelationships and the positive and negative effects they have in his spiritual development. Thus, the aim of the book can be summarized in the following: knowing the true nature of man, understanding spiritual significances in creation and clarifying their metaphysical implications for spiritual development.

From another perspective, it is a survey of divine manifestation as it occurs in various degrees of being. This work explores both the ontology of mysticism as well as its epistemological foundations, which is the nature of being according to the mystics and the way of spiritual attainment.

21 Guanzi, *Neiye* (Inner Cultivation), ch. 49, cited in Claude Larre and Elisabeth Rochat de la Vallée, *Rooted in Spirit: The Heart of Chinese Medicine* (Barrytown, 1995), 46.

قانون التناسب

المناسبة لغةً هي المشاكلة[1] ، والمراد هنا العلاقة والرابطة بين الموجودات عموماً، والتناسب قانون عام ونظام شامل للوجود ، فالإنسان له مناسبة مع الحق ومناسبة مع الخلق[2] بها تعرف صلته بالموجودات ، حينئذ يجتهد في جلبها وتقويتها إن كانت نافعة أو دفعها والاحتراز منها إن كانت ضارة بحسب حاله ومقامه الذي هو عليه ، وهذا ما يقرره المشايخ والمرشدون أو ما يطلع عليه السالك إن كان من أهل المشاهدة والقرار ، والإنسان الذي هو مختصر العالم وزبدته له مع كل آية حق وحقيقة[3].

تزيد النفس تكاملاً سلباً أو إيجاباً[4] ، وعلى ذلك لابد له من قراءة كتب[5] الحق تعالى ورؤية آياته الآفاقية والأنفسية والتدبر فيها والوقوف على مضامينها ومراد الحق

---

١ المشاكلة : هي اتفاق الشيئين في الخاصة ، وقد يراد منها التناسب ، وربما تلتبس مع المساواة والمماثلة ، والمضاهاة. (فالمساواة) هي الاتفاق في الكمية. (والمماثلة) هي الاتفاق في النوعية. و(المضاهاة) هي شعبة من الماثلة. و(المناسبة) اعم من الجميع.

٢ كمناسبة الإنسان مع الملك والفلك والجن والحيوان والنبات وكذلك مناسبة الإنسان مع أخيه الإنسان ، والمناسبة بين أعضاء الجسد الواحد ، وبين الصفات والأحوال وأخلاق الإنسان التي هي كالعائلة الواحدة ، والمناسبة بين العمل والجزاء وغيرها.

٣ إشارة إلى الآية المباركة : ﴿سَنُرِيهِمْ آيَاتِنَا فِي الآفَاقِ وَفِي أَنفُسِهِمْ حَتَّى يَتَبَيَّنَ لَهُمْ أَنَّهُ الْحَقُّ﴾ [فصلت:٥٣].

عن صالح بن مسمار أن رسول الله ﷺ قال لحارث بن مالك : كيف أنت ؟ أو : ما أنتَ يا حارث ؟ قال : مؤمن يا رسول الله ﷺ ، قال : مؤمن حقاً ؟ قال : مؤمن حقاً. قال : لكل حق حقيقة ، فما حقيقة ذلك ؟ قال : عزفت نفسي عن الدنيا ، فأسهرت ليلي ، وأضمأت نهاري ، وكأني انظر إلى عرش ربي عزّ وجلّ ، وكأني انظر إلى أهل الجنة يتزاورون فيها ، وكأني اسمع عواء أهل النار ، فقال رسول الله : « مؤمن نور الله قلبه » مفردات ألفاظ القرآن ص٢٤٧ / الراغب الأصفهاني.

٤ فان للنفس تكاملًا من جهة الفضيلة وتكاملًا من جهة الرذيلة ، قال الله تعالى : ﴿وَهَدَيْنَاهُ النَّجْدَيْنِ﴾ نجد الخير ونجد الشر / البحار / ج٥ / ص١٩٦ ، وقال تعالى : ﴿إِنَّا هَدَيْنَاهُ السَّبِيلَ إِمَّا شَاكِراً وَإِمَّا كَفُوراً﴾ [الإنسان (الدهر):٣].

٥ اعلم إن كتاب الله تعالى إما تكويني ، وإما تدويني ، فالتكويني آفاقي وانفسي ، والتدويني

The Law of Correspondence

Lexically, correspondence means "analogy,"[1] and what is intended here is the general correlation and connection between things. Correspondence is a universal law and an order that embraces existence. Man possesses a correspondence with God and another with creation by which he discerns his interrelationships with the entities.[2] As a result, he strives to attract and strengthen that correlation if it is beneficial, or repel and eschew it if it is harmful, according to his state and station. Sages and spiritual guides affirm this truth or the wayfarer himself perceives it if he is steadfast among the people of witnessing. The human being, who is the summation and quintessence of the world, has a share and reality of every divine sign.[3]

The soul increases in perfection either negatively or positively.[4] Thus, it is necessary to read the books[5] of God, discern His signs on the horizons and in

1 "Analogy" (*al-mushākala*) is the agreement of two things in an attribute. It may denote correspondence but may also convey equality (*al-musāwa*), similarity (*al-mumāthala*) or resemblance (*al-muḍāha*). Equality is agreement in quantity, similarity is agreement in quality and resemblance is a branch of similarity; analogy is the most general.

2 This includes the correspondences between man and the angels, celestial spheres, Jinn, animals and plants. Similarly, man himself has a correspondence with his fellow man, the limbs of a single body, between attributes, states and ethical qualities which are like a family, deeds and recompense, and so on.

3 This refers to the verse, "We will show them Our signs on the horizons and in themselves until it becomes clear that He is the Truth" (41:53).

It is related from Ṣāliḥ ibn Mismār from the Prophet that the Prophet asked Hārith b. Mālik, "How are you, or what is your state?" He replied, "Imbued with faith, O Prophet of God." He asked, "Are you truly imbued with faith?" He said, "Indeed!" The Prophet said, "For every truth there is a reality so what is the reality of (your faith)?" He replied, "I have abstained from the world and kept vigil during my nights and remained thirsty during my days. It is as if I am witnessing the Throne of my Lord, the Mighty and Magnificent. It is as if I see the people of paradise visiting each other and hear the wailing of the people of hell." The Prophet then said, "He is a believer whose heart God has illuminated." Rāghib, *Mufradāt alfāẓ al-Qur'ān*, 247.

4 The soul increases in perfection either in the direction of virtue or in the direction of vice. God says in the Qur'ān, "We have shown him two paths" (90:10), the path of virtue and the path of vice. Majlisī, *Biḥār al-anwār*, 5:196. "We have shown him the way, he is either grateful or ungrateful" (76:3).

5 Know that God's books are either existential or written. The existential refers to the "horizons" and "souls", and the written is between two covers. The existential book is

وبالأخص حين أوقفه عليها ومن ثم اتخاذها طريقاً للوصول إليه تعالى عز اسمه ، فان تلك الآيات تجلياته ومظاهر أسمائه ورسائله التي لا تنقطع يفصل فيها ويجمل أوامره ونواهيه وإرشاداته وحكمه لأصحاب البصر والبصيرة وأهل الخير والشر حتى يتبين لهم أنه الحق. كما قال تعالى : ﴿سَنُرِيهِمْ آيَاتِنَا فِي الآفَاقِ وَفِي أَنفُسِهِمْ حَتَّى يَتَبَيَّنَ لَهُمْ أَنَّهُ الْحَقُّ﴾ [فصلت:٥٣].

وقال[٦] أهل المعرفة في تجلي الحق تعالى واستخلاف آدم ، وإجمال الحقائق فيه : « فسبحان الذي تجلى بذاته لذاته[٧] ، فأظهر آدم[٨] ، واستخلفه على مظاهر أسمائه

هو ما بين الدفتين ، والآفاقي كتاب المحو والإثبات والكتاب المبين وأم الكتاب. ﴿يَمْحُو اللّهُ مَا يَشَاء وَيُثْبِتُ وَعِندَهُ أُمُّ الْكِتَابِ﴾ [الرعد:٣٩] ، ﴿وَلاَ رَطْب وَلاَ يَابِس إِلاَّ فِي كِتَاب مُّبِين﴾ [الأنعام:٥٩] والأنفسي عليبني وسجيني ﴿إِنَّ كِتَابَ الأَبْرَارِ لَفِي عِلِّيِّينَ﴾ [المطففين:١٨] ﴿وإِنَّ كِتَابَ الفُجَّارِ لَفِي سِجِّين﴾ [المطففين:٧] شرح منطق المنظومة / ص٢٦/ حسن زاده الآملي.

٦ مقدمة القيصري على فصوص الحكم / ص٥.

٧ إن الأسماء الإلهية التي هي تجلياته تعالى ، في المرتبة الواحدية منبعثة من الشؤون الذاتية المستجنة في غيب الذات وظهوراتها بلا تجاف عن مقامها الشامخ ألاحدي الجمعي ، كما أن الوجودات العينية من تجليات الأسماء وظهوراتها بلا تجاف عن مرتبتها الأسمائية بل النسبة في المقامين النسبة الظلية ، ولكل من الأسماء الإلهية مظهراً خاصاً يربيه إلا الاسم الجامع ، فان مظهره مظهر الكل كما أن نفسه كل الأسماء بنحو الوحدة الجمعية ، فعين آدم إمام أئمّة الأعيان بحكم الاتحاد ، فإظهار كل شي غير آدم بتوسط اسم خاص من الأسماء إلا آدم فانه يظهر في العين بلا توسط اسم خاص بل بكل الأسماء والشؤون.

وهذا معنى تجلى بذاته لذاته فأظهر آدم. أو معنى تجلى ذاته لذاته فرأى ذاته مبدأ لجميع الكمالات ، فأظهر تلك الكمالات بنحو الوحدة في المجلى الأتم والمشهد الأعظم ، أعني مرآة مشهد آدم لأنها قابلة لظهورها فيها دون غيرها من المرائي الكونية. (شرح الآشتياني على مقدمة القيصري / ص٨)

٨ إن الأحدية عبارة عن مجلى الذات ليس للأسماء ولا للصفات فيه ظهور أصلاً فالأحدية اسم لصرافة الذات المجردة عن الاعتبارات كلها؛ وليس لهذا المجلى مظهر في الأكوان أتم من الإنسان إذا استغرق في ذاته ونسى اعتباراته وانصرف عن ظواهره فكان هو في هو من غير أن ينسب إليه شي مما يستحقه من الأوصاف الحقية والخلقية ، وبالجملة مجرداً عن كل الإشارات والنسب والاعتبارات ، وهذه الأحدية في الحقيقة عين الكثرة المتنوعة لا باعتبار الكثرة كأحدية الجدار مثلاً ، فإنها اسم لتلك الهيئة الوحدانية الجدارية ، كما انك مثلاً عند استغراقك في ذاتك التي أنت بها ، أنت لا تشاهد إلا نفس هويتك ومحض إنيتك ولا يظهر لك في شهودك هذا شي من حقائقك المنسوبة إليك ، فمظهر الأحدية فيك هو ذاتك باعتبار عدم الاعتبارات

the souls, contemplate them, comprehend their significance and His intent therein, especially as one encounters them. Thereafter, he considers these signs the very path of attainment to God, for they are His theophanies, the manifestations of His names and His perpetual communications. In them, His commandments, prohibitions, instructions and decrees are detailed and summarized for the people of vision and inward perception and for both the virtuous and the wicked, so that it becomes evident that He is the Truth, as He has stated, "We will show them Our signs on the horizons and in themselves until it becomes evident that He is the Truth" (41:53).

With respect to God's theophany in Adam's vicegerency and the summarization of realities within him, the gnostics have said:[6] "Glory be to Him who revealed His Essence to Himself.[7] Then manifested Adam[8] and appointed him vicegerent over the manifestations of His names, described as the world.

---

the Tablet of Effacement and Establishment (*kitāb al-maḥw wa-l-ithbāt*), the Manifest Book (*al-kitāb al-mubīn*) and the Mother of the Book (*umm al-kitāb*), as referred to by the verses, "He effaces what He wishes and affirms what He wishes and to Him belongs the Mother of the Book" (13:39). "There is neither wetness nor dryness except that it is in the Manifest Book" (6:59). The books of the soul are either from the sublime or the ignoble, "Indeed the books of the righteous are in the sublime (*ʿillīyīn*)" (83:7,18) and "the books of the wicked are in the ignoble (*sijjīn*)" (83:7). Ḥasanzade Āmulī, *Sharh al-manẓuma*, 1:26.

6 Qayṣarī, *Muqaddimat al-Qayṣarī ʿalā fuṣūṣ al-ḥikam*, 5.

7 The divine names, which are His manifestations on the degree of Unity (*al-wāḥidiyya*) emanate from the theophany of the Essence, embraced in the unseen Essence, without being separate from their lofty, unitary and collective degree, just as individual entities, which are the theophanies and manifestations of the divine names are not separate from their plane. In both cases is that the latter is a shadow of the former. Each of the divine names governs a specific manifestation, except the Comprehensive Name (*al-ism al-jāmiʿ*), for its manifestation is complete and is identical with all the names in a unitary and comprehensive way. Thus, Adam is the comprehensive, foremost leader among the created beings, as everything besides Adam manifests through a specific name. In the outward realm, Adam is manifest without the intermediary of a specific name but through every name and reality.

This is the meaning of the statement, "The One who revealed Himself by His Essence for His Essence so He manifested Adam." Alternatively, it means His Essence revealed Itself so that God witnessed His own Essence as the origin of all perfections. So He singularly manifested those perfections in a perfect theophany, the greatest plane of reflection, which is the mirror of Adam because Adam had the receptivity for its manifestation to the exclusion of all other ontological mirrors. *Sharḥ muqaddimat al-Qayṣarī*, 8.

8 The Singularity (*al-aḥadiyya*) is the theophany of the Essence in which there is no manifestation of any divine name or attribute. It is called the Singularity insofar as the Essence is divested of all conditions. There is no manifestation for this theophany

المنعوته بالعالم ، وأجمل فيه جميع الحقائق وأبهم[٩] ، ليكون صورة اسمه الجامع[١٠] العزيز الأكرم ، وحامل أسرار العليم الأعلم ، فيدل به عليه ، فيعلم »[١١].

وللنسخة الإنسانية مناسبة ومطابقة مع العالم الكبير. قال القيصري: « لما علمت أن للحقيقة الإنسانية ظهورات في العالم تفصيلاً ، فأعلم أن لها أيضاً ظهورات في العالم الإنساني إجمالًا وأوّل مظاهرها فيه الصورة الرّوحية المجردة ، المطابقة للصورة العقلية.

ثم الصورة القلبية ، المطابقة للصورة التي للنفس الكلية ثم الصورة التي للنفس الحيوانية ، المطابقة للطبيعة الكلية ، وللنفس المنطبعة الفلكية وغيرها.

ثم الصورة الدخانية اللطيفة المسماة بـ « الروح الحيوانية » عند الأطباء المطابقة للهيولى الكلية.

ثم الصورة الدموية ، المطابقة لصورة الجسم الكل.

ثم الصورة الأعضائيه ، المطابقة لأجسام العالم الكبير ، وبهذه المتنزلات في المظاهر الإنسانية حصل التطابق بين النسختين.[١٢]

فأنت باعتبار حقيقتك أتم مظهر للأحدية.

٩ لوحدتها وبساطتها.

١٠ الله تعالى.

١١ مقدمة القيصري / ص١٣.

١٢ مقدمة القيصري / ص٩٩.

He summarized and concealed in him every reality,[9] so that he would be the form of His comprehensive name,[10] the Mighty and Magnanimous, and the bearer of mysteries of the knowing, the Omniscient, so He reveals [Himself] through him and thus becomes known."[11]

The human replica, therefore, has a correspondence and congruence with the Great World. Qayṣarī writes, "Since you have come to know that the human reality has particular manifestations in the cosmos, know that there are summarized manifestations in the human world.

The first such manifestation is the form of the immaterial spirit which corresponds to the form of the Intellect.

Then, the form of the heart corresponds to the form the Universal Soul.

Then, the form of the animal soul corresponds to Universal Nature and the Soul Imprinted on Celestial Bodies and others. Then, the subtle ethereal spirit which the physicians call the animal spirit, corresponds to Universal Prime Matter.

Then, the form of blood corresponds to the form of the Universal Body.

Then, the form of the limbs corresponds to the body of the Great World. Thus, it is through these descending degrees of manifestations on the human plane the correspondence between the two replicas is achieved."[12]

---

in the worlds more complete than man, should he become absorbed in His essence, remove all conditions and depart from his outwardness. He exists, in and of himself, without associating others with Him, either in relation to His real attributes or to those of creation. In short, he becomes divested of all indications, associations and conditions.

This is a singularity that is at one with multiplicity and not multiplicity qua multiplicity, such as, for example, the oneness of a wall. For it refers to a particular unified form, that is, of its being a wall. In the same way, for example, that you are immersed in yourself and do not see but your own identity and your own selfhood. In seeing yourself you cannot distinguish those realities attributed to you, so the manifestation of singularity in you is your very self without being conditioned by anything else. Thus, from the perspective of your reality, you are the complete manifestation of singularity.

9 Due to its unity and simplicity.

10 Allah.

11 *Muqaddimat al-Qayṣarī*, 13.

12 *Muqaddimat al-Qayṣarī*, 99.

وقال : «اعلم أن الروح الأعظم[١٣] الذي في الحقيقة هو الروح الإنساني ، مظهر الذات الإلهية[١٤] من حيث ربوبيتها[١٥] ، لذلك لا يمكن أن يحوم حولها حائم ، ولا أن يروم وصلها رائم ، الدائر حول جنابها يحار ، والطالب نور جمالها يتقيد بالأستار لا يعلم كُنهها إلا الله ، ولا ينال بهذه البغية سواه.[١٦] وكما أن له في

---

١٣ وهو العقل الأول ، والحقيقة المحمدية ، والنَّفس الواحد ، والحقيقة الأسمائية ، وهو أول موجود خلقه الله على صورته ، وهو الخليفة الأكبر ، وهو الجوهر النوراني ، جوهريته مظهر الذات ، ونورانيته مظهر علمها ، ويسمى باعتبار الجوهرية نفساً واحدة ، وباعتبار النورانية عقلاً أولاً. (الجرجاني / ص١١٨)

والروح الأعظم : يُعنى به العقل الأول ، ويقال له القلم الأعلى ، وذلك لان العقل الأول له ثلاثة وجوه معنوية كلية.

فالوجه الأول : أخذه الوجود والعلم مجملاً بلا واسطة وإدراكه وضبطه ما يصل إليه من حضرة غيب موجده ، فباعتبار هذا الوجه يسمى بالعقل الأول ، لأنه أول من عَقَل عن رَبّه وأول قابل لفيض وجوده.

والوجه الثاني : هو تفصيله لما أخذه مجملًا في اللوح المحفوظ بحكم : اكتب علمي في خلقي واكتب ما هو كائن ، ويسمى بهذا الوجه بـ : القلم الأعلى ، الذي به يحصل نقش العلوم في ألواح الذوات القابلة قال تعالى : ﴿عَلَّمَ بِالْقَلَمِ﴾ [العلق:٤] وبهذا الوجه هو نفس محمد ﷺ ، المشار إليه بقوله ﷺ : « والذي نفس محمّد بيده... » ولهذا نطق بجوامع الكلم التي لم يؤتها من سواه من العالمين.

الوجه الثالث : كونه حاملاً حكم التجلي الأول ومنسوباً إلى مظهريته في نفسه لغلبة حكم الوحدة والبساطة عليه ، وبهذا الاعتبار هو حقيقة الروح الأعظم المحمدي ونوره ، لكونه جامعاً لجميع التجليات ، الإلهيات منها والكونيات ومنشأ لجميع أرواح الكائنات. (لطائف الإعلام / ص٣٠٣ / الكاشاني).

١٤ الذات : وجود الشيء وحقيقته ، وذات الله سبحانه وتعالى عبارة عن نفسه التي هو بها موجودٌ لأنه قائم بنفسه ، وذات الله تعالى غيب الأحدية ، والذات عبارة عن الوجود المطلق بسقوط الاعتبارات والإضافات والنسب والوجوهات. (الجيلي / ج١ / ص١٤ / ٤٧)

١٥ الرَّب : اسم للحق عز اسمه باعتبار نَسَب الذات إلى الموجودات الغيبية أرواحاً كانت أو أجساداً ، فإن نَسَب الذات إلى الأعيان الثابتة هي منشأ الأسماء الإلهية فالقادر ، والمريد ، ونَسَبُها إلى الأكوان الخارجية هي منشأ الأسماء الربوبية فالرزاق والحفيظ ، فالرب اسم خاص يقتضي وجود المربوب وتحققه ، والإله يقتضي ثبوت المألوه وتعينه ، وكل ما يظهر من الأكوان فهو صورة اسم رباني يُربّيه الحق به يؤخذ وبه يفعل ما يفعل ، وإليه يُرجع فيما يحتاج إليه ، وهو المعطي إيّاه ما يطلبه منه. (الكاشي / ص١٤٤)

١٦ مقدمة القيصري /ص١٣٧.

He says, "Know that the Supreme Spirit,[13] which in reality is the human spirit, is the manifestation of the divine Essence[14] from the aspect of Lordship.[15] It is not possible for the hoverer to circle it nor is it possible for the seeker to attain it. The circumambulator is perplexed in its presence and the seeker of

---

13 The Supreme Spirit is the First Intellect, the Muḥammadan Reality, the Unified Soul, the reality of the divine names and the first thing that God created in His form. It is the greatest vicegerent, the luminous Substance whose substantiveness is the manifestation of the Essence and whose luminosity is the manifestation of His knowledge. It is called the Unified Soul with respect to its being a substance and the First Intellect with respect to its being luminous. *Kitāb al-taʿrifāt,* 118.

The Supreme Spirit is the First Intellect and is also called the Supreme Pen because the First Intellect has three universal, spiritual aspects: The first aspect is that it receives existence and knowledge in summary form, without intermediary. It perceives and determines that which arrives from its origin, the degree of the Unseen. It is called the First Intellect because it is the first to perceive its Lord and the first to receive the emanation of His Being.

The second aspect involves the specifics in the Guarded Tablet of that which it receives in summary form through the command, "Record My knowledge of My creation and record all that exists." This aspect is called the Supreme Pen through which knowledge is inscribed on the tablets of receptive essences, mentioned by the verse, "He taught by the Pen" (96:4). In this aspect it is the Muḥammadan Soul, as indicated by his statement, "By He who holds Muḥammad's soul in His hands..." It is from this aspect that the Prophet articulated the most comprehensive discourse (Qurʾān), not transmitted by any individual in any other world.

The third aspect is that it embraces the first theophany attributed to divine self-manifestation caused by the ascendency of oneness and simplicity. From this perspective it is the reality of the Greatest Spirit of the Muḥammadan Light for it encompasses every theophany, divine or created, and is the origin of every spirit in existence. *Laṭāʾif al-iʿlām,* 303.

14 "Essence" is the existence of a thing and its reality. The Essence of God, the Glorified, refers to His very existence because He exists through Himself. His Essence is the Unseen Singularity (*ghayb al-aḥadiyya*). It also means absolute Being divested of conditions, attributes and entities. Jīlī, 1:13.

15 "Lord" is a name of God that indicates the relationship between the Essence and Unseen existence, whether spirits or bodies. The relationship of the Essence to the Permanent Archetypes (*al-aʿyān al-thābita*) gives rise to the divine names.

The names, the Able (*al-Qādir*) and the Willing (*al-Murīd*), along with their association with the external worlds gives rise to the names of Lordship, such as the Nourisher (*al-Razzāq*) and the Protector (*al-Ḥafīẓ*). For example, Lord (*al-Rabb*) is a name that entails the existence and realization of its subjects, and the Deity necessitates the existence of worshippers. Whatever enters existence is the canvas for one of the names of Lordship and is nurtured by God. He takes and does what He wills with them; they address their needs to Him and He gives them what they desire. *Laṭāʾif al-iʿlām,* 144.

العالم الكبير[١٧] مظاهر وأسماء ، من العقل الأول[١٨] والقلم الأعلى[١٩] والنور[٢٠] ، والنفس الكلية[٢١] ، واللوح المحفوظ[٢٢] ، وغير ذلك على ما نبهنا عليه من

---

١٧ العالم الكبير : يراد به جميع الكائنات. العالم الصغير : يراد به الإنسان ، عند الأكثرين ، وعند الشيخ الأكبر إن العالم الكبير هو الإنسان الكامل ، والإنسان الصغير هو العالم ، وذلك لكون الإنسان الكامل قد جمع كل ما في العالم ، وليس في العالم عند قطع النظر عن الإنسان الكامل كل ما فيه. (لطائف الإعلام / ص٣٨٦).

١٨ هو أول جوهر قَبِل الوجود من ربّه ، ولهذا سمي بـ « العقل الأول » لأنه أول من عقل عن ربه وقبل فيض وجوده.

والعقل محل لشكل العلم الإلهي في الوجود ، لأنه القلم الأعلى ، ثُمَّ يتنزل منه العلم إلى اللوح المحفوظ ، فهو إجمال اللوح ، واللوح تفصيله ، والعقل الأول الإمام المبين. (الجيلي / ج٢ / ص١٧).

١٩ القلم الأعلى : القلم علم التفصيل ، فإن الحروف التي هي مظاهر تفصيلها مجملة في مِدادِ الدَّواة لا تقبل التفصيل ما دامت فيها ، فإذا انتقل المِداد منها إلى القلم تفصلت الحروف به في اللوح المحفوظ ، وتفصيل العلم بها إلى لا غاية ، كما أنَّ النطفة التي هي مادة الإنسان ما دامت في ظهر آدم ، مجموع الصور الإنسانية مجملة فيها ، ولا تقبل التفصيل ما دامت فيها ، فإذا انتقلت إلى لوح الرَّحِم بالقلب الإنساني تفصلت الصورة الإنسانية.(الجرجاني / ص١٨٧)

والقلم الأعلى : هو العقل الأول ، يسمى بالقلم الأعلى من جهة كونه هو الواسطة بين الحق في إيصال العلوم والمعارف إلى جميع الخلق ، المشار إلى ذلك بقوله : اكتب علمي في خلقي واكتب ما هو كائن. (مطابق الإعلام / ص٤٧٧) والقلم الأعلى هو العقل الأول ، مثاله : قضى الحق بإيجاد زيد على الهيئة الفلانية في الزمان الفلاني. والأمر الذي اقتضى هذا التقدير في اللوح هو القلم الأعلى ، وهو المسمى بالعقل الأول ، والمحل الذي وجد فيه بيان هذا الاقتضاء هو اللوح المحفوظ المعبر عنه بالنَّفس الكلي. (التهانوي / ص١٢٩٢).

٢٠ النور : اسم من أسماء الله تعالى ، وهو تجليه باسمه الظاهر ، اعني الوجود الظاهر في صور الأكوان كُلِّها والنور عبارة عن الوجود الحق باعتباره ظهوره في نفسه وإظهاره لغيره في العلم والعين ويسمى شمساً أيضاً. (التهانوي / ص١٣٩٤).

٢١ النفس الكلية : جوهرة روحانية فاضت من العقل ، وهي نفس العالم بأسره ربطت بالجسم الكلي المطلق الذي هو جملة العالم سارية فيه ومدبرة له ومحركة ، وأن مثل النفس الكلية كجنس الأجناس ، والأنفس البسيطة كالأنواع لها ، والأنفس التي دونها كنوع الأنواع ، والأنفس الجزئية كالأشخاص مرتبة بعضها تحت بعض ، والنفس الكلية التي هي نفس العالم مؤيدة للنفوس البسيطة والعقل الكلي مؤيد للنفس الكلية والباري جل ثناؤه مؤيد للعقل الكلي ، والحق تعالى مبدعها كلها ومدبر لها من غير ممازجة ولا مباشرة ، فتبارك الله أحسن الخالقين. (رسائل إخوان الصفا / بتصرف)

٢٢ اللوح المحفوظ : اللوح هو الكتاب المبين والنفس الكلية ، والألواح أربعة : لوح القضاء السابق على المحو والإثبات وهو لوح العقل الأول ، ولوح القدر أي لوح النفس الناطقة الكلية التي يفصل فيها كليات اللوح الأول ويتعلق بأسبابها وهو المسمى باللوح المحفوظ ، ولوح النفس

the light of its beauty is fettered by veils. None fathoms its quintessence save God, and none reaches its limit except Him."[16]

Just as God has planes of manifestation and divine names in the Great World[17] that include the First Intellect,[18] the Supreme Pen ,[19] the Light,[20] the Universal Soul,[21] the Guarded Tablet,[22] and others, the human reality is

---

16 *Muqaddimat al-Qayṣarī*, 137.

17 The Great World refers to the entirety of creation and the Small World refers to man. But in the view of the Greatest Shaykh (Ibn al-ʿArabī), the Great World refers to the Perfect Human (*al-insān al-kāmil*), and the Small World refers to the cosmos. This is because man exemplifies all that is in the cosmos, but if the Perfect Human being is excluded from the world, then it does not contain all of creation. *Laṭāʾif al-iʿlām*, 386.

18 It is the first essence to accept existence from its Lord. That is why it is called the First Intellect, for it was the first to perceive its Lord and accept the effusion of His Being.

The Intellect is the vessel for the shape of divine knowledge in existence because it is the Supreme Pen. Knowledge then descends to the Guarded Tablet. It is the undifferentiated form of Tablet, and the Tablet is its elaboration. The First Intellect is also the Manifest Imām. Jīlī, 2:17.

19 The Pen is discrete knowledge, for letters are the expression of its detail which is condensed in the inkwell, as long as the ink remains in it. Thus, if the ink transfers to the Pen, the letters become distinct on the Guarded Tablet and knowledge is elaborated through it, ad infinitum. When the seed or the substance of man, remains in the loins, it contains the summary of all forms of humanness. It is not differentiated as long as it is inside of him, but if it transfers to the tablet of the womb—in a human transformation—it differentiates into the form of a human. *Kitāb al-taʿrifāt*, 187. The Supreme Pen is the First Intellect. Through the Supreme Pen, God conveys knowledge and realities to the rest of creation, expressed as, "Write My knowledge in My creation and write all that exists." *Muṭābiq al-iʿlām*, 477.

The Supreme Pen being the First Intellect is explained in the following: God ordained that Zayd should be created in a particular fashion at a particular time. The Supreme Pen or the First Intellect writes this decree on the Tablet. This decree appears in the Guarded Tablet, also called the Universal Soul. Tahānawī, 1292.

20 Light is one of the divine names. It is the theophany of His name, the Manifest, that is, manifest existence in the forms of the worlds. It refers to God's existence with respect to His self-manifestation and manifesting others, in knowledge and reality; it is also called the Sun. Tahānawī, 1394.

21 The Universal Soul is a spiritual substance emanating from the Intellect. It is the Soul of the world connecting with the Absolute Universal Body that pervades, governs and moves it. The Universal Soul is like primary genera, simple souls that are its species, subsidiary souls such as primary species and particular souls such as individuals, one after another. The Universal Soul, which is the soul of the world, supports the simple souls, the Universal Intellect supports the Universal Soul and the Almighty Originator supports the Universal Intellect. The Real creates and governs them all without admixing or immediacy. Glory to the Best of Creators! *Rasāʾil ikhwān al-ṣafā*.

22 The Guarded Tablet is the Manifest Book and the Universal Soul. There are four tablets: The Tablet of Decree (*al-qaḍāʾ*) that is prior to the Tablet of Effacement and

أن الحقيقة الإنسانية هي الظاهرة بهذه الصور في العالم الكبير ، كذلك له في العالم الصغير مظاهر وأسماء ، بحسب ظهوراته ومراتبه في الاصطلاح أهل الله وغيرهم ، وهي السر[٢٣] ، والخفي[٢٤] ، والروح[٢٥] ، والقلب[٢٦] ، والكلمة[٢٧] ، والرُّوع[٢٨] ، والفؤاد[٢٩] والصدر[٣٠] ، والعقل[٣١] والنفس[٣٢] ، كقوله تعالى :﴿فَإِنَّهُ يَعْلَمُ السِّرَّ وَأَخْفَى﴾ [طه:٧]، ﴿قُلِ الرُّوحُ مِنْ أَمْرِ رَبِّي﴾ [الإسراء : ٨٥] ، ﴿إِنَّ فِي ذَٰلِكَ لَذِكْرَىٰ لِمَن كَانَ لَهُ قَلْبٌ﴾ [ق:٣٧] ، ﴿بِكَلِمَةٍ مِّنَ اللَّهِ﴾ [آل عمران:٣٩] ، في عيسى عليه السلام ﴿مَا كَذَبَ الْفُؤَادُ مَا رَأَىٰ﴾ [النجم :١١] ، ﴿أَلَمْ نَشْرَحْ لَكَ صَدْرَكَ﴾ [الانشراح :١] ، ﴿وَنَفْسٍ وَمَا سَوَّاهَا﴾ [الشمس : ٧].

الجزئية السماوية التي ينتقش فيها كل ما في هذا العالم بشكله وهيئته ومقداره ، وهو المسمى بالسماء الدنيا ، وهو بمثابة خيال العالم ، كما أن الأول بمثابة روحه ، والثاني بمثابة قلبه ، ولوح الهيولى القابل للصورة في عالم الشهادة. (الجرجاني / ص٢٠٤)

واللوح المحفوظ : عبارة عن نور إلهي حَقي متجل في مشهد خلقي انطبعت الموجودات فيه انطباعاً أصلياً فهو أُمّ الهيولى لان الهيولى لا تقتضي صورة إلّا وهو منطبع في اللوح المحفوظ ، فإذا اقتضت الهيولى صورة ما وجد في العالم على حسب ما اقتضته الهيولى من الفَورِ والمُهلة. لان القلم الأعلى جرى في اللوح المحفوظ بإيجادها حَسَب ما اقتضته الهيولى. (التهانوي / ص١٢٩٢).

٢٣ السِّر : باعتبار أن الروح الأعظم تُدرك أنواره لأرباب القلوب والراسخين في العلم بالله ، دون غيرهم.

٢٤ الخفي : لخفاء حقيقته على العارفين وغيرهم.

٢٥ الروح : باعتبار ربوبيته للبدن ، وكونه مصدر الحياة الحسية ، ومنبع فيضانها على جميع القوى النفسانية.

٢٦ القلب : لتقلبه بين الوجه الذي يلي الحق ، فيستفيض منه الأنوار ، وبين الوجه الذي يلي النفس الحيوانية ، فيفيض عليها ما استفاض من موجدها على حسب استعدادها.

٢٧ الكلمة : باعتبار ظهورها في النفس الرحماني ، كظهور الكلمة في النفسى الإنساني.

٢٨ والرُّوع : باعتبار خوفه وفزعه من قهر مبدعه القهّار ، إذ أخذه من الرُّوع وهو الفزع.

٢٩ الفؤاد : باعتبار تأثره من مبدعه ، فان الفأد هو الجرح والتأثر لغةً.

٣٠ الصدر : باعتبار الوجه الذي يلي البدن ، لكونه مصدر أنواره وتصدّره عن البدن.

٣١ العقل : لتعقله ذاته وموجده ، وتقيده بتعين خاص ، وتقييده ما يُدرِكه ويضبطه بحصره إيّاها فيما تصوّره.

٣٢ النفس : لتعلقه بالبدن وتدبيره إيّاه. (مقدمة القيصري / ص١١٢)

manifest by these forms in the Great World. He has planes of manifestation and divine names in the Small World, according to degrees, which correspond to those in the Great World, in the terminology of the divine sages. These correspond to the mystery (*sirr*),[23] the hidden (*khafī*),[24] the spirit (*rūḥ*),[25] the heart (*qalb*),[26] the word (*kalima*),[27] the mind (*rūʿ*)[28]—the inner heart (*fuʾād*),[29] the breast' (*ṣadr*),[30] the intellect (*ʿaql*),[31] the soul (*nafs*),[32] as in: "He knows the secret and the hidden" (20:7); "Say, the spirit is a command from

---

Establishment (*al-maḥw wa-l-ithbāt*); it is the Tablet of the First Intellect.
The Tablet of Destiny (*al-qadr*) is the Tablet of the Universal Rational Soul. It differentiates universals found in the first Tablet being affiliated with their causes; it is called the Guarded Tablet.

The Tablet of the Heavenly Particular Soul is inscribed with all the forms of this world, structure and quantity; it is called the firmament of the world. It is equivalent to the imagination of the world, just as the first (Tablet) is equivalent to its spirit and the second is equivalent to its heart. The Tablet of Prime Matter is capable of receiving form in the visible world. *Kitāb al-taʿrīfāt,* 204.

The Guarded Tablet signifies the theophany of God's light in the reflection of creation whereby entities are essentially imprinted upon it. It is the mother of prime matter because prime matter does not beget a form except that there is already an impression of it in the Guarded Tablet. If prime matter requires a certain form, it is found in the world according to immediacy and measure. This is because the Supreme Pen impresses on the Guarded Tablet engendering forms according to the requisites of prime matter. Tahānawī, 1292.

23 It is called the mystery because none perceives its lights except the people of heart and those firm in knowledge, to the exclusion of others.

24 It is called the hidden because its reality is concealed from the gnostics and others.

25 It is called the spirit on account of its lordship over the body, the origin of sensory life and the source of effusion for the powers of the soul.

26 It is called the heart because of its fluctuation from the side which faces the Lord, receiving illumination thereby, and the side which faces the animal soul. It emanates to the soul what it has received from its source, according to its capacity.

27 It is called the word due to its appearing in the breath of the Merciful like words expressed through human breath.

28 It is called the mind (*rūʿ*) because of the fear and trepidation of its origin which is the divine name, the Subduer (*al-Qahhār*), since the etymology of the word indicates fear.

29 It is called the inner heart due to its being affected by its source, since *fàd* lexically means smitten and injured.

30 It is called the breast with respect to the face that adjoins the body, for it is the source of its light and occupies the foremost position in the body.

31 It is called the Intellect because it conceives its origin and Engenderer, and because of its delimitation and particular individuation, since it binds and contains that which it perceives and delimits the objects of its cognition.

32 It is called the soul because of its attachment to the body and its governance.

وفي الحديث الصحيح : « أن روح القدس نفث في رُوعي : أن نفساً لن تموت حتى تستكمل رزقها ».

واعلم أن المناسبة بين الحق والخلق هي أسمائه المتجلية في العالمين الكبير والصغير وهي عينها حاصلة بين العالمين.

قال الفيض الكاشاني (قدس سره) : « والله سبحانه وإن كان بذاته غنياً عما سواه كما قال عزّ وجلّ : ﴿فَإِنَّ اللهَ غَنِيٌّ عَنِ الْعَالَمِينَ﴾ [آل عمران :٩٧] ولكن أسماؤهُ الغير المتناهية تقضي أن يكون لكل منها مظهر في الخارج يظهر فيه أثر ذلك الاسم ومعناه ، ويتجلى المسمّى الذي هو الذات تعالى شأنه بذلك الاسم لأهل التوحيد حتى يعرف الله بصفات الكمال كلها ، ولذلك إنما يخلق الله ويدبر ويربي كل نوع من أنواع العالم باسم من أسمائه كما أشير إليه في أدعية أهل البيت (عليهم السلام) بالاسم الذي خلقت به العرش وبالاسم الذي خلقت به الكرسي ، وبربّ كذا وبربّ كذا إلى غير ذلك ».[٣٣]

وإنما اختص كل مخلوق باسم بسبب غلبة ظهور الصفة التي دلّ عليها ذلك الاسم فيه كما أشير إليه في الحديث القدسي : « يا آدم هذا محمّد وأنا الحميد المحمود في فعالي شققت له اسما من اسمي وهذا عليّ وأنا العلي العظيم شققت له اسماً من اسمي »[٣٤] ، فمظهر الرحمن مثلاً من يجري على يديه الرّحمة لمن يستحق الرحمة ثم من يجري عليه الرحمة ، ومظهر القهار من يجري على يديه القهر لمن يستحق القهر ثم من يجري عليه القهر إلى غير ذلك ، فانه لو لم يكن في الخارج راحم ومرحوم لم يظهر الرحمانية ، ولو لم يكن قاهر ومقهور لم يظهر القهّارية وقس عليه سائر الأسماء.

ولما كانت الأسماء كلها تحت حيطة اسم الله الجامع لها المحيط بها فمظهره مظهر الكل ، ومظهر الكل خليفة الله المفيض لجميع الكمالات من اسم الله على ما سواه.

---

٣٣ قرة العيون / ص٣٤٦.

٣٤ البرهان في تفسير القرآن / ج١ / ص٨٨.

my Lord" (17:85); "In it is a reminder for him who possesses a heart" (50:37); "A Word from God, noble, chaste and a prophet among the righteous" (3:39), referring to Jesus; "The heart did not deny what it saw" (53:11); "Did we not expand your breast?" (94:1); "By the soul and that which rectifies it" (91:7).

In a sound narration, "The Holy Spirit was blown into my mind (*rūʿ*): A soul does not die until its provision is completed."

Know that the correspondence between God and creation is the theophany of His names in both the Great and Small Worlds and is equally accessible in each world.

Fayḍ Kāshānī writes, "God the most glorified, even if He is independent of all others—as He states, 'Indeed, God is independent of the worlds" (3:97), His infinite names necessitate that each should have a manifestation in the external world that displays the imprint and meaning of a particular name. The Essence, which is the Named, manifests through a particular name to the monotheists (*ahl al-tawḥīd*) until they attain gnosis of God through all of the attributes of perfection. For this reason, God creates, directs, and lords over every species in the world by one of His names, as indicated in the supplications of the Prophet's family (*ahl al-bayt*), "By the name through which You created the Throne (*ʿarsh*) and by the name through which You created the Pedestal (*kursī*), and by the Lord of... and so forth."[33]

Each entity is governed by the dominant divine attribute exhibited in the entity, as mentioned in the hadith *qudsī*, "O Adam, this is Muḥammad and I am the One who Praises and is Praised (*al-Ḥamīd, al-Maḥmūd*) in my acts; I reserved a name for him from amongst My names. This is ʿAlī and I am the Most High and the Mighty; I reserved a name for him from amongst My names."[34]

So the manifestation of the Merciful (*al-Raḥmān*), for example, is to show mercy to the worthy and the manifestation of the Subduer (*al-Qahhār*) is to subdue one who merits it. If neither the merciful nor one shown mercy existed in the external world, the attribute of mercy would not become manifest. Similarly, if neither the subduer nor the subdued existed, the attribute of subdual would not become manifest. The same applies for every other divine name.

Since all of the divine names are subsumed under the all-encompassing name *Allah*, the complete manifestation is God's vicegerent, to the exclusion of others, who is the recipient of all perfections embraced by this name.

---

33 *Qurrat al-ʿuyūn*, 346.

34 *al-Burhān fi tafsīr al-Qurʾān*, 1:88.

وقال في تربية الأسماء للمخلوقات « كل مخلوق يدعو بلسان استحقاقه الفايض عليه من اسم الله ما يستحق له وإعطاؤه سبحانه الاستحقاق دعاء منه إلى الطلب ، فالطلب بهذا الاعتبار إجابة لدعوة الحق ، أجيبوا داعي الله ، وهو باعتبار آخر سؤال من الله سبحانه يسأله من في السموات والأرض ، وهذا السؤال إنما هو بلسان الحاجة والافتقار وعلى وجه الذل والاضطرار ، وإنما هو اسم من أسمائه سبحانه مناسب لحاجة السائل ، فالفقير مثلاً يدعو باسم المغني والمريض باسم الشافي والمظلوم باسم المنتقم ، وعلى هذا القياس فكل ذرة من ذرات العالم يدعو الله اضطراراً بلسان حاله اسم من أسمائه تعالى وهو يجيب دعوته في حضرة ذلك الاسم الذي دعاه به كما قال : ﴿أَمَّن يُجِيبُ الْمُضْطَرَّ إِذَا دَعَاهُ﴾ [النمل :٦٢] ».[٣٥]

ومطالب الكل على حسب مسؤولاتهم مبذولة دائماً وحوائجهم مقضية أبداً ﴿وَآتَاكُم مِّن كُلِّ مَا سَأَلْتُمُوهُ﴾ [إبراهيم:٣٤] لا يخيب منه أحد قط إلا من كان على بصيرته غشاوة من استعداده ، فأخذ يدعوه بلسان المقال ما يدعو بلسان الحال ، فلذلك يخيب قولاً وان استجيب حالاً وهو قوله سبحانه ﴿وَمَا دُعَاءُ الْكَافِرِينَ إِلاَّ فِي ضَلاَلٍ﴾ [الرعد :١٤] وهذا الذي ذكرناه أحد معاني قوله سبحانه : ﴿كُلَّ يَوْمٍ هُوَ فِي شَأْنٍ﴾ [الرحمن:٢٩] وبذلك يظهر أن سر المناسبة بين الإنسان والحق تعالى من جهة ، وبين الإنسان والموجودات من جهة أخرى هي لأسمائه قال تعالى : ﴿وَعَلَّمَ آدَمَ الأَسْمَاء كُلَّهَا﴾ [البقرة:٣١].

وذكر فيض الكاشاني (قدس سره) : أن المراد بتعليمها آدم كلها خلقه من أجزاء مختلفة وقوى متباينة حتى استعد لإدراك أنواع المدركات من المعقولات والمحسوسات والمتخيلات والموهومات ، وإلهامه معرفة ذوات الأشياء ، وخواصها وأصول العلم وقوانين الصّناعات وكيفية آلاتها والتمييز بين أولياء الله وأعدائه فتأتي بمعرفة ذلك كله مظهريّته لأسمائه تعالى كلها وجامعيّته جميع كمالات الوجود اللايقة به حتى صار منتخبا لكتاب الله الكبير الذي هو العالم الأكبر كما قال أمير المؤمنين عليه السلام.

دواؤك فيك وما تشعر   وداؤك منك وما تبصر
وتزعم أنك جرم صغير   وفيك انطوى العالم الأكبر
وأنت الكتاب المبين الذي   بأحرفه يظهر المضمر

---

٣٥ قرة العيون / ص٣٤٧.

With respect to the divine names nurtuinge creation, "Every entity seeks its measure through the tongue of their inherent worthiness to receive grace and effusion from the name *Allah*. God's bestowal of worthiness is His invitation to seek (Him). From this perspective, the very act of seeking is their response to God's appeal in the verse, 'Respond to God's summoner' (46:31).

From another perspective, their seeking of God is simply an expression of need, indigence, humility and necessity, as in, "All in the heavens and the earth call upon Him," and relates to the divine name that corresponds to the need of the seeker. Hence, the impoverished asks through the name, the Needless (*al-Mughnī*), the ill asks through the name, the Healer (*al-Shafī*), and the oppressed through the name, the Avenger (*al-Muntaqim*). In this manner every particle in the universe is compelled to implore God, expressing its state by one of His names. He, therefore, answers their supplication through the very name by which they call upon Him, as stated in the verse, 'Who else answers the call of the distressed when he calls upon Him?' (27:62)."[35]

All that they seek is granted and their needs always fulfilled, "And you are given everything you ask for" (14:34). None is disappointed except one whose receptivity occludes his insight. So a person sets out asking through words but not the language of his state. For that reason his verbal asking is without success though his desires are granted through his state, as He says, "The supplication of the unbelievers is only misguidance" (13:14). This is what we intended as one meanings of verse, "Every day He is in manifestation" (55:29). Thus, the mystery of the correspondence between man and God, and man and creation is conveyed in the divine names, as He says, "We taught Adam all the names" (2:31).

Fayḍ Kāshānī writes, "What is meant by 'teaching Adam all the names' is his genesis from different parts and multiple powers enabling him to perceive the various rational, sensory, imaginative, and delusory objects of perception. It is to gain awareness of essences, their specifics, the principles of knowledge, the axioms of construction, the use of instruments and the distinction between the friends of God and His enemies. With the sum of this knowledge he is the locus of manifestation of every divine name and the recipient embracing every ontological perfection, until he became designated as Great Book of God, which is the Greatest World, mentioned by Imām 'Alī:

Your cure is in you but you do not sense it — Your illness is from you but you do not see it
You reckon yourself a small mote — While within you the Universe is enfolded
You are the open book whose — Letters disclose the hidden

35 *Qurrat al-'uyūn*, 347.

وإنما تعرف الملائكة حقائق الأشياء كلها لاختلافها وتباينها وكونهم وحدانية الصفة ليس في جبلتهم خلط وتركيب ، ولهذا لا يفعل كل صنف منهم إلا فعلاً واحداً فالراكع منهم راكع أبداً ، والساجد منهم ساجد أبداً ، والقائم منهم قائم أبداً كما حكى الله عزّ وجلّ عنهم بقوله : ﴿وَمَا مِنَّا إِلاَّ لَهُ مَقَامٌ مَّعْلُومٌ﴾ [الصافات :١٦٤].

ولهذا ليس لهم تنافس وتباغض ، بل مثالهم مثال الحواس ، فان البصر لا يزاحم السمع في إدراك الأصوات ولا الشم يزاحمها ولا هما يزاحمان الشم فلا جرم مجبولون على الطاعة لا مجال للمعصية في حقهم ﴿لاَ يَعْصُونَ اللهَ مَا أَمَرَهُمْ وَيَفْعَلُونَ مَا يُؤْمَرُونَ﴾ [التحريم :٦] وقوله تعالى : ﴿يُسَبِّحُونَ الَّيْلَ وَالنَّهَارَ لاَ يَفْتُرُونَ﴾ [الأنبياء :٢٠].

فكل صنف منهم مظهر لاسم واحد من الأسماء الإلهية لا يتعداه ففاقهم آدم بمعرفته الكاملة ومظهريته الشاملة ، فمعنى قوله تعالى سبحانه : ﴿أَنبِئْهُم بِأَسْمَآئِهِمْ﴾ [البقرة :٣٣] أخبرهم بالحقائق المكنونة عنهم والمعارف المصوّرة عليهم ليعرفوا جامعيتك لها وقدرة الله على الجمع بين الصفات المتباينة والأسماء المتناقضة ومظاهرها بما فيها من التضاد في مخلوق واحد كما قيل :

ليس على الله بمستنكر ... أن يجمع العالم في واحد

وروي عن الإمام الصادق عليه السلام أنه قال : « إن الصورة الإنسانية أكبر حجة الله على خلقه ، وهي الكتاب الذي كتبه بيده وهي الهيكل الذي بناه بحكمته ، وهي مجموع صور العالمين ، وهي المختصر من العلوم في اللوح المحفوظ ، وهي الشاهد على كل غائب ، وهي الحجّة على كل جاحد ، وهي الطريق المستقيم إلى كل خير ، وهي الصراط الممدود بين الجنة والنار ».[٣٦]

فالنفس الإنسانية مجموع صور العالمين وهي جسر ممدود بين الدنيا والآخرة من حيث إنها جوهر روحاني له تعلق بالبدن الطبيعي وعالم الشهادة ، والإنسان من شأن الدنيا والآخرة ، فمن عرف النفس حق المعرفة فقد عرف النشأتين وأدرك العالمين والأثر والتأثر بهما والمناسبة الحاصلة بينهما.

---

٣٦ تفسير الصافي / ج١/ ص٩٢.

The angels are aware of realities discretely and distinctly and they are singular in attribute indicating that their nature is not admixed or compound. For this reason each class of angels performs only one task; those that are bowing (*rukūʿ*) are always bowing, those that are prostrating (*sujūd*) are always in prostration, and those that are standing (*qiyām*) are always standing, as the Almighty describes them, "We do not have but a specified station" (37:164).

For this reason, they do not compete with one another nor do they harbor mutual animosity. In this they resemble the senses; sight does not vie with hearing to perceive sound, nor does the sense of smell vie with the other senses, and so forth. Obedience is intrinsic to the angels and there is no scope for defiance, "They do not disobey God's commands and perform what they have been commissioned" (66:6). "The night and day glorify Him and are not remiss" (21:20).

Since each class of angel is a manifestation of a single divine name, Adam surpasses them because of the totality of his knowledge and the inclusiveness of his manifestation. This is the meaning of the verse, "So inform them of their names" (2:33) that is, reveal to them those realities concealed from them, the knowledge of their own forms so that they may realize your comprehensiveness and God's power to combine divergent attributes, contrary names and opposing manifestations in a single created thing, as it is said,

None can deny that God Can gather the world into a single thing

It is related that Imām al-Ṣādiq said, "The human form is the greatest proof of God for His creation. It is the book that He wrote by His own hand, the edifice that He constructed by His wisdom and the totality of the forms of the worlds. It is the summation of knowledge in the Guarded Tablet, the evidence for all who do not bear witness, and the testament against every disbeliever. It is the straight path to every good and the bridge spanning paradise and hell."[36]

The human soul is the totality of the forms of every world, the bridge spanning this world and the hereafter, for it is a spiritual substance but has an attachment with the natural body and the visible world. Human affairs concern both the world and the hereafter, so he who truly knows himself, knows both dimensions and perceives both worlds, their causes and effects and the correspondences between them.

36 *Tafsīr al-ṣāfī*, 1:92.

روي أن أعرابياً سأل أمير المؤمنين عليه السلام عن النفس فقال له : عن أي نفس تسأل

فقال : يا مولاي هل النفس أنفس عديدة ؟

فقال عليه السلام : نعم نفس نامية نباتية ، ونفس حسّية حيوانية ، ونفس ناطقة قدسية ، ونفس إلهية ملكوتية كلية.

قال : يا مولاي ما النامية النباتية ؟

قال : قوة أصلها الطبائع الأربع بدو إيجادها مسقط النطفة ، مقرّها الكبد ، مادتها من لطائف الأغذية ، فعلها النمو والزيادة ، وسبب فراقها اختلاف المتولدات ، فإذا فارقت عادت إلى ما منه بدأت عود ممازجة لا عود مجاورة.

فقال : يا مولاي وما النفس الحسّية الحيوانية ؟

قال : قوة فلكية وحرارة غريزية أصلها الأفلاك بدو إيجادها عند الولادة الجسمانية فعلها الحياة والحركة ، والظلم والغشم والغلبة واكتساب الأموال والشهوات الدنيوية مقرها القلب سبب فراقها اختلاف المتولدات ، فإذا فارقت عادت إلى ما منه بدأت عود ممازجة لا عود مجاورة فتعدم صورتها ويبطل فعلها ووجودها ويضمحل تركيبها

فقال : يا مولاي وما النفس الناطقة القدسية ؟

قال : قوة لاهوتية بدو إيجادها عند الولادة الدنيوية ، مقرّها العلوم الحقيقية الدينيّة ، موادّها التأييدات العقليّة ، فعلها المعارف الرّبانية ، سبب فراقها تحلل الآلات الجسمانية، فإذا فارقت عادت إلى ما منه بدأت عود مجاورة لا عود ممازجة.

فقال : يا مولاي وما النفس اللاهوتية الملكوتية الكلية ؟

فقال : قوة لاهوتية جوهرة بسيطة حية بالذات أصلها العقل منه بدت وعنه دعت وإليه دلت وأشارت وعودتها إليه إذا كملت وشابهته ، ومنها بدأت الموجودات وإليها تعود بالكمال فهو ذات الله العليا وشجرة طوبى وسدرة المنتهى وجنة المأوى ، من عرفها لم يشق ، ومن جهلها ضلّ سعيه وغوى.

فقال السائل : يا مولاي وما العقل ؟

قال : العقل جوهر درّاك محيط بالأشياء من جميع جهاتها ، عارف بالشيء قبل كونه ، فهو علّة الموجودات ونهاية المطالب.(٣٧)

---

٣٧ كتاب الحقائق / الفيض الكاشاني / ص٣٦٣.

It is related that a Bedouin asked Amīr al-Mu'minīn about the soul, to which he replied, "Which soul are you asking about?"

The Bedouin asked, "My master, are there many souls?"

He responded, "Yes, there is the growing vegetative, the sensory animal, the sacred rational, and the universal angelic divine soul."

The Bedouin asked, "My master, what is the growing vegetative soul?"

He replied, "It is a power originating from the four elements that begins at conception; it resides in the liver; its substance is derived from rarified nutrients; its activity is growth and increase; the cause of its separation is the inconsistency of its constituents. When it separates it returns to its origin, reintegrating without having independent existence."

Then he asked, "My master, what is the sensory animal soul?"

He replied, "It is a celestial power and a fire of instinct whose origin is the celestial spheres; its genesis occurs at physical birth; its activity is life and movement, oppression, tyranny, domination, acquiring wealth and worldly desires; it resides in the heart and the cause of its separation is the inconsistency of its constituents. Thus, when it separates it returns to its origin, reintegrating without having independent existence, so its form is destroyed, its activity and existence cease and its composition disintegrates."

He asked, "My master, what is the sacred rational soul?"

He replied, "It is a divine power that originates at the time of birth in this world. Its seat is true religious knowledge; its substance is the intellect's affirmation; its activity is gnosis of the divine. The reason for its separation is the dissolution of the physical apparatus. When it separates it returns to its origin, remaining independent and does not recombine."

He asked, "My master, what is the divine universal angelic soul?"

He replied, "It is a divine power, a simple substance, alive through its own essence; its origin is the intellect from which it appears, summoning it, indicating and pointing to it, returning to it when it is complete and resembling it. The entities originate from it and return to it perfected. It is the lofty Essence of God, the Blessed Tree (*shajarat tūbā*), the Farthest Lote Tree (*sidrat al-muntahā*) and paradise. He who knows it will not be wretched and he who is ignorant of it goes astray and is lost.

He asked, "My master, what is the intellect?"

He replied, "The intellect is an essence that perceives, encompassing things in every aspect, cognizant of things before their becoming; it is the reason for being and the goal of pursuits."[37]

---

37 *Kitāb al-haqā'iq*, 363.

وعن كميل بن زياد قال : سألت مولانا عليّاً أمير المؤمنين عليه السلام ، فقلت : يا أمير المؤمنين أريد أن تعرفني نفسي فقال عليه السلام : يا كميل وأي الأنفس تريد أن أعرفك ؟

فقلت : يا مولاي هل هي إلا نفس واحدة ؟

فقال عليه السلام : يا كميل إنما هي أربعة : النامية النباتية ، والحسيّة الحيوانية ، والناطقة القدسيّة ، والكلية الإلهية ، ولكل واحدة من هذه خمس قوى وخاصيّتان.

فالنامية النباتية لها خمس قوى : ماسكة ، وجاذبة ، وهاضمة ، ودافعة ، ومربية ، ولها خاصيتان : الزيادة والنقصان وانبعاثها من الكبد.

والحسيّة الحيوانية لها خمس قوى : سمع ، وبصر ، وشمّ ، وذوق ، ولمس ، ولها خاصيتان : الشهوة ، والغضب ، وانبعاثها من القلب ، والناطقة القدسيّة لها خمس قوى : فكر ، وذكر وعلم ، وحلم ونباهة ، وليس لها انبعاث وهي أشبه الأشياء بالنفوس الملكية ولها خاصيتان : النزاهة والحكمة. والكلية الإلهية لها خمس قوى : بقاء في فناء ، ونعيم في شقاء ، وعز في ذل ، وفقر في غناء ، وصبر في بلاء ، ولها خاصيتان : الرِّضا والتسليم ، وهذه التي مبدؤها من الله وإليه تعود ، وقال الله تعالى :﴿وَنَفَخْتُ فِيهِ مِن رُّوحِي﴾ وقال تعالى : ﴿يَا أَيَّتُهَا النَّفْسُ الْمُطْمَئِنَّةُ ۞ ارْجِعِي إِلَى رَبِّكِ رَاضِيَةً مَّرْضِيَّةً﴾ والعقل وسط الكل.[٣٨]

وروي عن أمير المؤمنين عليه السلام : « إن للأنبياء وهم السابقون خمسة أرواح روح القدس ، وروح الإيمان ، وروح القوة ، وروح الشهوة ، وروح البدن.

فبروح القدس بعثوا الأنبياء وبها علموا الأشياء ، وبروح الإيمان عبدوا الله ولم يشركوا به شيئاً ، وبروح القوة جاهدوا عدوهم وعالجوا معاشهم ، وبروح الشهوة : أصابوا لذيذ الطعام ونكحوا الحلال من شباب النساء ، وبروح البدن دبّوا ودرجوا .قال : « وللمؤمنين وهم أصحاب اليمين الأربعة الأخيرة ، وللكفار وهم أصحاب الشمال الثالثة الأخيرة كما للدواب في لفظ هذا معناه ».[٣٩]

---

٣٨ كتاب الحقائق / الفيض الكاشاني / ص٣٦٣.

٣٩ كتاب الحقائق / الفيض الكاشاني / ص٣٦٣.

Kumayl b. Ziyād relates, "I asked our master 'Alī, 'O Amīr al-Mu'minīn, I want you to describe my soul to me.'

He replied, 'O Kumayl, which of the souls should I describe?'

I said, 'My master, is there not but one soul?'

He said, 'O Kumayl, there are four souls: the growing vegetative, the sensory animal, the sanctified sacred, and the divine universal soul. Each one of them has five powers and two special attributes.

The growing vegetative soul has five faculties: grasping, attracting, digesting, repelling and preserving. It has two special attributes, increase and decrease; it arises from the liver.

The sensory animal soul has five faculties: hearing, sight, smell, taste and touch. It has two special attributes, desire and anger; it arises from the heart.

The sacred rational soul has five faculties: thought, remembrance, knowledge, forbearance and intelligence. It does not arise from anything and is the closest in resemblance to the spirits of the angels. It has two special attributes, virtue and wisdom.

As for the divine universal soul, it has five powers: subsistence in annihilation, experiencing comfort in distress, maintaining honor in humiliation, feeling indigent in prosperity and having patience in adversity. It has two special attributes, contentment and submission. It is the one whose origin and return is God, as He states, "I blew into him of My spirit" (15:29), and "O tranquil soul, return to your Lord, contented and having pleased your Lord" (89:27-28). The intellect is the center of it all.'"[38]

It is related that Amīr al-Mu'minīn said, "The prophets who are the foremost possess five spirits, the sanctified spirit, the spirit of faith, the spirit of strength, the spirit of desire and the corporeal spirit. By the sanctified spirit they were commissioned to be messengers and had knowledge of matters. Through the spirit of faith they worshipped God and did not associate anything with Him. Through the spirit of strength they fought their enemies and amended their relationships. Through the spirit of desire they took pleasure in food and married the lawful among the young women. Through the corporeal spirit they moved forward and walked."

He said, "The believers who are the people of the right possess the last four spirits, whereas, the unbelievers who are the people of the left possess the last three, as do the animals."[39]

---

38 *Kitāb al-haqā'iq*, 363.
39 *Kitāb al-haqā'iq*, 363.

ولولا تلك المناسبة بين الحق والإنسان ما ربط السفير الأعظم الإلهي معرفة الرّب بمعرفة النفس فقال : « من عرف نفسه فقد عرف ربه » فإن من عرف نفسه فوق ما يعرف بالتنزيه والتشبيه ، وجمع في معرفتها بينهما ، ووجدها موصوفة بهما أيضاً ، فقد جمع في معرفة ربه بينهما كذلك ، ونال بمعرفة نفسه درجة الكمال في العلم بالله تعالى في ذاته وصفاته وأفعاله ، وذلك لان باطن النفس الإنسانية تنزيه وظاهرها تشبيه ، وهي عالية في دنوّها ودانية في علوها ، فعن إمام الملك والملكوت صادق آل محمد صلوات الله وسلامه عليهم : « الجمع بلا تفرقة زندقة ، والتفرقة بدون الجمع تعطيل ، والجمع بينهما توحيد » وقد أجاد الحكيم الرباني (أنباذ قلس) في شأن النفس حيث قال : « إن من رام أن يعرف الأشياء من العلو . أعني الجوهر الأول . عسر عليه إدراكها ، ومن طلبها من أسفل عسر عليه إدراك العلم الأعلى لانتقاله من جوهر كثيف إلى جوهر في غاية اللطف ، ومن طلبها من المتوسط . وعرف المتوسط كنه المعرفة . أدرك به علم الطرفين وسهل عليه الطلب »[٤٠].

٤٠ شرح المنظومة / حسن زاده الآملي / ج٥/ ص١٣-١٤.

Were it not for this correspondence between God and man, the greatest divine emissary could not have accomplished gnosis of the Lord through gnosis of the self, as indicated by the statement, "He who knows himself knows his Lord."

Therefore, he who knows his soul beyond the lens of transcendence and immanence, his consciousness having unified both aspects—finds that the soul can be described by both. Thus, he unifies both aspects in the gnosis of His Lord. Through the gnosis of his soul he achieves a degree of perfection in knowing God's Essence, attributes and acts.

This is because the inward aspect of the human soul is transcendent and the outward aspect is immanent. It is sublime in its lowliness, and low in its sublimity, as mentioned by the Imām of the Kingdom and Dominion, the Veracious (al-Ṣādiq) of the progeny of Muḥammad, "Unifying without individuating is heresy and individuating without unifying is suspension (of the intellect)—combining the two is monotheism."

The divine sage, Empedocles, skillfully described the soul in the following, "Whoever seeks knowledge from above—the first substance—finds it difficult to grasp, and whoever seeks knowledge from below, finds it difficult to comprehend sublime knowledge due to the problem of conveying the utterly insubstantial from the dense. Thus, he who seeks it from the middle, and knows it to its fullest extent—attains knowledge of both aspects and his seeking becomes effortless."[40]

40 Ḥassanzade Āmulī, *Sharḥ al-manẓūma*, 5:13-14.

الباب الأوّل

التناسب بين الإنسان والملك

إن بين الإنسان والملائكة مناسبة وعلاقة تتلخص بالعقل والفعل والتدبير. أما العقل[1] : فقد ورد عن عبد الله بن سنان قال : سألت أبا عبد الله جعفر بن محمد الصادق عليه السلام فقلت: الملائكة أفضل أم بنو آدم ؟

---

١ عن الإمام الصادق عليه السلام : « إن الله خلق الملائكة من نور » / الاختصاص / ص١٠٩ وعنه عليه السلام : « والذي نفسي بيده ، لملائكة الله في السماوات أكثر من عدد التراب في الأرض ، وما في السماء موضع قدم إلا وفيها ملك يُسبحه ويقدسه ، ولا في الأرض شجر ولا مَدَر إلا وفيها ملك موكل بها » البحار / ج٥٩ / ص١٧٦ / ح٧ و الملك باصطلاح الحكماء هو العقل ، وقد يطلق العقل على القوة العاقلة الإنسانية.
والعقل جوهر مجرد في ذاته وفعله أي لا يكون جسماً ولا جسمانياً ولا يتوقف أفعاله على تعلقه بجسم ، وهو جوهر مجرد غير متعلق بالجسم تعلّق التدبير والتصرف ، وإن كان متعلق بالجسم على سبيل التأثير.
والملك : جوهر بسيط ذو حياة ونظر وعقل ، وأن الاختلاف بين الملائكة والجن والشياطين كالاختلاف بين الأنواع ، والملائكة جواهر مقدسة عن طلب الشهوة وكدورة الغضب.
قال سيد الأوصياء عليه السلام في صفة الملائكة « هم أعلمُ خلقك بك ، وأخوفهم لك ، وأقربهم منك ، لم يسكنوا الأصلاب ، ولم يُضمَّنوا الأرحام ، ولم يُخلَقوا من ماء مهين ، ولم يتشعَبهم ريب المنون ، وإنّهم على مكانهم منك ، ومنزلتهم عندك واستجماع أهوائِهم فيك ، وكثرة طاعتهم لك ، وقلة غفلتهم عن أمرك ، لو عاينوا كُنه ما خفي عليهم منك لحقروا أعمالهم ». (نهج البلاغة / خ١٠٩)
وعن الإمام الصادق عليه السلام : « إن الملائكة لا يأكلون ولا يشربون ، ولا ينكحون وإنما يعيشون بنسيم العرش » تفسير القمي / ج٢ / ص٢٠٦.
وأما أصناف الملائكة فلا يعرفهم غير خالقهم كما قال تعالى : ﴿وَمَا يَعْلَمُ جُنُودَ رَبِّكَ إِلاَّ هُوَ﴾ [المدثر :٣١] والملائكة منهم : « حملة العرش ، وإسرافيل وميكائيل ، وجبرائيل ، وعزرائيل والكروبيون ، وملائكة سبع سماوات ، والحفظة ، والمعقبات ، ومنكر ونكير ، والسياحون ، وهاروت وماروت وغيرهم (عليهم السلام) ».
وفي كتاب اليواقيت والجواهر « الملائكة لهم عقل ، وليس لهم فكرة ، ففاتهم ثواب الفكر في مصنوعات الله ، وعدموا كون الحق تعالى سمعهم وبصرهم ». (اليواقيت والجواهر / ص٣٩٨ /

CHAPTER 1

The Correspondence Between Man and Angel

The correspondence and relationship between the human being and the angels can be summarized by intelligence, activity and governance.[1] As for intelligence, ʿAbdallāh b. Sinān relates that he asked Imām al-Ṣādiq, "Which are superior the angels or the children of Adam?"

---

1 It is related from Imām al-Ṣādiq, "God created the angels from light." (*al-Ikhtiṣāṣ*, 109). It is also related, "By Him who holds my life in His hands, the angels of God in the heavens are more numerous than the grains of sand on the earth. There is not a place to tread in the heavens but an angel glorifies and sanctifies Him, nor is there a tree or clod of earth but that an angel is its guardian." *Biḥār al-anwār*, 59:176, no. 7.

Angel in the terminology of the philosophers signifies intellect, but it may also refer to the faculty of rationality in man. The intellect is an immaterial substance in essence and in actuality, that is, it is neither a body nor bodily in nature, nor do its activities require attachment to a body. It is an immaterial substance whose association with bodies is by way of influence, not by way of management or employment.

The angel is a simple substance, possessing life, reflection and intellect. The difference between angels, Jinn and satans is akin to the variation between different species, although the angels are substances that are unadulterated by the urges of desire or contaminated by anger.

Imām ʿAlī in description of the angels says, "They are the most knowledgeable of You among your creation, the most apprehensive of You and the nearest to You among your creation. They never dwelled in loins, nor within the womb, nor were they created by a contemptible fluid. They did not diversify through the uncertainty of trials, rather they hold distinct places with You and stations near You. Their aspiration is directed towards You, their obedience to You is great and neglect of your command is slight. If they were to behold Your reality which is hidden from them, they would find their own deeds paltry. *Nahj al-balāgha*, sermon 109.

A tradition related from Imām al-Ṣādiq says, "The angels do not eat, drink, or procreate, rather they live by the breeze of the Throne." *Tafsīr Qummī*, 2:206.

None know the types of angels except their Creator, as He says, "None know the soldiers of Your Lord except Him" (74:31). Among them are the Bearers of the Throne, Isrāfīl, Mīkā'īl, Gabriel, Izrā'īl, Karrubī, the angels of the seven heavens, the Protectors, the Punishers, Munkar and Nakīr, Harūt, Mārūt and others.

In *Yawaqīt wa-l-jawāhir*, Shaʿrānī writes, "The angels have intellect but do not reflect. Thus, they are deprived of the reward of contemplating God's handiwork and are unable to become His hearing and His sight. Shaʿrānī, *Yawaqīt wa-l-jawāhir*, 398.

فقال : قال أمير المؤمنين علي بن أبي طالب عليه السلام « إن الله عزّ وجلّ ركب في الملائكة عقلًا بلا شهوة ، وركب في البهائم شهوة بلا عقل ، وركب في بني آدم كليهما ، فمن غلب عقله شهوته فهو خير من الملائكة ، ومن غلب شهوته عقله فهو شر من البهائم ».

وقال عليه السلام : « إن الله خص الملك بالعقل دون الشهوة والغضب ، وخص الحيوانات بهما دونه وشرّف الإنسان بإعطاء الجميع ، فان انقادت شهوته وغضبه لعقله صار أفضل من الملائكة لوصوله إلى هذه المرتبة مع وجود المنازع والملائكة ليس لهم مزاحم ».

وقال النراقي (رحمه الله) : « ولما كانت القوة العاقلة من سنخ الملائكة ، والواهمة من حزب الأبالسة والغضبية من أفق السباع ، والشهوية من عالم البهائم ، فبحسب غلبة واحدة منها تكون النفس إما ملكاً أو شيطاناً أو كلباً أو خنزيراً ، فلو كانت الغلبة والسلطنة لقهرمان العقل ظهر في مملكة النفس أحكامه وآثاره ، وانتظمت أحوالها ، ولو كانت لغيره من القوى ظهر فيها آثاره فتهلك النفس ويختل معاشها ومعادها .

ثم المنشأ للتنازع والتجرد والبقاء في النفس الإنسانية انما هو قوتها العقلية لأن التدافع انما بينها وبين سائر القوى ، فليس في نفوس سائر الحيوانات لفقدانها العاقلة تنازع وتجاذب وإن اختلفت في غلبة ما فيها من القوى ، فان الغلبة في الشياطين للواهمة ، وفي السباع للغضب ، وفي البهائم للشهوة ، وأما الملائكة فتنحصر قوتها بالعاقلة فليس فيها سائر القوى فلا يتحقق فيها تدافع وتنازع.

فالجامع لعوالم الكل هو الإنسان وهو المخصوص من بين المخلوقات بالصفات المتقابلة ، ولذلك صار مظهراً للأسماء المتقابلة الإلهية وقابلاً للخلافة الربانية ، وقائماً بعمارة عالمي الصورة والمعنى والملائكة وإن كانوا مخصوصين بالجنة الروحانية ولوازمها من الإشراقات العلمية وتوابعها من اللذات العقلية ، إلا أنه ليس لهم جهة جسمانية ولوازمها بخلاف الإنسان فانه محيط بجميع المراتب المختلفة ، وسائر في الأطوار المتباينة من الجمادية والنباتية والحيوانية والملكية ، وان له الترقي عن جميع تلك المراتب بأن

الشعراني / ط دار إحياء التراث / مؤسسة التاريخ العربي)

He replied, "Amīr al-Mu'minīn 'Alī b. Abī Ṭālib said, 'God Almighty composed the angels of intellect but without desire and composed the animals of desire but without intellect, yet composed man of both. Thus, he whose intellect dominates his desire is superior to the angels and he whose desire dominates his intellect is worse than the animals.'

He also said, "God endowed the angels with intellect but without desire and anger, and endowed the animals with both but without intellect, yet He ennobled man with all three.

Thus, if his desire and anger obey his intellect, he becomes superior to the angels, for he arrives at this station in the midst of conflict, whereas there is no such strife in the angels.'"

Narāqī says, "Since the faculty of intellect is from the class of angels, the imagination from the party of satans, anger from the horizon of predators and desire from the world of beasts, whichever one predominates, the soul becomes either angel, satan, dog or pig. However, if the intellect dominates and governs the kingdom of the soul its laws and effects appear therein and its states become orderly, but if the soul is stewarded by the other powers, their effects appear and the soul is thus destroyed, its life and hereafter ruined.

The origin of conflict, immateriality and subsistence in the human soul is the intellect which is driven forward by the opposition between the intellect and the other faculties. There is no such conflict and contention in the souls of animals for they lack intellect and differ only with respect to their dominant faculty. In the satans the dominant faculty is the imagination, in the predators it is anger, and in the beasts it is desire. As for the angels, the sole faculty is the intellect to the exclusion of the othes, so no conflict and contention arises within them.

That being which comprises every world is the human being, who is distinguished among all creation to possess contrary properties. For this reason, the human being is the locus of manifestation of contrary divine names and worthy of divine vicegerency, upholding the edifice of both the world of form and the world of meaning. Even if the angels have been assigned to spiritual paradise along with its associated realities, such as illuminative knowledge and their subsequent intellectual pleasures, they do not possess a bodily aspect nor its concomitants.

In contrast, the human being encompasses all the differing degrees of existence and moves through the various stages of mineral, vegetal, animal and angelic realms. Once he advances past all of these degrees through the realization of pure unitary witnessing, he surpasses the angelic horizon. Thus, he becomes the comprehensive replica of the realities of the Kingdom

تتحقق له مرتبة مشاهدة الوحدة الصرفة ، فيتجاوز عن أفق الملائكة ، فهو النسخة الجامعة لحقائق الملك والملكوت ، والمعجون المركب من عالمي الأمر والخلق.

ولما كان الإنسان ذو جنبه روحانية يناسب بها الأرواح الطيبة والملائكة القادسة ، وذو جنبة جسمانية يشابه بها السباع والأنعام ، فبالجزء الجسماني أقيم في هذا العالم الحسي مدة قصيرة ، وبالجزء الروحاني ينتقل إلى العالم العلوي ، ويقيم فيه أبداً في مصاحبة الأرواح القدسية ، بشرط أن يتحرك بقواه نحو كمالاته الخاصة ، حتى يغلب الجزء الروحاني على الجسماني ، وينفض عن نفسه كدورات الطبيعة ، وتظهر فيه آثار الروحانيات من العلم بحقائق الأشياء والأنس بالله تعالى والحب له والتحلي بفضائل الصفات ، وحينئذ يقوم بغلبة روحانيته بين الملأ الأعلى يستمد منهم لطائف الحكمة ، ويستنير بالنور الإلهي ويزيد ذلك بحسب دفع العلائق الجسمية ، حتى إذا ارتفعت عنه حجب الغواسق الطبيعية بأسرها ، وأزيلت عنه أستار العوائق الهيولانية برمتها ، خلى عن جميع الآلام والحسرات ، وكان أبداً مسروراً بذاته ، مغتبطاً بحاله مبتهجاً بما يرد عليه من فيوضات النور الأول ، ولا يُسرّ إلا بتلك اللذات ، ولا يغتبط إلا بها ، ولا يهش إلا بإظهار الحكمة الحقة بين أهلها ولا يرتاح إلا بمن ناسبه وأحب الاقتباس منه ، ولا يبالي بمفارقة الدنيا وما فيها ، ويرى جسمه وماله وجميع خيرات الدنيا وبالاً وكلاً عليه إلا ما هو ضروري يحتاج إليه بدنه الذي يفتقر إليه في تحصيل كماله ، ويحن أبداً إلى مصاحبه الذوات النورية... »(٢)

وعلى ذلك فهو يطلب المناسبة بينه وبين الملك على أساس حكومة العقل وقانونه حتى يمتلئ من المعارف الإلهية ، والشوق الإلهي والبهجة الإلهية والشعار الإلهي وتتقرر الحقائق في عقله كتقرر القضايا الأولية فيه ، بل يكون علمه بها اشد إشراقاً وظهوراً من علمه بها ، وإذا بلغ هذه الغاية فقد استعد للوصول إلى المرتبة القصوى ، ومجاورة الملأ الأعلى ، فيصل إلى ما لا عين رأت ، ولا أذن سمعت ، ولا خطر على قلب بشر ، و يفوز بما أشير إليه في الكتاب الإلهي بقوله تعالى :﴿فَلَا تَعْلَمُ نَفْسٌ مَّا أُخْفِيَ لَهُم مِّن قُرَّةِ أَعْيُنٍ﴾ [السجوة:١٧]

---

٢ جامع السعادات / ج١ / ص٣٤ « بتصرف ».

(*al-mulk*) and Dominion (*al-malakūt*) and the fusion of the two worlds, the Command (*al-amr*) and Creation (*al-khalq*).

Since the human being corresponds to the virtuous spirits and sanctified angels through his spiritual aspect and resembles the predators and beasts through his corporeal aspect, he subsists in this world for a short time by the latter and he transcends to the higher world by the former, subsisting in it eternally in the company of sanctified spirits. This is on the condition that he moves through his faculties in the direction of his specific perfection so that his spiritual aspect dominates his corporeal aspect. As a consequence, he casts from himself the impurities of nature and the effects of spirituality emerge, particularly, knowledge of realities, intimacy and love of God and the adornment of virtuous qualities.

Then, through his victorious spiritual aspect, he stands among the Higher Plenum (*al-mala᾽ al-aʿlā*), receiving from them the subtleties of wisdom. He becomes illuminated by a divine light which increases in proportion to the dispelling of corporeal attachments. When the dusky veils of nature are completely removed and the occluding curtains of primordial matter are entirely lifted, he is devoid of all pains and regrets and remains eternally joyous in his being, delighted in his state and exultant in that which arrives from effusions of the First Light. He finds joy in nothing but that Essence, delights in nothing else and finds pleasure only in the disclosure of true wisdom from among its folk. He finds serenity only with those who are in harmony with it and love to acquire it. His parting with the world and all that it contans is of no consequence since he sees his body, wealth and all the world's treasures loathsome and tedious, except for what is necessary for the maintenance of his body, requisite for the attainment of his perfection. So, he yearns endlessly for communion with the luminous spirits."[2]

In light of this, he seeks a correspondence to the angels based on the intellect's governance and sovereignty until he becomes infused with divine realizations, fervor, splendor and a distinguishing mark. Realities become established in his intellect as a priori knowledge; in fact, his knowledge of those realities is more intensely luminous and manifest. If he arrives at this extremity, he is prepared to reach the ultimate end and keep company with the Higher Plenum, for he attains what no eye has seen nor ear has heard, nor that which transpires in the heart of man. This triumph is mentioned in the divine book of the Almighty, "The soul does not know what coolness of the eyes are hidden from it" (32:17).

---

2 *Jāmiʿ al-saʿdāt*, 1:34.

ولما علمت أن الإنسان يناسب الملائكة في اللذة العقلية ، وفي السبعية والبهيمية والشيطانية يناسب السباع والبهائم والشياطين ، فأعلم أن من غلب عليه إحدى اللذات الأربع كانت مشاركته لما يُنسب إليه أكثر حتى إذا صارت الغلبة تامة لكان هو ولا تظن أن ما يفوت عن النفس من الصفاء والبهجة لأجل ما يعتريها من الكدرة الحاصلة من معصية من المعاصي يمكن تداركه ، فان ذلك محال ، إذ غاية الأمر أن تتبع تلك المعصية ، فلا تزداد بتلك الحسنة إشراقاً وسعادة ، ولو جاء بها من دون سيئة لزاد بها نور القلب وبهجته ، وحصلت له درجة في الجنة ، ولما تقدمت السيئة سقطت هذه الفائدة وانحصرت فائدتها في مجرد عود القلب إلى ما كان عليه قبلها ، وهذا نقصان لا حيلة لجبره ، ومثال ذلك أن المرآة التي تدنست بالخبث والصدأ إذا مسحت بالمصقلة وإن زال به هذا الخبث ، إلا أنه لا تزيد به جلاء وصفاء بخلاف ما إذا لم تتدنس أصلاً ، فان التصقيل يزيدها صفاء وجلاء وإلى ما ذكر أشار النبي ﷺ بقوله : « من قارف ذنباً فارقه عقل لم يعد إليه أبداً »[٣].

وأما الفعل :فقدر ورد عن الرسول الأكرم ﷺ[٤] : « إن العبد إذا توضأ أو غسل مع ذكر المستحبات المبينة في محلها ، خلق الله تعالى بعدد كل قطرة من قطرات وضوئه أو غسله ملكاً يسبح الله ، ويقدسه ، ويهلّله ، ويكبره ، ويصلي على محمد وآله الطيبين ، وثواب ذلك لهذا المتوض ، ثم يأمر الله بوضوئه وغسله ، فيختم عليه بخاتم من خواتيم العزّة... ».

وكذلك ما ورد عن سيد الأوصياء عليه السلام أنه قال : « من توضأ مثل وضوئي وقال مثل قولي ، خلق الله له مع كل قطرة ملكاً يقدسه ، ويسبحه ، ويكبّره فيكتب الله له ثواب ذلك إلى يوم القيامة ».[٥]

فهذه الروايات الشريفة والأنفاس الطاهرة وأمثالها تبين المناسبة بين فعل العبد والملك ، ومن هنا اهتم أهل الله بجلب الملائم لما فيه من الأجر والثواب وتكامل النفس ورقيها وعلى العكس فانهم دفعوا المنافر ، فقد ورد عن أبي عبد الله عليه السلام انه قال : « إذا توضأ أحدكم ولم يسم كان للشيطان في وضوئه شرك ، وإن أكل

٣ جامع السعادات / ج١ / ص٤٦.
٤ وسائل الشيعة / ج١ / ص٣٩٨ / ١٠٤٠/ أبواب الوضوء.
٥ وسائل الشيعة / ج١ / ص٤٠١ / ١٠٤٦ / باب استحباب الدعاء بالمأثور.

Having realized that the human being corresponds with the angels with respect to intellectual pleasures and corresponds with the predators, beasts and satans with their respective pleasures, then know that whichever of the four pleasures gains ascendency, his correspondence to it strengthens until it completely dominates him.

Let it not be supposed that it is possible to redress the lost purity and splendor of the soul from the tarnish of accumulated sins. It is impossible because persistence in sin prevents good deeds from increasing in luminosity and felicity in the soul. If a good deed is performed without being followed by a sin, the heart's light and splendor intensify and one attains a degree in paradise. But if followed by a sin, its benefit is nullified and the heart returns to its previous condition; this loss cannot be redressed. For example, polishing a mirror that has been sullied by an impurity or tarnished by rust will not increase the mirror's luster even if the impurity is removed. In contrast, a mirror that has never been tarnished will only increase in clarity and luster when polished.

The Prophet alludes to this in his statement, "One who is tempted by sin, (an aspect) of his intellect departs from him never to return again."[3]

It has been related from the Prophet, "If the servant makes ablution (*wuḍū'*) or bathes (*ghusl*) while performing the supererogatory acts in their proper place, God creates an angel for every drop of water of his ablution or bath, glorifying Him, sanctifying Him, exalting Him, magnifying Him and sending blessings on Muḥammad and his pure progeny. The reward of all that belongs to this servant. Then, God consecrates his ablution and bath and seals him with the seal of honor."[4]

It is also related by the Master of Trustees (Imam ʿAlī),"Whoever makes ablution as I do and recites as I recite, God creates an angel that sanctifies Him and magnifies Him for every drop of water and records his reward till the Day of Resurrection."[5]

These lofty narrations and pure utterances illustrate the correspondence between man and the angels. For this reason, the people of God devote themselves to securing that which is harmonious with divine reward, the spirit's perfection and ascent and renounce that which contravenes it.

It is related from Abū Abdallāh (al-Ṣādiq), "If one makes ablution and does not mention (God's) name, Satan partakes in it. If one eats, drinks or wears

3 *Jāmiʿ al-saʿādāt*, 1:46.

4 *Wasāʾil al-shīʿa*, 1:398.

5 *Wasāʾil al-shīʿa*, 1:401.

أو شرب أو لبس وكل شي صنعه ينبغي له أن يسمي عليه ، فإن لم يفعل كان للشيطان فيه شرك ».[٦]

وهذا الكلام لا ينحصر في الوضوء ، بل كل أفعال الخير لها مناسبة ومسانخة مع الملائكة كما انه كل أفعال الشر لها مناسبة ومسانخة مع إبليس والشياطين من الجن والأنس.

قال صادق أهل البيت عليه السلام[٧] : « والذي نفسي بيده ، لملائكة الله في السماوات أكثر من عدد التراب في الأرض ، وما في السماء موضع قدم إلا وفيها ملك يُسبحه ويقدسه ، ولا في الأرض شجر ، ولا مَدَر ، إلا وفيها مَلك موكل بها » وقال سيد الأوصياء عليه السلام في ذم أتباع الشيطان[٨] :

« اتخذوا الشيطان لأمرهم ملاكاً ، واتخذهم له أشراكاً ، فباضَ وفرّخ في صدورهم ، ودَبّ ودَرَج في جحورهم ، فنظر بأعينهم ، ونطق بالسنتهم ، فركب بهم الزَّلل ، وزين لهم الخطل ، فعل من قد شركه الشيطان في سلطانه ، ونطق بالباطل على لسانه ».

وعلى ذلك فالمتفرس إذا رأى نفسه أو السالك في الحال التي هو عليها بحاجة إلى أمر ما من تقديس أو تسبيح أو تكبير أو تهليل أو غيرها من الاذكار أمر نفسه والمريد أوجب عليهما ذلك الأمر الذي يتمم دائرة تكامل النفس ورقيها كإدامة الوضوء مثلًا مع الشرائط المعروفة والاستحبابات المذكورة فتحصل المناسبة بينه وفعل الخير وبالتالي بينه وبين الملك الموكل به يؤيده ويسدده بأذن الله تعالى ، عن رسول الله صلى الله عليه وآله « أتاني جبرئيل عليه السلام فقال : يا محمد ، كيف ننزل عليكم وأنتم لا تستاكون ولا تستنجون بالماء ولا تغسلون براجمكم ».[٩]

وعن الإمام الباقر عليه السلام : قال جبرئيل عليه السلام : « يا رسول الله ، إنا لا ندخل بيتاً فيه صورة إنسان ، ولا بيتاً يُبال فيه ، ولا بيتاً فيه كلب ».[١٠]

وهكذا فالمناسبة لا تحصل بين الملك وبيت الإنسان الحقيقي الذي هو وجوده وبيته الصوري الذي يسكن فيه وكذا يفعل المتفرس على العكس إذا رأى ضعف

---

٦ وسائل الشيعة / ج١ / ص٤٢٦ / ١١١٥ / باب تأكيد استحباب التسمية والدعاء بالمأثور.

٧ البحار / ٥٩ / ١٧٦ / ٧.

٨ نهج البلاغة / الخطبة ٧.

٩ النهاية : ١/ ١١٣.

١٠ الكافي / ٣ / ٣٩٣ / ٢٦ .

something, or performs any other action, he must mention (God's) name. If he does not then Satan partakes in it."[6]

This does not strictly pertain to ablution, but every good deed has a correspondence and relationship with the angels, just as every evil deed has a correspondence and relationship with Iblīs and the satans among the men and Jinn.

Imām al-Ṣādiq said, "By Him, who holds my life in His hands, the angels of God in the heavens are more numerous than the sands on the earth. There is not a place to tread in the heavens but that an angel glorifies and sanctifies Him, nor is there a tree or clod of earth but that an angel is its guardian."[7] In disparaging the followers of Satan, Imām 'Alī says, "They have made Satan the basis for their affairs and he has taken them as his cohorts. He has laid eggs and hatched them in their breasts. He creeps and crawls in their laps, he sees through their eyes and speaks through their tongues. He compels them to err and commit folly; Satan has indeed made of them minions in his domain, uttering falsehoods through their tongues.[8]

Thus, if a wayfarer or a person of spiritual insight is in need of sanctifying, glorifying, magnifying, extolling or another form of litany in given state, he prompts himself to do so. The aspirant (*murīd*) is in greater need of assistance in completing the circle of the soul's perfection and ascent, such as being in a constant state of ablution with its specific conditions and performing supererogatory acts. As a result, a correspondence forms between him and the good deed, then between the angel commissioned to him who further strengthens and supports him by God's permission.

The Prophet mentions, "Gabriel came to me and said, 'O Muḥammad, how can we descend to your people when none of you brush your teeth, nor wash your privates with water, nor wash the dirt from your knuckles?"[9]

It is related from Imām al-Bāqir that Gabriel said, "O Prophet of God, we do not enter a house in which there is a picture of a human, one urinates or there is a dog."[10]

In this case, a correspondence cannot be established between the angel and either the true abode of man, his being, or his formal house, his residence. However, if one imbued with spiritual insight feels vulnerable to Satan's intrusion concerning any matter, utterance, or thought, he compels himself

6 *Wasā'il al-shī'a*, 1:426.

7 *Biḥār al-anwār*, 59:176.

8 *Nahj al-balāgha*, sermon 7.

9 *Al-Nihāya*, 1:113.

10 *Al-Kāfi*, 3:393, no. 26.

النفس من جهة مشاركة الشيطان مثلًا في كل فعل وقول وفكر أمر أو أوجب ذكر التسمية في الليل والنهار أو في أوقات معلومه أو أذكار أخرى من تهليل وتسبيح ، قال الإمام الصادق عليه السلام : « قال إبليس : خمسة أشياء ليس لي فيهن حيلة وسائر الناس في قبضتي وذكر منها ، مَن كَثُر تسبيحه في ليله ونهاره ».

وأيضاً للإنسان مناسبة مع الملك من حيث فعل العبودية والقيام لله تعالى فالناس عبيد اختيار واضطرار ، والملائكة عبيد اضطرار ، والمناسبة من حيث الاضطرار ، فالملائكة عليهم السلام ، منهم سجود لا يركعون ، ومنهم ركوع لا ينتصبون ، وصافون لا يتزايلون ، ومسبحون لا يسأمون ، لا يغشاهم نوم العيون ولا سهر العقول ، ولا فترة الأبدان ، ولا غفلة النسيان ، فليس لهم من الأمر إلا الاضطرار دون الاختيار.[١١]

وأما الاضطرار عند الإنسان ، فانه لما كانت الصفات الحميدة كأفراد العائلة الواحدة والصفات الذميمة مثلها ، فمن أدرك فرداً منهما أدت به إلى الأخرى إلا مع عارض ومانع يمنعه ولا يزال العبد يدخل في أبواب الخير ويثاب رغم انفه حتى يقبضه الله تعالى عليه.

وقد ورد عن الرسول الأكرم صلى الله عليه وآله : « إذا أراد الله بعبد خيراً عَسَله ، قيل : وما عَسَلَه ؟ قال : يفتح له عملاً صالحاً قبل مَوتِهِ ثم يقبضه عليه »[١٢]. وعنه صلى الله عليه وآله : « من يزرع خيراً يوشك أن يحصد خيراً »[١٣]. وعن الإمام علي عليه السلام : « غارس شجرة الخير يجتنيها أحلى ثمرة »[١٤]. وعنه عليه السلام : « فعل الخير ذخيرةٌ باقية وثمرة زاكية »[١٥].

وعلى أساس تلك المناسبة بين عبيد الاختيار والاضطرار وعبيد الاضطرار من حيثية الاضطرار تجد أن العارفين بالله يحيون الليل ويقيمون النهار أو أقل من ذلك أو أكثر منهم سجود لا يركعون ، ومنهم ركوع لا ينتصبون وصافون لا يتزايلون ،

---

١١ نهج البلاغة / الخطبة ١.
١٢ كنز العمال : ٣٠٧٦١.
١٣ البحار / ٧٧ / ٧٦ / ٣.
١٤ غرر الحكم / ٦٤٤٢.
١٥ غرر الحكم /٦٥٤٥.

to repeat God's name day and night, or at special times, or other invocations glorifying and extolling Him. Imām al-Ṣādiq states, "Iblīs said, 'There are five things for which I have no deception, otherwise humanity is in my grasp. One among them is the person who frequently glorifies God throughout his day and night.'"

There is also a correspondence between man and the angels with respect to servitude and the upholding of God's commandments. Human beings are servants—willingly or unwillingly—but the angels are servants by necessity. The correspondence that exists is in this latter aspect of necessity. Imām 'Alī says, "There are angels who are in prostration and never rise to bow, those who are bowing and never stand, those who are standing and never cease, and those who are glorifying and never tire. They are not overcome by sleepiness of the eyes, slip of wit, fatigue of the body nor the neglect of forgetfulness. They have no affair except that it is prescribed and compulsory."[11]

Praiseworthy or blameworthy attributes that are like members of a single family give rise to compulsion in the human being. One who apprehends even a single attribute is lead to the others, unless there is an impediment hindering him. The servant continues entering doors of virtue and is rewarded in spite of himself until God takes his life in the midst of it. It is related from the noble Messenger, "If God wishes his servant success he sweetens him (with honey)." It was asked, "What is to be 'sweetened with honey'?" He replied, "He inspires him to perform a good deed before his death, then He takes his life in the midst of it."[12] He also said, "Whoever plants goodness, all but reaps goodness."[13] Imām 'Alī says, "He who plants a tree of goodness picks the sweetest fruit."[14] He also said, "A good deed is a lasting treasure and a wholesome profit."[15]

On the basis of the correspondence between the servants who are both compelled and have freewill and those who are simply compelled, the gnostics of God keep vigil at night and discharge their obligations by day. Many of them are in a state of prostration and do not bow, or bow and do not stand, or stand and never cease. There are those who glorify Him and never grow weary; neither sleepiness of the eyes, nor vigilance of the intellect, nor fatigue of the body nor the neglect of forgetfulness overcomes them. This excludes

---

11 *Nahj al-Balāgha*, sermon 1.
12 *Kanz al-'ummāl*, no. 30761.
13 *Biḥār al-anwār*, 77/76, no. 3.
14 *Ghurar al-ḥikam*, no. 7442.
15 *Ghurar al-ḥikam*, no. 6545.

ومسبحون لا يسأمون لا يغشاهم نوم العيون ولا سهر العقول ، ولا فترة الأبدان ، ولا غفلة النسيان ، إلا بما أوجب الله تعالى عليهم تشريعاً وتكويناً[١٦] وهذه الأعمال والرياضات[١٧] لا تدرك إلا بنور الفراسة أو ما يضاهيها يُرشد إليها الشيخ ويقول بها المؤمن المتفرس : ﴿وَاللَّهُ يَقُولُ الْحَقَّ وَهُوَ يَهْدِي السَّبِيلَ﴾.

فاعلم انه ما من ذرة من ذرات العالم إلا وقد وكل بها ملك أو ملائكة ، وما من قطرة إلا ومعها ملك ينزل بها من السحاب ويدعها في المكان الذي قدر الله تعالى ، كما هو صريح روايات أهل بيت العصمة سلام الله عليهم فهذا حال الذرات والقطرات فما ظنك بالأفلاك والكواكب والهواء والغيوم والرياح والأمطار والجبال والقفار والبحار والعيون والأنهار والمعادن والنبات والحيوان وما هو أعلى من ذلك .

والإنسان الجامع شتات العالم ومختصر تفصيله وكَلَ الله تعالى به ملائكة تدبر مملكته وتحفظها في الليل والنهار كما قال تعالى في كتابه العزيز:

﴿وَهُوَ الْقَاهِرُ فَوْقَ عِبَادِهِ وَيُرْسِلُ عَلَيْكُم حَفَظَةً حَتَّىَ إِذَا جَاء أَحَدَكُمُ الْمَوْتُ تَوَفَّتْهُ رُسُلُنَا وَهُمْ لاَ يُفَرِّطُونَ﴾ [الأنعام:٦١]. وعن الإمام الباقر عليه السلام في قوله تعالى : « له معقباتٌ من بين يديه ومن خلفه يحفظونه من أمر الله ».[١٨]

بأمر الله من أن يقع في ركِيٍّ ، أو يقع عليه حائط أو يصيبه شي ; حتى إذا جاء القدر خَلّوا بينه وبينه يدفعونه إلى المقادير ، وهما ملكان يحفظانه بالليل وملكان يحفظانه بالنهار يتعاقبان. وفي تفسير القمي[١٩] : « وإن عليكم لحافظين ».

قال : الملكان الموكلان بالإنسان ، « كراماً كاتبين » يكتبون الحسنات والسيئات.

فبالملائكة التدبير وصلاح العالم بتقدير العزيز الحكيم فمنهم من وكل بإدارة الأفلاك وحركات الكواكب ، وما تحت فلك القمر من العناصر والمولدات (المعادن والنبات والحيوان) وهو الروح الأمين عليه السلام ومنهم نافخ الأرواح في الأجساد وهو إسرافيل عليه السلام ، ومنهم أمير الوحي وهو جبرئيل عليه السلام ، ومنهم من وكل بالأرزاق وهو ميكائيل عليه السلام ،

---

١٦ تشريعاً أي الالتزام بأوامر ونواهيه الحق تعالى وما إليها. تكويناً : أي التعامل مع الأمور كالطعام والشراب وغيرها لحاجة لا لشهوة.

١٧ الرياضة : رضت الدابة ذللتها ، ورياضة النفس مأخوذة من رياضة البهيمة وهي منعها عن الإقدام على حركات غير صالحة لصاحبها.

١٨ البحار / ٥٩ / ١٧٩ / ١٦.

١٩ تفسير القمي / ٢ / ٤٠٩.

the natural (*takwīn*) and divine law (*tashrīʿ*) that God has ordained.[16] These practices and disciplines cannot be fathomed except through clairvoyance (*firāsa*) or by emulating the example of a spiritual master (*shaykh*); yet the clairvoyant (*mutafarris*) believer says, "God speaks the truth and He guides the way" (33:4).[17]

Know that there is no particle in the universe but that an angel is commissioned to it, nor is there a drop of water but an angel brings it down from the clouds and places it where God has determined, as explicitly stated by the infallible progeny of the Prophet. If such is the case with particles and drops of water, then surely it is true of planets, stars, air, clouds, winds, rains, mountains, deserts, oceans, springs, rivers, minerals, plants, animals and all that is higher.

The human being is the collectivity of disparate things in the universe and the summary of its individuation, for whom God has appointed angels. They administer His kingdom and protect it day and night, as He mentions in the following verse, "He is the Supreme, above His servants, and He sends sentinels for you until the time death draws near; Our messengers take his life and they are not remiss" (6:61). It is related from Imām al-Bāqir that the verse, "'For each person there is a succession of angels preceding him and in his wake. They guard him by the command of God' (13:11).[18]

It means that should the will of God cause one to fall down a well, or be stricken by a collapsing wall or fall victim to some calamity, the angels safeguard him until fate takes its course; there are two angels successively protecting him through the night and two protecting him during the day." In Tafsīr Qummī, the verse, "They are guarding over you" (82:10) refers to the two angels appointed for man, the "Noble Scribes" (82:11), who record good and evil deeds.[19]

The angels regulate and maintain the structure of the world by the decree of the Almighty and Wise. Among the angels, the Trusted Spirit (*al-rūḥ al-amīn*) is appointed to orchestrate heavenly bodies, stars and the sublunary realm, such as the elements and compositions (the minerals, plants and animals). Isrāfīl infuses spirits into bodies. Gabriel is entrusted with revelation. Mīkāʾīl is appointed to issue provision. ʿIzrāʾīl separates souls from their bodies. The

---

16 *Tashrīʿ* refers to the commandments and prohibitions of God. *Takwīn* refers to affairs related food, drink and other bodily needs.

17 Discipline means training an animal and "discipline of the self" originates from this meaning. It is to prohibit movements that are harmful to its performer.

18 *Biḥār al-anwār*, 59:179.

19 *Tafsīr al-Qummī*, 2:409.

ومنهم مفرق الأرواح من الأجساد وهو عزرائيل عليه السلام ، ومنهم الحفظة وهم الكرام الكاتبون عليه السلام ، ومنهم المعقبات عليه السلام ، وهم الذين ينزلون بالبركات ويصعدون بأرواح بني آدم ، ومنهم منكر ونكير عليه السلام يسألان في القبر ، ومنهم السياحون عليه السلام يحبون مجالس الذكر ويشهدون لهم ، ومنهم هاروت وماروت عليه السلام يعلمان السحر ليدفع به ، ومنهم ملائكة التسخير عليه السلام المسخرون لنا بالعروج ليلاً ونهاراً من حضرة الحق إلينا ومن حضرتنا إلى الحق ، ومنهم ملائكة الاستغفار المستغفرين لمن في الأرض ، والمستغفرين للمؤمنين خاصة.

وعن سيد الأوصياء عليه السلام في خلق الملائكة قال[٢٠] : « ومنهم أمناء على وحيه ، وألسنة إلى رسله ، ومختلفون بقضائه وأمره ، ومنهم الحفظة لعباده ، والسَّدَنَة لأبواب جنانه ، ومنهم الثابتةُ في الأرضين السفلى أقدامهم ، والمارقة من السماء العليا أعناقهم ، والخارجة من الأقطار أركانهم ، والمناسبة لقوائم العرش أكتافهم ، نَاكسَةُ دونه أبصارهم ، متلفِّعون تحته بأجنحتهم ، مضروبة بينهم وبين من دونهم حجب العزة ، وأستار القدرة ، لا يتوهمون ربهم بالتصوير ، ولا يجرون عليه صفات المصنوعين ، ولا يحدونه بالأماكن ، ولا يشيرون إليه بالنظائر ».

وعن رسول الله صلى الله عليه وآله[٢١] : « خلق الله الملائكة من نور وأن منهم لملائكة أصغر من الذباب » فإذا أهتم السالك بأمر النفس وتهذيبها ، وذكرها بالله وأسمائه وآياته بعد نسيانها أو خشية نسيانها تنزلت عليه الملائكة وأيدته ، وقضت حاجته وخدمته وثبتته على فعل الخير وجهاد النفس. قال تعالى: ﴿الْحَمْدُ لِلَّهِ فَاطِرِ السَّمَاوَاتِ وَالْأَرْضِ جَاعِلِ الْمَلَائِكَةِ رُسُلاً﴾ [الفاطر:١] وقال تعالى : ﴿إِذْ يُوحِي رَبُّكَ إِلَى الْمَلَائِكَةِ أَنِّي مَعَكُمْ فَثَبِّتُوا الَّذِينَ ءَامَنُوا﴾ [الأنفال:١٢]. وهكذا فالمتفرس والشيخ المرشد إذا نظر في نفس السالك والمريد بحسب الحال التي يقتضيها حاجةً إلى التأييد والتسديد أرشده إلى جملة من الأعمال والاذكار فيتجلى له الملك في النوم واليقظة يقوي عزيمته ويرفع همته ويبشره ويقضي حاجته ، وما يتنزل عليه إلا بحكم المناسبة.

---

٢٠ نهج البلاغة / ص٤١.

٢١ كنز العمال / ح١٥١٧٤.

guardians are the Noble Scribes (*al-kirām al-kātibīn*) and the Successors (*al-mu'aqibāt*) are those who descend with blessings and ascend with human spirits. Munkar and Nakīr interrogate in the grave, the Roamers (*al-sayyāḥūn*) are those who love gatherings of remembrance, bearing witness to them. Hārūt and Mārūt (Gog and Magog) know magic so that they may ward it off. There are angels of service acting as conduits from the divine presence to man and ascending with man's deeds, day and night. There are angels of forgiveness, pardoning those on earth and in particular, the believers.

It is related that Imām 'Alī said about the creation of the angels, "Among them are trustees of His revelation, heralds for His messengers, bearers of his decree and command, protectors of His creatures and sentinels of the gates to His gardens. Among them are those whose feet are firmly planted in the lowest world but whose necks extend into the highest heaven, limbs extending from all sides, shoulders proportioned to the pillars of the Throne, eyes cast down before it, enwrapped in their wings beneath it. There is a barrier between them and all others, veils of glory and curtains of might. They do not envision their Lord through representation of form, nor ascribe to Him attributes of createdness; they do not limit Him to place nor allude to Him through similitudes."[20]

The Prophet states, "God created the angels from light and some are smaller than flies."[21] When the wayfarer realizes the gravity of his soul's edification, he remembers God, His names and His signs, after its neglect or the fear of neglect, then the angels descend and assist him, fulfill his needs, serve him and strengthen him to perform good deeds in order that he may combat his soul.

The Almighty says, "All praise belongs to God, the Originator of the heavens and the earth, Maker of the angels as His messengers" (35:1), and "Then your Lord revealed to the angels, 'I am indeed with you; so fortify the believers'" (8:12).

Hence, when the clairvoyant (*mutafarris*) and guiding *shaykh* looks into the soul of the wayfarer or the aspirant, he directs him to a set of acts or litanies commensurate with the support or assistance he needs. Then an angel reveals himself either during his sleep or wakefulness and strengthens his resolve, raises his determination, encourages him and fulfills his needs. However, this only occurs through a certain correspondence.

---

20 *Nahj al-Balāgha*, sermon 1.

21 *Kanz al-'ummāl*, no. 15174.

قال تعالى : ﴿إِنَّ الَّذِينَ قَالُوا رَبُّنَا اللَّهُ ثُمَّ اسْتَقَامُوا تَتَنَزَّلُ عَلَيْهِمُ الْمَلَائِكَةُ﴾ [فصلت: ٣٠]. لذلك ورد كثير على لسان أهل الله تعالى انهم يسألون الحق تعالى تسخير خادم الاسم الشريف ، فانه لكل آية واسم وخير سَدَنه من الملائكة.

قال البوني (رحمه الله) في ذكر الاسم القدوس : وأما الذكر القائم به تقول : « البسملة ، الهي قدسني من شبهات الأغيار ، وأشرح صدري بنور الأنوار ، وأكشف لي عن عالم الملك والملكوت لأحظى بالسر الأقدس النفيس الأنفس ، واكشف عن قلبي حجاب الغفلة وقربني إليك زلفى يا سبوح يا قدوس ، ومدني برقيقة من رقائق اسمك القدوس لأقدس بها وجودي بتقديس الأبرار الكاملين الأخيار من الأنبياء والصالحين ، وسخر لي خادم هذا الاسم لأتحلى بالتحقيق والتمكين ، يا مالك يوم الدين ، أجب أيها السيد (لقائيل) وأعوانك بحق اسمك القدوس ».[٢٢]

---

٢٢ شمس المعارف الكبرى / الشيخ احمد بن علي البوني (رحمه الله) / ص٤٥٧.

God says, "Indeed those who say, 'Our Lord is God!' and then remain steadfast, the angels descend upon them ..." (41:30). For this reason, many a petition has been made from the divine sages asking God to grant access to the keeper of a noble name because for every sign, name and bounty there are gatekeepers of angels.

Būnī writes that the invocation related to the name, the Sanctified (*al-Quddūs*) is the following: In the name of God, the Beneficent, the Merciful, O God, sanctify me from the obscurities of otherness, expand my breast through the light of lights, unveil for me the worlds of Kingdom (*mulk*) and Dominion (*malakūt*) so that I may relish the hallowed secret of the precious souls, remove from my heart the veil of negligence and bring me close to Thee. O Glorified, O Sanctified! Extend to me a shred of subtlety from Your name, the Sanctified, so that I may hallow my existence through it like the sanctification of the virtuous, the perfect and the chosen from your Prophets and the righteous. Enable me to serve this name so that I may become infused with it through its realization and investiture. O Possessor of the Day of Judgment! Respond, O Master to (me) and your assistants, in the name of Your name, the Sanctified (*al-Quddūs*).[22]

22 Būnī, *Shams al-maʿārif al-kubrā*, 457.

الباب الثاني

التناسب بين الإنسان والفلك

اعلم أنه يكفينا لمعرفة المناسبة بين الإنسان والفلك كون الإنسان مختصر العالم وزبدته ، ومع ذلك نذكر ما جاء على لسان إخوان الصفاء[1] وخلان الوفاء في رسائلهم عند بيان تركيب جسد الإنسان ، وأن فيه أمثلة وإشارات إلى تركيب الأفلاك وأبراجها والسماوات وأطبقاها ، وجعل سريان قوى النفس في مفاصل جسده ، واختلاف أعضائه كسريان قوى الملائكة وقبائل الجن والإنس والشياطين في أطباق السماوات والأرض ، في أعلى عليين إلى أسفل السافلين.

وأما مماثلة تركيب جسد الإنسان بتركيب الأفلاك :[2]

---

١ رسائل إخوان الصفاء وخلان الوفاء / ج٢ / ص٤٦٣.

٢ الأفلاك : ذهب الجمهور من الحكماء القدماء إلى أن الأرض وما حولها من العنصريات محاطة بجسم عظيم فلكي دائم الحركة لا ينفك عن صفاته كما قال الشيخ الرئيس : إن الفلك مطلقاً جسم كروي بسيط شفاف فيه مبدأ الميل المستدير فقط ، فلا يقبل خرقاً ولا لتئاما ولا كوناً ولا فساداً ولا زوال عن حيزه أبداً ولا تضاد فيه ولا مضاد له ولا فيه سكون عن حركته ولا تغيير في صفته ، وكذلك الأجرام المركوزة فيه كالشمس والقمر ، والنجوم أجسام كروية من جنس جوهر الفلك الذي لا يتكون ولا يفسد... الخ. (الفصل الرابع من الفن الثاني من طبيعيات كتاب الشفاء / ابن سينا).

وأما الهيئة المتأخرة ، فقد انكر أصحابها وجود الجسم الفلكي رأساً ولم يؤمنوا بحقيقته فضلاً عن الإيمان بصفاته ، فهم يطلقون اسم الفلك على المدارات الفرضية للأجرام السماوية ، إذ كل جرم سماوي فهو متحرك عندهم في فراغ الفضاء في مدار معين يباين مدار الجرم المماثل له على نسب متناسقة نظمها ناموس الجاذبية بقدرة إلهية ،كما قال أمير المؤمنين عليه السلام : « ووشج بينها وبين أزواجها ».

فالوشيج اشتباك القرابة والأزواج استعارة بمعنى الأمثال أي أوجد الله سبحانه روابط متناسبة بين الأجرام وبين أمثالها حفظاً لنظامها الصالح.

وبالجملة فان الجرم السماوي متحرك لديهم على نظام دوري رجعي مستمر ، وكل جرم متحرك

CHAPTER 2

The Correspondence Between Man and the Celestial Spheres

Know, it suffices that man is the epitome and quintessence of the universe to recognize his correspondence with the celestial spheres. Nevertheless, we will mention what the Brethren of Purity (*Ikhwān al-ṣafā' wa khillān al-wafā'*)[1] have said in their Epistles regarding the composition of the body of man, for which there are illustrations and allusions pointing to the composition of the celestial spheres, constellations, the heavens and its strata insofar as the powers of the soul permeate through the articulations of the body and its various members like the flowing of angelic hosts and tribes of Jinn, men and satans in the heavenly and earthly strata—from the highest of the high to the lowest of the low.

The composition of the human body resembles the composition of the celestial spheres:[2]

---

1 *Rasā'il Ikhwān al-ṣafā' wa khillān al-wafā'*, 2:463.

2 The celestial spheres: Some of the philosophers of antiquity maintained that the earth and its surroundings, including the elements, are enveloped by a great celestial body that is in constant motion and cannot be divested of its attributes. Ibn Sīnā writes, "The celestial sphere is an absolute spherical body that is simple, transparant and constantly in orbit. It cannot be pierced nor yield to contact, generation or corruption, nor relinquish its domain. There is neither incompatibility in it, nor a contrary for it, nor stillness in its movement, nor any change in its attributes. Similarly, the firm celestial bodies in them, such as the Sun, Moon, stars and spherical bodies are of the substance of the celestial sphere which are not generated or corrupted." Ibn Sīnā, *Ṭabī'iyāt kitāb al-shifā'* (The Book of Healing: The Natural World, the Second Science), ch. 4.

The later astronomers rejected the very existence of the great celestial body, let alone its attributes. They stated that the term "celestial sphere" refers to the movement of the heavenly bodies since each of those bodies are moving in space in a particular orbit that differs from the orbit of their like in a well-measured way, according to the law of gravity, as Imām 'Alī states, "He closely connected (*washaja*) them and their companions (*azwāj*)." *Washīj* means involvement of similars and *azwāj* means likes. So, God created corresponding relationships between celestial bodies and their kind to maintain its sound order.

According to them, celestial bodies are constantly revolving. Each body is continuously in motion and it is only the imagination that considers its course and orbit to

فلما كانت الأفلاك تسع طبقات مركبة بعضها في جوف بعض[٣] ، كذلك

على نهج مستمر ، فان الوهم يفرض لمسيره مجرى على حسب سيره ، وذلك المجرى والمدار يسميه المتأخرون (فلكاً) ولا يختص ذلك عندهم بالنيرين والنجوم بل يثبت للأرض والسحب والشهب والرجوم.

وقد ورد عن أهل البيت (عليهم السلام) ففي حديث أبي بصير المروي في آخر فصل من كتاب الإرشاد للشيخ المفيد انه قال للإمام الصادق عليه السلام : إن الناس يقولون إذ تغير الفلك فسد ؟ فقال : ذلك قول الزنادقة وأما المسلمون ، فليس لهم إلى ذلك سبيل. والشرع الإسلامي لم يخالف الحكماء في أصل الفلك واسمه ، وإنما خالفهم في حقيقته ولوازمه كما قال تعالى ﴿وَكُلٌّ فِي فَلَكٍ يَسْبَحُونَ﴾ [يس:٤٠] أي أن الأجرام السماوية تسبح وتجري في الفلك لا ثابتة في ثخن الأفلاك لا تنتقل من مواضعها قط ، وقد ذكر ذلك فخر الدين الرازي في تفسيره وقال : إن الذي يدل عليه ظاهر القرآن هو أن تكون الأفلاك واقفة والكواكب تكون جارية فيها كما تسبح السمكة في الماء. (الهيئة والإسلام / السيد هبة الدين الشهرستاني / ص٤٩ و٥٣).

٣ الأفلاك التسعة هي : فلك القمر ، وفلك عطارد ، وفلك الزهرة ، وفلك الشمس (النير الأعظم) ، وفلك المريخ ، وفلك المشتري ، وفلك زحل ، وفلك البروج (فلك الثوابت) ، وفلك الأفلاك (الأطلس) وأما ما دون فلك القمر فتسمى كرة النار ، وكرة الهواء ، وكرة الماء ، وكرة الأرض ، فالأفلاك تسعة والكرات أربعة فتكون عشر كرة متلاصقة كما في الهيئة القديمة.

قال الشيخ بهاء الدين محمد العاملي في كتاب تشريح الأفلاك ص ٦ : « العالم الجسماني كرة منضدة من ثلاث عشرة كرة متلاصقة ، أعلاها الأطلس وهو كاسمه غير مكوكب ، ثم فلك الثواب ، وكلها مركوزة في ثخنه بحيث يماس سطح اعظمها سطحية وهذان هما العرش والكرسي بلسان الشرع ثم السماوات السبع للسيارات السبع المشهورة ، كل في فلك يسبحون ، وترتيبها عن السّلف مأثور والكلام فيه مشهور ».

العالم : اسم لما يعلم به الشيء ، وفي عرف الحكماء اسم لكل وجود وينقسم إلى روحاني وجسماني ، فالجسماني ما حواه السطح الظاهر من الفلك الأعلى.

منضدة : مرتبة.

الأطلس : فلك الأفلاك ، فهو اطلس غير منقوش وخالي من الكواكب غير مكوكب : لا يحيط به شيئ.

فلك الثوابت : أي الفلك المشتمل على الكواكب الثابتة.

مركوزة في ثخنة : أي ثابتة في غلظه. سطحية : أي السطح المقعر والمحدب.

هما العرش والكرسي : أي الفلك الأطلس ، وفلك الثوابت.

السماوات السبع للسيارات السبع المشهورة ، فلك القمر ، وفلك عطارد ، وفلك الزهرة ، وفلك الشمس ، وفلك المريخ ، وفلك المشتري ، وفلك زحل. كما قال (تحفة الأحباب شرح فارسي بر تشريح الأفلاك / سيد محمد جواد تهراني).

Just as the celestial spheres are composed of nine strata each in the interior of the other,[3] the human body is composed of nine substances [organs], each

---

be a celestial sphere. It is not specific to the two luminaries or the stars but it exists for the earth, clouds and meteorites.

It has been related by Abū Baṣīr in the last section of *Kitāb al-irshād* of Shaykh al-Mufīd that Imām al-Ṣādiq states, "People claim that if the celestial sphere changes, it will fall apart. This is the claim of the unbelievers and they have no proof for it. The Muslims, however, do not hold that particular view and Islamic doctrine does not contradict the philosophers with respect to the principles of astronomy and its nomenclature. It opposes them only in describing its reality along with its concomitants as it says in the Qur'ān, 'Each is floating in a celestial body'"(36:40), that is, the bodies float and drift in the celestial sphere. They are not stationary in its medium and do not deviate from their trajectory.

Fakhr al-dīn al-Rāzī mentions in his commentary, "What is gleaned from the apparent meaning of the Qur'ān is that the celestial spheres are stationary while the planets are moving in it just as fish swim in the sea." Shahrastānī, *Islamic Astronomy*, 49, 53.

3 The celestial spheres are nine: the spheres of the Moon (*al-qamar*), Mercury (*uṭārid*), Venus (*al-zuhra*), the Sun (*al-shams*), Mars (*al-mirrīkh*), Jupiter (*al-mushtarī*), Saturn (*al-zuḥal*), the constellation (*al-burūj*), the ultimate sphere (*al-aṭlas*). As for the sublunary region, it is called the globe of fire, the globe of wind, the globe of water, the globe of earth. Thus, the celestial spheres are nine and the globes are four so there are ten globes adjacent to one another in the ancient system of astronomy.

Shaykh Bahā al-Dīn 'Āmilī in the book, *Tashrīḥ al-aflāk* (An Elucidation of Astronomy) writes, "The physical world consists of thirteen concentric spheres adjacent to one another, the highest of them is *al-aṭlas* (lit. effaced). As its name suggests, it does not contain any stars. Then there is the sphere of *al-thawāb* (lit. stationary) which is established in its dense stratum and whose ceiling comes in contact with the former. Together they are called the Throne (*al-arsh*) and the Pedestal (*al-kursī*), respectively, in the terminology of Revelation. The seven heavens and the seven planets (*sayyārāt*, lit. travellers) follow, as mentioned in the verse, 'Each is floating in a celestial sphere' (21:33). Their order has been established by the ancients and is considered common knowledge.

"World" (*al-'ālam*) denotes that through which something is known. In the philosophical tradition, it refers to all creation, spiritual and material. The material is that which is enveloped by the outward ceiling of the highest celestial sphere."

munḍada: arranged.

al-Aṭlas, the ultimate sphere, is uninscribed, void of stars and not enveloped by anything.

The stationary sphere (*al-thawāb*) is the one that contains fixed stars, secured in its medium, that is, firm in its dense stratum. Its ceiling is dome-shaped.

The spheres of *al-aṭlas* and *al-thawāb* are the Throne and the Pedestal, respectively. The seven heavens for the seven known planets are the following: the spheres of the Moon, Mercury, Venus, the Sun, Mars, Jupiter Saturn. Sayyid Muḥammad Jawād Tehrānī, *Tuḥfat al-aḥbāb sharḥ farsī bar tashrīḥ al-aflāk*.

وُجد في ترتيب جسد الإنسان تسع جواهر بعضها جوف بعض ، ملتفات عليها مماثلة لها ، وهي العظام ، والمخ ، واللحم ، والعروق ، والدم ، والعصب ، والجلد ، والشعر ، والظفر ، فجعل المخ في جوف العظام مخزوناً لوقت الحاجة إليه ، ولف العصب على مفاصله كيما يمسكها فلا تنفصل ، وحشا خلَلَ ذلك باللحم صيانة لها ، ومد في خلل اللحم العروق والأوردة الضاربة لحفظها وصلاحها ، وكسا الكل بالجلد ستراً لها وجمالاً لها ، وأنبت الشعر والظفر من فضل تلك المادة لمأربها ، فصار مماثلًا لتركيب الأفلاك بالكمية والكيفية جميعاً ، لأنها تسع طبقات ، وهذه تسع جواهر ، وتلك بعضها جوف بعض وهذه مثال ذلك ولما كان الفلك مقسوماً اثني عشر برجاً ، وجد في بنية الجسد اثنا عشر ثقباً مماثلاً له ، وهي العينان ، والأذنان ، والمنخران ، والثديان ، والفم ، والسُرّة ، والسبيلان.

ولما كانت الأبراج ستة منها جنوبية(٤) ، وستة منها شمالية كذلك وجدت ست ثُقب في الجسد في الجانب اليمين ، وستُ في الجانب الشمال مماثلة له بالكمية

---

٤ إن البروج ستة منها شمالية ، وستة جنوبية ، وستة مستقيمة الطلوع ، وستة معوجة الطلوع ، وستة ذكور ، وستة إناث ، وستة نهارية ، وستة ليلية ، وستة فوق الأرض ، وستة تحت الأرض ، وستة تطلع بالنهار ، وستة تطلع بالليل ، وستة صاعدة ، وستة هابطة ، وستة يمنة ، وستة يسرة ، وستة من حيز الشمس ، وستة من حيز القمر.

أما الستة الشمالية ، فهي الحمل ، والثور ، والجوزاء ، والسرطان ، والأسد ، والسنبلة وإذا كانت الشمس في واحد منها يكون الليل أقصر والنهار أطول. وأما الستة الجنوبية : فهي الميزان ، والعقرب ، والقوس ، والجدي ، والدّلوَ ، والحوت وإذا كانت الشمس في واحد منها ، يكون الليل أطول والنهار أقصر. وأما المستقيمة الطلوع : فهي السرطان ، والأسد ، والسنبلة ، والميزان ، والعقرب ، والقوس.

وكل واحد منها يطلع في أكثر من ساعتين. وإذا كانت الشمس في واحد منها ، تكون هابطة من الشمال إلى الجنوب ، ومن الأوج إلى الحضيض ، والليل آخذ من النهار.

وأما المعوجّة الطلوع : فهي الجدي ، والدّلو ، والحوت ، والحمل ، والثور ، والجوزاء ، وكل واحد منها يطلع في أقل من ساعتين. وإذا كانت الشمس في واحد منها ، تكون صاعدة من الجنوب إلى الشمال ، ومن الحضيض إلى الأوج ، والنهار آخذ من الليل.

وأما الستة الذكور النهارية : فهي الحمل ، والجوزاء ، والأسد ، والميزان ، والقوس ، والدّلو.

وأما الستة الإناث الليلية : فهي الثور ، والسرطان ، والسنبلة ، والعقرب ، والجدي والحوت.

وأما الستة التي تطلع بالنهار : فهي من البروج الذي فيه الشمس إلى البرج السابع منها.

والستة التي تطلع بالليل : هي من البرج السابع إلى البرج الذي فيه الشمس.

in the interior of the other, being enwrapped by a substance similar to it. These are the bones, marrow, flesh, veins, blood, nerves, skin, hair and nails. Marrow is in the interior of bones, stored for use in times of need. Nerve fibers sheath articulations connecting bones together so they cannot disjoin. Flesh fills the interstices and protects them. Pulsating veins and arteries extend throughout the fissures in the flesh securing it and ensuring its well-being. It is all clothed by the skin which covers and beautifies it. Hair and nails grow out of the excess of this material as its final end.

Thus, the human being resembles the composition of the celestial spheres in quantity and quality because it also comprises of nine strata. These nine substances are like those strata, each of which subsist in the interior of the other.

Just as the celestial spheres are divided into twelve constellations, the human body also has twelve orifices: two eyes, two ears, two nostrils, two nipples, a mouth, an umbilicus and two nether orifices. Just as there are six southern constellations and six northern,[4] there are six orifices that are on

---

4 There are six northern and six southern constellations, six whose rising is straight and six whose rising is curved, six male and six female, six daytime and six nighttime, six above the earth and six below the earth, six that rise during the day and six that rise during the night, six rising, six setting, six on the right and six on the left, six in the solar mansion and six in the lunar mansion.

The six northern constellations: Aries, Taurus, Gemini, Cancer, Leo and Virgo. If the Sun is among them, then the night is shorter than the day. The six southern constellations are Libra, Scorpio, Sagittarius, Capricorn, Aquarius, and Pisces. If the Sun is in them, then the night is longer than the day.

The six whose rising is straight: Cancer, Leo, Virgo, Libra, Scorpio and Sagittarius. Each one of them rises more than two hours. If the Sun is in them, they set from the north to the south, from the apex to the nadir, and the night is longer than the day.

The six whose rising is curved: Capricorn, Aquarius, Pisces, Aries, Taurus and Gemini. Each one of them rises for less than two hours. If the Sun is in them, they rise from south to the north, from the nadir to the apex, and the day is longer than the night.

The six masculine diurnal ones: Aries, Gemini, Leo, Libra, Sagittarius, and Aquarius.

The six feminine nocturnal ones: Taurus, Cancer, Virgo, Scorpio, Capricorn and Pisces.

The six that rise in the day are from the constellations that contain the Sun until the seventh.

The six that rise at night are from the seventh until that which contains the Sun.

The six in the solar mansion are the constellations from Leo to Capricorn.

The six in the lunar mansion are the constellations from Aquarius to Cancer.

From another perspective these constellations can be divided into four categories: Three which occur in spring, rising from the north with increasing daylight; they are

والكيفية جميعاً. ولما كان في الفلك سبعة كواكب سيارة بها تجري أحكام الفلك والكائنات ، وكذلك وجدت سبع قوى في الجسد فعّاله بها يكون صلاح الجسد.

ولما كانت هذه الكواكب ذوات نفوس وأجسام لها أفعال جسمانية في الأجسام ، وأفعال روحانية في النفوس كذلك وجدت في الجسد سبع قوى جسمانية ، وهي القوة الجاذبة(٥) ، والماسكة(٦) ، والهاضمة(٧) ، والدافعة(٨) ، والغاذية(٩) ، والنامية(١٠) ،

وأما الستة التي من حيز الشمس : فهي من برج الأسد إلى برج الجدي.

والستة التي من حيز القمر : هي من برج الدلو إلى برج السرطان.

ومن وجه آخر هذه البروج تنقسم أربعة أقسام منها : ثلاثة ربيعية صاعدة في الشمال ، زائدة النهار على الليل ، وهي الحمل ، والثور ، والجوزاء وثلاثة صيفية هابطة في الشمال ، آخذة الليل من النهار ، وهي السرطان ، والأسد ، والسنبلة. ومنها ثلاثة خريفية هابطة في الجنوب ، زائدة الليل على النهار ، وهي الميزان والعقرب والقوس ، ومنها ثلاثة شتويّة صاعدة من الجنوب ، آخذة النهار من الليل ، وهي الجدي ، والدلو ، والحوت.

وتنقسم هذه البروج من جهة أخرى أربعة أقسام : ثلاثة منها مثلثات ناريات حارات يابسات شرقيات على طبيعة واحدة وهي : الحمل ، والأسد ، والقوس ، وثلاثة منها مثلثات ترابيات باردات يابسات جنوبيات على طبيعة واحدة وهي : الثور ، والسنبلة ، والجدي ، وثلاثة منها مثلثات هوائيات حارات رَطبات غربيات على طبيعة واحدة وهي : الجوزاء والميزان والدّلو ، ومنها مثلثات مائيات باردات رطبات شماليات على طبيعة واحدة هي السرطان والعقرب والحوت.

وكذلك من جهة أخرى تنقسم هذه البروج ثلاثة أثلاث :

أربعة منها منقلبة الزمان ، وهي : الحمل ، والسرطان ، والميزان ، والجدي ، وأربعة منها ثابتة الزمان ، وهي : الثور ، والأسد ، والعقرب ، والدّلو ، وأربعة منها ذوات الجسدين : وهي الجوزاء ، والسنبلة ، والقوس ، والحوت. (رسائل إخوان الصفا / ج١ / ص١١٧).

٥ القوة الجاذبة : وهي التي تجذب النافع من الغذاء ، وهي موجودة في سائر الأعضاء لان كل عضو يجذب ما يوافقه ، وغذاء كل عضو يخالف غذاء الآخر.

٦ القوة الماسكة : وهي التي تسمك الغذاء ، ريثما تتصرف فيها القوة المغيرة ، وذلك بأن تجعل العضو محتوياً على الغذاء بحيث لا تترك فرجة.

٧ القوة الهاضمة : وهي التي تحيل ما جذبته وأمسكته الماسكة إلى مزاج صالح يجعل بعضها جزءاً من المغتذي وبعضها فضلاً.

٨ القوة الدافعة : وهي التي تدفع الفضل الذي لا يصلح أن يكون غذاء أو زادا على قدر الكفاية.

٩ القوة الغاذية : وهى التي تحيل الغذاء إلى مشابهة المغتذي ليخلف بدل ما يتحلل.

١٠ القوة النامية : وهي التي تزيد في أقطار الجسم على التناسب الطبيعي ليبلغ به تمام النثوى ، والفرق بينها وبين الغاذية أن الغاذية تورد الغذاء تارة مساوياً وتارة زائد وتارة ناقصاً ، وأما النامية

the right side of the body and six that are on the left side corresponding to the constellations in both quantity and quality. Just as there are seven planets which sustain the celestial spheres and the cosmos, there are seven faculties which preserve the well-being of the body.

Just as these seven planets possess both form and soul which undergo physical activity and spiritual activity, respectively, the human body has seven corporeal faculties: attraction,[5] retention,[6] digestion,[7] expulsion,[8] nutrition,[9] growth[10] and imagination,[11] and seven spiritual or sensory faculties: vision, hearing, taste, smell, touch, speech[12] and intellect.

Aries, Taurus and Gemini. Three which occur in summer, setting in the north, the daylight longer than the night; they are Cancer, Leo and Virgo. Three which occur in autumn, setting in the south, with increasing night; they are Libra, Scorpio and Sagittarius. Three which are in the winter, rising from the south, the night longer than the day; they are Capricorn, Aquarius and Pisces.

From another perspective, these constellations can be further divided into four categories: Three of them, Aries, Leo and Sagittarius are characterized by fire, heat, dry and east. Three of them, Taurus, Virgo and Capricorn are characterized by earth, cold, dry and south. Three of them, Gemini, Libra and Aquarius are characterized by air, heat, wet and west. Three of them, Cancer, Scorpio and Pisces are characterized by water, cold, wet and north.

These constellations can also be divided into thirds: Four that are changing in time, Aries, Cancer, Libra and Capricorn; four that are fixed in time, Taurus, Leo, Scorpio and Aquarius; four that have two bodies, Gemini, Virgo, Sagittarius and Pisces. *Rasāʾil Ikhwān al-ṣafāʾ wa khillān al-wafāʾ*, 1:117.

5 The faculty of attraction absorbs nutrients from food and is present in every organ. Each organ absorbs that which is beneficial for it and the nourishment of one organ differs from that of another.

6 The faculty of retention holds food during its processing by another faculty so that it is not expelled immediately and its contents made accessible.

7 The faculty of digestion transforms what the faculty of retention absorbs and retains, into a wholesome mixture, rendering it part nourishment and part waste.

8 The faculty of expulsion is responsible for expelling waste, either because it is not suitable for nourishment or the nourishment is in excess quantity.

9 The faculty of nutrition transforms food into that which resembles nutrients rather than dissolved food.

10 The faculty of growth supplies the regions of the body with nutrition so it inheres organically. The difference between the faculty of nutrition and the faculty of growth is that the former supplies nutrition either in equal, greater or lesser proportion than what is needed, whereas the latter only supplies nutrition from the excess of dissolved food.

11 The faculty of imagination issues form and design, namely, that of shape, roughness and smoothness, etc.

12 The faculties of speech and intellect: The human being is composed of a body and a soul. God conferred upon man speech and intelligence, outwardly and inwardly.

والمصوّرة[١١] وسبع قوى أخرى روحانية ، وهي القوى الحساسة أعني : الباصرة ، والسامعة ، والذائقة ، والشامة ، واللامسة ، والقوة الناطقة[١٢] ، والقوة العاقلة.

والقوة الحساسة مناسبة للخمسة المتحيرة[١٣] ، والقوة الناطقة مناسبة للقمر ، والقوة العاقلة مناسبة للشمس ، وذلك أن لكل واحد من الكواكب الخمسة بيتين في الفلك ، أحدهما في حيز الشمس ، والثاني في حيز القمر ، والنيران[١٤] لكل واحد منهما بيت ، كذلك وجد في بنية الجسد لكل واحد من القوى الحساسة مَجريان ، أحدهما في الجانب الأيمن ، والآخر في الجانب الأيسر ، فالقوة الباصرة مجراها في العينين ، والقوة السامعة مجراها في الأذنين ، والقوة الشامّة مجراها في المنخرين ، والقوة اللامسة مجراها في اليدين ، والقوة الذائقة الشهوانية مجراها في الفم بالجانب الأيمن أشبهُ والفَرْج بالجانب الأيسر أشبهُ.

وأما القوة الناطقة فمجراها الحلقوم إلى اللسان ، والقوة العاقلة فمجراها وسط الدماغ ، ونسبة القوة الناطقة إلى القوة العاقلة كنسبة القمر إلى الشمس وذلك أن القمر يأخذ نوره من الشمس في جريانه من منازل القمر الثمانية والعشرين ، وذلك أن القوة الناطقة من العقل تأخذ معاني ألفاظه بجريانه في الحُلقوم ، فيعبّر عنها بثمانية وعشرين حرفاً. ونسبة ثمانية وعشرين حرفاً للقوة الناطقة كنسبة ثمانية وعشرين منزلاً للقمر.

فلا تورد إلا زائداً من المتحلل.

١١ المصورّة : وهي التي يصدر عنها التخطيط والتشكيل والملاسة والخشونة وأمثال ذلك.

١٢ القوة الناطقة والعاقلة : اعلم أن الإنسان مركب من النفس والبدن ، خصه الله تعالى بالنطق والعقل سراً وعلناً وزين ظاهره بالحواس والحظ الأوفر وباطنه بالقوى وما هو أشرف وأقوى ، وهيأ للنفس الناطقة الدماغ وأسكنه أعلى محل وأوفق رتبة ، وزينه بالفكر والذكر والحفظ ، وسلط عليه الجواهر العقلية لتكون النفس أميره والعقل وزيره والقوى جنوده والحس المشترك مريده والأعضاء خدمه والبدن محل مملكته والحواس يسافرون في جميع الأوقات في عالمهم ويلتقطون الأخبار الموافقة والمخالفة ويعرضونها على الحس المشترك الذي هو واسطة بين النفس والحواس وهو يعرضها على القوة العقلية لتختار ما يوافق وتطرح ما يخالف.

١٣ المتحيرة هي عطارد ، والزهرة ، والمشتري ، والمريخ ، وزحل. ومعنى التحير هي حركتها نحو المغرب وأخرى التوقف ، وأخرى نحو المشرق ، فيعرض لها الاستقامة والإقامة والرجوع.

١٤ الشمس والقمر (النير الأعظم والنير الأصغر).

The sensory faculties correspond each of the five moving planets (*al-mutaḥayyira*),[13] the faculty of speech to the Moon and the intellectual faculty to the Sun. This is because each of the five planets has two houses in the celestial spheres, one in the domain of the Sun and the other in the domain of the Moon. The two luminaries (*nīrān*) each have a house.[14] Similarly, in the edifice of the body, there are two channels for each of the sensory faculties, one on the right side and the other on the left. The channel for vision is the eyes, for hearing the ears, for smelling the nostrils, for touch the hands, the mouth resembles the right side of the carnal appetite the privates resembles the left.

The channel for the faculty of speech extends from the throat to the tongue. The channel for the faculty of intellect is the center of the brain. The relationship between speech and intellect is like that of the Moon to the Sun, since the Moon derives its light from the Sun in its twenty-eight lunar mansions. Similarly, the faculty of speech conveys the meaning of words by its movement in the throat; these are known as the twenty-eight letters of the alphabet. Thus, the twenty-eight letters of the alphabet correspond to the twenty-eight phases of the Moon.

Just as the constellations have two nodes, an apogee and a perigee that are hidden in essence but manifest in activity, and by which there is either felicity or misfortune, there are two hidden aspects in the body that manifest in activity. It is through these aspects that the body's constitution is rectified and the activities of the soul flourish; they are soundness of disposition or its lack thereof. If the body's disposition is harmonious, the limbs will be sound and the activities of the soul will be upright and conducted naturally. If the

---

He beautified him outwardly with an ample provision of senses and inwardly with faculties of greater strength and nobility. He fashioned the brain, a seat for the rational soul, and housed it in the highest place and appropriate station. Then, he adorned it with thought, remembrance and memory and made it subject to intellectual substanstances so that the intellect is sovereign and the soul its minister. The faculties are its soldiers, the *sensus communis* (*al-ḥiss al-mushtarak*) its attendent, the limbs its servants and the body the domain of its kingdom. The senses travel at all times in their respective realms bringing back agreeable or disagreeable news and presenting it to the *sensus communis*, which is the intermediary between the soul and the senses. Then, the soul presents it to the faculty of intellect so that it may accept what is agreeable and discern what is disagreeable .

13 The five moving planets (*al-mutaḥayyira*): Mercury, Venus, Jupiter, Mars and Saturn. *Taḥayyur* means moving towards the west, remaining still, then moving towards the east. Thus, they are subject to directional movement, rest and return.

14 *Nīrān* refers to the Sun and the Moon, the greater and lesser luminaries, respectively.

وكما كان في الفلك عُقدتان وهي الرأس والذنب ، وهما خفيًا الذات ، ظاهر الأفعال ، بهما سعادات الكواكب ونحوساتها ، كذلك وجد في الجسد أمران خفيان للذات ، ظاهر الأفعال ، بهما صلاح بنية الجسد وصحةُ الأفعال للنفس ، وهما صحة المزاج وسوءُ المزاج ، وذلك أنه إذا صح مِزاج أخلاط الجسد ، صحت أعضاؤه ، واستقامت أفعال النفس وجَرت على الأمر الطبيعي وإذا فسد المزاج اضطربت البنية وعِيقت أفعال النفس عن جريها على السَّداد ، وأضرُّ ما يكون نحوسة العُقدتين على النيِّرين ، لأنها أوكَدُ الأسباب في كسوفهما ، وكذلك أضرُّ ما يكون سوءُ المزاج على القوة الناطقة والقوة العاقلة لأنه يعوقهما من أفعالهما أكثر وأشدّ والعينان في الجسد مناسبتان لبيتي المشتري في الفلك ، والأذنان في الجسد مناسبتان لبيتي عُطارد في الفلك ، والمنخران في الجسد والثّديان مناسبتان في الجسد لبيتي الزّهرة ، والسبيلان لبيتي زُحَل والفم لبيت الشمس والسُّرّة لبيت القمر. والسُّرّة كانت باب الغذاء في الرَّحِم قبل الولادة ، والفم باب الغذاء في الدنيا ، والسبيلان مقابلان لهما كتقابل بيتي زحل لبيتي النيِّرين.

وكما أن في الفلك بروجاً فيها حدود ووجوه ودرجات لها أوصاف مختلفة ، كذلك للجسد أعضاء ومفاصل وعروق وأعصاب وعظام يطول شرحها ومناسبتها بحدود الفلك.

وبهذه المناسبة يتبين ارتباط الإنسان بالأفلاك ، أي ارتباط الآية الإجمالية الإنسانية بالآية التفصيلية الفلكية ويتجلى هذا أكثر وضوحاً حين الاذكار والقيام بالرياضات المناسبة المختصة بتلك الآية الأنفسية المناسبة للآية الفلكية ولذا تجد بعض السالكين يتوجهون إليها وهو عين التوجه إلى النفس فإنه لا فرق بين العالم الصغير والعالم الكبير وآياتهما إلا بالإجمال والتفصيل وخصوصاً عند تجلي المناسبة وعلى ذلك ينصح المشايخ مريدهم حين الاذكار والأعمال المخصوصة النظر إلى الكواكب كالشمس والقمر وغيرها أو التطلع إلى مدار الفلك المعين ومثله النظر إلى الشجر والحجر والماء والأرض والسماء وغيرها من آيات الله الآفاقية والأنفسية مما يزيد النفس قوةً وثباتاً واقتراب من الحق والحقيقة.

﴿سَنُرِيهِمْ ءَايَاتِنَا فِي الآفَاقِ وَفِي أَنفُسِهِمْ حَتَّى يَتَبَيَّنَ لَهُمْ أَنَّهُ الْحَقُّ﴾ [فصلت:٥٣] ولا يعني التوجه إلى تلك الآيات هو توجه إلى غير الحق (والعياذ بالله) بل أنها تجلي الحق ومظاهر أسمائه أُمر الإنسان أن يتدبرها ويفكر بها ، كما قال تعالى : ﴿الَّذِينَ

disposition is corrupted and its foundation disturbed, the activities of the soul will be compromised and lead to obstruction.

The most harmful effect on the nodes is that which occurs during the eclipses of the two luminaries. Likewise, the most harmful state of a corrupted disposition is that which affects the faculty of speech and the faculty of intellect because the body's activities are more intensely impeded.

The eyes correspond to the two houses of Jupiter, the ears to the two houses of Mercury, the nostrils and the nipples to the two houses of Venus, the two lower orifices to the two houses of Saturn, the mouth to the house of the Sun, and the umbilicus to the house of the Moon. The umbilicus is the source of nourishment in womb and the mouth is the source of nourishment in the world. The two lower orifices are contraries in the way that the two houses of Saturn oppose the two luminaries.

Just as there are constellations in the celestial spheres with defined limits, aspects and degrees and various qualities, the body possesses limbs, joints, veins, nerves and bones. Further elaboration of their interrelationships with the celestial spheres would be prolix.

Through this correspondence the relationship between the summarized signs in the human being and the detailed signs of the celestial spheres are elucidated. These correspondences become all the more evident during appropriate invocations and spiritual practices that correspond specifically to the signs in the soul and their counterparts in the celestial spheres. For this reason, you will find some wayfarers turning their attention towards them, which is, in reality turning one's attention to the soul since there is no difference between the Great World and the Small World. The signs of each world are either summarized or individuated, particularly during the very manifestation of the correspondence.

Therefore, spiritual preceptors instruct their disciples that during their invocations and special practices they should look at the heavenly bodies such as the Sun, Moon and others, or observe the movement of a particular constellation. Similarly, they instruct them to observe trees, rocks, water, earth and sky from among the divine signs of the horizons and the souls, all of which increase the soul in strength, resolve and nearness to Truth and Reality.

"We shall show them Our signs on the horizons and within themselves until it becomes manifest to them that He is the Truth" (41:53). Turning one's attention to these signs does not mean orienting oneself to other than God—in whom we seek refuge. They are God's theophanies and the manifestations of His names. Man has been commanded to ponder and reflect on these signs, as God says, "Those who remember God, standing, sitting, and reclining, and reflect on the creation of the heavens and the earth, saying, 'Our Lord, You

يَذْكُرُونَ اللهَ قِيَاماً وَقُعُوداً وَعَلَىٰ جُنُوبِهِمْ وَيَتَفَكَّرُونَ فِي خَلْقِ السَّمَاوَاتِ وَالْأَرْضِ رَبَّنَا مَا خَلَقْتَ هَٰذَا بَاطِلاً سُبْحَانَكَ فَقِنَا عَذَابَ النَّارِ﴾ [آل عمران:١٩١].

فان الله سبحانه وتعالى سخر لنا ما في السماوات وما في الأرض جميعاً إن في ذلك لآيات لقوم يتفكرون كما قال تعالى في كتابه العزيز : ﴿وَهُوَ الَّذِي مَدَّ الْأَرْضَ وَجَعَلَ فِيهَا رَوَاسِيَ وَأَنْهَاراً وَمِن كُلِّ الثَّمَرَاتِ جَعَلَ فِيهَا زَوْجَيْنِ اثْنَيْنِ يُغْشِي الَّيْلَ النَّهَارَ إِنَّ فِي ذَالِكَ لَآيَاتٍ لِّقَوْم يَتَفَكَّرُونَ﴾ [الرعد:٣].

وقال تعالى : ﴿كَذَالِكَ نُفَصِّلُ الْأَيَاتِ لِقَوْم يَتَفَكَّرُونَ﴾ [يونس:٢٤].

وقال تعالى : ﴿إِنَّ فِي ذَالِكَ لَآيَةً لِّقَوْم يَتَفَكَّرُونَ﴾ [النحل:١١].

وقال تعالى : ﴿أَفَلاَ يَتَدَبَّرُونَ الْقُرْءَآنَ أَمْ عَلَى قُلُوب أَقْفَالُهَا﴾ [محمد:٢٤].

هذا والكثير من الآيات والرويات التي تحث على هذا الموضوع.

والله يقول الحق وهو يهدي السبيل.

have not created this in vain. Glory be to You! Preserve us from the torment of the Fire'" (3:191).

God, the Almighty, has made everything in the heavens and earth pliant to us—in that there are signs for people who reflect, as He states in the Holy Book, "It is He who spread out the earth and placed therein firm hills and flowing streams, and for every fruit He made pairs. He covered the night with the day. Indeed, in that there is a sign for people who reflect" (13:3).

"Thus, do we expound the signs for people who reflect" (10:24).

"Indeed, in that there is a sign for people who reflect" (16:11).

"Will they then not meditate on the Qur'ān, or are there locks upon the hearts?" (47:24). These and many other verses and narrations emphasize this subject.

God speaks the truth and guides the way.

الفصل الثالث

التناسب بين الإنسان والأجرام

قال إخوان الصفا : أن نسبة جرم الجسد كنسبة جرم الشمس[1] من العالم بأسره ، وذلك أنه لما كان مركز جرمها في وسط الأفلاك ، هكذا جعل الباري تعالى جرم القلب[2] في وسط الجسد ، وكما أن من جرم الشمس ينبث النور والشعاع في جميع العالم بأسره ، ومنها تسري قوى روحانياتها في جميع أجزاء العالم ، وبها حياة العالم وصلاحه ، كذلك ينبث من جرم القلب الحرارة ، وتسير في العروق الضوارب إلى سائر أطراف البدن ، وبها تكون حياة الجسد وصلاحه.

وأيضاً إن نسبة جرم الطّحال[3] من الجسد كنسبة زُحل من العالم ، وذلك أن جرم زُحل تنبث مع شعاعه قوى روحانيته ، وتسري في جميع أجزاء العالم ، وبها

---

١ اختلفوا في أن الشمس هل هي بذاتها مصدر الحرارة مثلما أنها ينبوع النور ، كما تقرر في الفلسفة الجديدة أو هي بالذات منبع النور فقط ، وليست بذات حرارة ولا نارية كما تقرر في الفلسفة القديمة.

وزبدة دعوى القدماء أن الشمس بذاتها ليست بحارة ولا باردة ولا رطبة ولا يابسة لأن هذه الأمور تخص العنصريات والأجرام بأسرها مقدسة عن العوارض العنصرية ومنزهة من آثار العالم السفلي ، فالحرارة المشهودة من الشمس أو اليبوسة أو الإحراق ليست عندهم من نفس الشمس بل النور الشمسي ذو خصوصية في الوجود تقتضي بعد السطوع على سطوح الأرضيات ثم الانعكاس عنها إحداث الحرارة ونحوها من الآثار فنسبة صدور الحرارة إلى المستنير أحق وأولى من نسبته إلى المنير ، وإنما المنير سبب إعدادي يوجب ظهور الحرارة من الأرضيات ، وليست الحرارة ثائرة من نفس النور أو الشمس بل المنير مثار النور فقط ، والمستنير مثار النار.

وأما عند المتأخرين فالشمس كالسراج مصدر النور والنار معاً ، ومرسلهما بالإشعاع إلى كل سيار ، وان كرتها مركبة من طبقات نارية وبخارية لا تبرح عن الثوران والاشتعال ، وشبهوها ببحر عظيم من نار تلاطمت أمواجه وشعله ، وقد يبلغ طول ألسنتها وزبانيتها نحو خمسون ألف فرسخ ، وربما انحرفت عن حافته كانحراف شعلة الشمع إذا لاعبتها الريح. (الهيئة والإسلام / الشهرستاني / ص١٩٣).

٢ القلب : جسم صنوبري الشكل لحمي الجوهر له جوف يحوي الدم ، أعلاه غليظ لأنه منبت الشرايين وأسفله مستدق ليبعد عن عظام الصدر من جهاته ، ولحمه قوي لئلا يتناثر من المؤذيات ، وقد وضع في وسط البدن. (حياة الحيوان / الدميري / ج٢ / ص٢٢٠ / بتصرف).

٣ الطّحال : وهو جسم لحمي طويل الشكل موضوع في الجانب الأيسر يحوي دماً سوداوياً

CHAPTER 3

The Correspondence Between Man and the Celestial Bodies

The Ikhwān al-Ṣafā' write, "The human body is like the Sun[1] in relation to the entire cosmos given that it is at the center of the celestial spheres. For this reason, the Almighty Creator has made the heart[2] the center of the human body. Just as the Sun radiates rays and light, infusing its spiritual powers and giving life and vitality to all parts of the cosmos, heat emanates from the heart pulsating through veins and reaching all parts of the body, giving it life and vitality.

The relationship of the spleen[3] to the human body is like that of Saturn to the cosmos. That is because Saturn emanates its spiritual powers with its

---

1 There are differing opinions as to whether the Sun itself is the source of heat as well as the source of light as posited by modern philosophy, or that the Sun is only the source of light but not heat and light as held by ancient philosophy.

The ancients believed that the Sun is neither hot, cold, wet, nor dry because these attributes are specific to the elements. However, the celestial bodies are impervious to the accidental qualities of the elements and the effects of the lower world. Therefore, the heat, dryness, or fire derived from the Sun does not belong to the Sun directly, rather its rays possess a special existential property inducing heat and other effects on when they radiate and reflect on the plane of terrestrial bodies. Heat is attributed to the reflected thing rather than the luminary itself. The luminary is a preparatory cause for the origination of heat from terrestrial bodies. It does not emanate from light or the Sun, which is solely the source of light, but from terrestrial bodies.

Subsequent thinkers held that the Sun, like a lamp, is the source of both light and fire casting its rays upon all moving bodies. Its sphere contains strata of fire and gases that are constantly igniting and combusting. It resembles a tempestuous ocean of fire with waves of flares whose length is greater than fifty thousand leagues. This flare may stray from its course like the wind making the flame of a candle flicker. Shahrastānī, *Islamic Astronomy*, 193.

2 The heart is a hollow, fleshy conical organ that holds blood. Its upper part is thick because it is the origin of the arteries and its lower part is thin so it does not collide with the bones in the chest. Its flesh is strong in order to be protected from harm; it is located in the center of the body. Damīrī, *Ḥayāt al-ḥayawān*, 2:220.

3 The spleen is a long fleshy organ located in the left side of the body. It contains blood which is blackish in color and has two channels originating from it. One channel connects to the liver, extracting the blackish compound from the blood and purifying

تماسُك الصور في الهيولى وبقاؤها بإذن الله ، فهكذا ينبث من جرم الطحال قوة الخلط السوداوي البارد اليابس ، وتجري مع الدم في العروق الواردة إلى سائر أطراف الجسد ، وبها يكون جمود رطوبة الدم ، وتماسك أجزائه.[٤]

وأيضاً إن نسبة جرم الكبد[٥] مع الجسد كنسبة جرم المشتري من العالم ، وذلك أنه ينبث من جرمه مع شعاعه قوى روحانيته ، وتسري في أجزاء العالم ، وبها يكون

ينبت منه قناتان أحدهما تتصل بتقعير الكبد تجذب الخلط السوداوي من الدم لئلا ينفذ الدم مع السوداء بل يصفو عن الخلط الردئ ، والقناة الثانية تتصل بفم المعدة وتثبته على شهوة الغذاء. (حياة الحيوان / الدميري / ج٢ / ص٢٢١ /).

٤ أن أصل علم النجوم هو معرفة ثلاثة أشياء ، وهي الكواكب والأفلاك والبروج. فالكواكب أجسام كريات مستديرات مضيئات منها سبعة يقال لها السيّارة وهي زحل والمشتري والمريخ والشمس والزُّهرة وعطارد والقمر ، والباقية يقال لها ثابتة ، ولكل كوكب من السبعة السيارة فلك يخصُّه.

والأفلاك هي أجسام كرُيات مُشفّات مجوفات وهي تسعة أفلاك مركبة بعضها في جوب بعض كحلقة البصل ، فأدناها إلينا فلك القمر وهو محيط بالهواء من جميع الجهات كإحاطة قشرة البيضة ببياضها ، والأرض في جوف الهواء كالمُحّ في بياضها ، ومن وراء فلك القمر فلك عطارد ، ومن وراء فلك عطارد فلك الزهرة ، ومن وراء فلك الزهرة فلك الشمس ، ومن وراء فلك الشمس فلك المريخ ، ومن ورائه فلك المشتري ، ومن ورائه فلك زُحل ، ومن ورائه فلك الكواكب الثابتة ومن ورائه فلك المحيط. وذلك أن الفلك المحيط دائم الدوران كالدولاب يدور من المشرق إلى المغرب فوق الأرض ، ومن المغرب إلى المشرق تحت الأرض ، في كل يوم وليلة دورة واحدة ، ويدير سائر الأفلاك والكواكب معه ، كما قال الله عزّ وجلّ « وكلٌّ في فلك يسبحون » وهذا الفلك المحيط مقسومٌ باثني عشر قسماً كجزر البطيخة ، كل قسم منها يسمى برجاً وهذه أسماؤها : الحمل ، والثور ، والجوزاء ، والسرطان ، والأسد ، والسنبلة ، والميزان ، والعقرب ، والقوس ، والجدي ، والدّلو ، والحوت. فكل برج ثلاثون درجة ، جملتها ثلاثمائة وستون درجة ،وكل درجة ستون جزءاً ، كل جزء يسمى دقيقة ، جملتها أحد وعشرون ألفا وستمائة دقيقة ، وكل دقيقة ستون جزءاً يسمى ثانية ، وكل ثانية ستون جزءاً ، وكل جزء يسمى ثالثة ، وهكذا إلى الروابع والخوامس وما زاد ، بالغاً ما بلغ. (رسائل إخوان الصفا / ج١ / ص١١٦)

٥ الكبد : وهو جسم لحمي ألين من القلب وأرطب ، يحمل روحاً طبيعياً ودماً غذائياً ينفذ منه في العروق إلى سائر الأعضاء ، وهو موضوع في الجانب الأيمن تحت الضلوع العالية من ضلوع الخلف ، وشكله هلالي وتقعيره في الجانب الذي يلي المعدة وحدبته إلى الحجاب ، وهو مربوط برباطات تتصل بالغشاء الذي عليه ، وينبت من مقعره قناة تنقسم إلى أقسام منها ما يأتي قعر المعدة وإلى الأمعاء ، وبهذه الفوهات تجذب الغذاء إلى الكبد ويصير في الكبد ما ينضجه ، وفي جذبة الكبد عروق تسمى الأوردة يجري فيها الدم إلى سائر الأعضاء ، وخلق جرم الكبد شبيهاً بالدم الجامد ليحيل الكيلوس فيه إلى شبه جوهرة. (حياة الحيوان / ج٢ / ص٢٢٠)

rays and infuses the rest of the universe.[4] Forms within prime matter (*al-hayūla*) are held together through it and remain by God's permission. The spleen emits the power of the black, cold and dry humor which flows with the blood in the arteries, reaching all parts of the body. The wetness of blood congeals through it and its parts are held together.

The relationship of the liver[5] to the human body is like that of Jupiter to the cosmos. Jupiter emanates its spiritual powers infusing the rest of the universe, regulating its parts and harmonizing its pillars. Through it, the

---

it, and the second channel connects to the opening of the stomach and secures the appetite. Damīrī, *Ḥayāt al-ḥayawān*, 2:221.

4 The principles of astronomy are based in knowing three things: the planets, the celestial spheres and the constellations. The planets, also called the *movers*, are the following seven luminary spherical bodies: Saturn, Jupiter, Mars, the Sun, Venus, Mercury and the Moon. The rest of the celestial bodies are considered stationary. Each of the seven movers possesses a distinct celestial sphere. The celestial spheres are concave spherical bodies, nine hollow spheres that envelop one another like the skins of an onion. We are in the innermost celestial sphere, that of the Moon, which is surrounded by a ubiquitous wind like whiteness permeating an eggshell. The earth is in nucleus of this wind like the yolk in the egg. Exterior to the celestial sphere of the Moon is that of Mercury, then Venus, the Sun, Mars, Jupiter and Saturn. Beyond these are the stationary stars then the outermost celestial sphere (*al-falak al-muḥīṭ*). The outermost celestial sphere is constantly rotating like a wheel, from the east to the west above the earth and from the west to the east under the earth. It completes one rotation in a single day and night. The rest of the celestial spheres and planets move in conjunction with it, just as God mentions in the Qurʿān, "Each floats in a celestial sphere" (36:40).

The outermost celestial sphere is divided into the twelve signs of the Zodiac: Aries, Taurus, Gemini, Cancer, Leo, Virgo, Libra, Scorpio, Sagittarius, Capricorn, Aquarius and Pisces. Each sign comprises thirty degrees totalling three-hundred and sixty. Each degree has sixty parts which are termed minutes. In total there are twenty-one thousand and six hundred minutes. Each minute has sixty parts termed seconds. Each part is referred to as a third, fourth, fifth and so on. *Rasāʾil Ikhwān al-ṣafāʾ wa khillān al-wafāʾ*, 1:116.

5 The liver is a fleshy organ that is softer than the heart and more damp. It contains the natural spirit and nutrient-rich blood that reaches all of the organs through the arteries. It is located on the right side of the body under the rib cage. Its shape is like a crescent and its bottom end is on the side facing the stomach; it is covered by connective tissue. Channels originate from its interior and branch off, such as one that connects the stomach to the intestines. Through these openings nutrition is absorbed into the liver where it is ripened. In the liver there are arteries that carry blood to all of the organs. The organ of the liver resembles coagulated blood, transforming its substances into what it resembles. *Ḥayāt al-ḥayawān*, 2:220.

ترتيب أجزائه ، واعتدال أركانه ، ومناسبة موجوداتها التي في العالم على أفضل الحالات وأكمل الصفات.

وأيضاً فإن نسبة جرم المرارة(٦) من الجسد كنسبة جرم المريخ من العالم ، وذلك أنه تنبث من جرمه مع شعاعه قوى روحانية ، وتسري في جميع أجزاء العالم ، وبها تكون عزمات الموجودات وبلوغ النهايات ، فهكذا ينبث من جرم المرارة قوى الخلط الصفراوي ، وتجري مع الدم إلى سائر أطراف الجسد وهي الملطِّفة للأخلاط ، المعيدة لها إلى أقصى مدى غاياتها ومنتهى نهاياتها.

وأيضاً نسبة جرم المعدة(٧) إلى الجسد كجرم الزهرة في العالم ، وذلك أنه ينبث من جرمها مع شعاعها قوى روحانيتها ، وتسري في جميع أجزاء العالم ، وهي المفرّحة الملذذة المُسِرّة جميع الخلائق الجسمانية والروحانية التي في العالم ، وبها زينة الموجودات ومحاسن الكائنات في العالم ، أعني عالم الأفلاك والأمهات أي الأركان الأربعة وهي (الماء ، والنار ، والهواء ، والتراب) ، فهكذا ينبث من جرم المعدة القوة الشهوانية الطالبة للغذاء الذي هو مادة الجسد وهيولى الأخلاط ، وبها تكون حياة الجسد ولذَة العيش ، وقوام البدن في الأجسام البشرية والأجسام الطبيعية.

---

٦ المرارة : وهي وعاء المرة الصفراء موضوعة في قعر الجانب الأعلى من الكبد ، ولها مجريان أحدهما يتصل بتقعير الكبد والآخر يتشعب فيتصل بالأمعاء العليا وبأسفل المعدة ، فالمرارة تجذب من مقعر الكبد المرة الصفراء وتقذفها إلى الأمعاء ، أما الجذب فلتصفية الدم عن المرة الصفراء ، وأما القذف فلتنقية الأمعاء من الفضول وينصب منها إلى عضلة المخرج فيثبته على الحاجة ، ولما كانت المعدة والأمعاء محتاجة إلى التنقية من الفضول لما بقي فيها من بقية الغذاء فضلة لزجة يتلطخ بها جعل للمرة مجرى ضيقاً إلى المعدة فتنصب إليها المرة وتجلوها من الخلط البلغمي وتغسلها ، فان البلغم لا يزال يتولد في المعدة عند خلاء المعدة واشتداد الجوع ، فلو كان انصبابها وقت امتلاء المعدة لاختلطت بالغذاء وأفسدتها.

٧ المعدة : وهي شبيه بقرعة طويلة العنق مركبة بثلاث طبقات مركبة من شظايا دقاق شبيهة بشظايا العصب تسمى الليف يحيط بها لحم وليف أحد الطبقات بالطول والأخرى بالعرض والأخرى بالورب ، فالليف الطولاني يجذب الغذاء ، والليف الذي بالعرض يدفعها والمورب يمسكها ربما تؤثر فيه الحرارة وتنضجها ، ووضعت تحت القلب وبين الكبد والطحال يميناً ويساراً ولحم الصلب من خلف لينال من حرارة هذه الأعضاء فينهضم فيها الغذاء وجعل أمامها إلى صفاق البطن ليمدد إذا امتلأت من الغذاء ، وخلقت مستديرة الشكل لتسع غذاء كثيراً ، وقعرها أوسع من أعلاها لان قامة الإنسان منتصبة وما يتناوله من الطعام والشراب ثقيل فميل الجميع إلى جهة قعر المعدة فوجب أن يكون أوسع. (حياة الحيوان / ج٢ / ص٢٢١)

correspondences between the entities in the cosmos are maintained in optimal order in keeping with the most perfect qualities.

The relationship of the gallbladder[6] to the human body is like that of Mars to the cosmos. Since its rays emanate its spiritual powers to the rest of the universe, the entities possess resoluteness and reach their endpoints. The gallbladder releases yellow humor which circulates with the blood assisting it in reaching the farthest extent of the limbs; it is the lightest of the humors.

The relationship of the stomach[7] to the human body is like that of Venus to the cosmos. When Venus emanates its spiritual powers, it exhilarates, delights and gives joy to all physical and spiritual entities in the cosmos. It adorns and beautifies all creatures in existence, particularly, those in the celestial world and their "mothers," which are the four elements: earth, water, air and fire. Thus, the faculty of desire arises from the stomach which seeks nourishment and forms the material body along with the substance of the humors. Through it, the body is alive, derives pleasure in living and sustains the human and other natural bodies.

---

6 The gallbladder is the storage site of yellow bile and is located in a cavity below the liver. It has two ducts, one that connects to the liver and one that is branched and connects to the small intestines and the stomach. The gallbladder absorbs yellow bile from the interior of the liver then discharges it to the intestines. As for absorption, its function is to purify blood from yellow bile. As for discharging, its function is to cleanse the intestines from waste. It is released when needed by a sphincter. When the stomach and intestines need to be cleared of the waste product from digested food, especially as it clings and constricts the intestinal tract, bile is released in order to form a phlegm-like mixture, which causes it to clear out. Phlegm continues to form in the stomach even when empty or in extreme hunger. But if it were to be released when the stomach is full it would combine with the food and spoil it.

7 The stomach resembles a gourd with a long neck. It is composed of three precise layers similar to the layers of nerves which are fibers covered by muscles. The fibers of one layer are vertical, of another layer horizontal and of another layer oblique. The vertical fibers attract food, the horizontal fibers repel it and the oblique fibers hold it, perhaps to heat and ripen it. It is placed below the heart and between the liver and spleen to its right and left, respectively, and the flesh of the spinal column from behind, so that it receives the heat of these organs and is digested properly. The skin which covers it is able to distend when it is filled with food. Its shape is round so that it encompasses more food. Its bottom is wider than its top because the human being stands upright so when he eats and drinks the contents will settle at the bottom of the stomach. Thus, it is necessary that its bottom should be wider. (Damīrī, *Ḥayāt al-ḥayawān*, 2:221.

وأيضاً إن نسبة جرم الدماغ[8] كنسبة جرم عطارد من العالم ، وذلك أنه ينبث من جرمه مع شعاعه قوى روحانيته التي تسري في جميع أجزاء العالم ، وبها يكون الحس والشعور والعرفان في جميع الخلائق من العالمين جميعاً ، من الملائكة والناس أجمعين ، والجن والشياطين والحيوانات أجمع فهكذا ينبث من وسط الدماغ قوة بها يكون الحس والشعور والذهن والفكر والرّوية والمعارف أجمع.

وأيضاً إن نسبة جرم الرئة[9] كنسبة جرم القمر من العالم ، وذلك أنه ينبث من جرمه مع شعاعه قوى روحانيته التي تسري في عالم الأركان تارة ، وفي عالم الأفلاك تارة ، وذلك أن جرم القمر نصفه أبداً ممتلئ نوراً ، ونصفه الآخر مظلم ، وهو تارة يقبل بوجهه الممتلئ من النور نحو عالم الأركان من أول الشهر ، وتارة نحو عالم

---

٨ الدماغ : وهو جسم محويّ في غشائين منبع للروح النفساني ومنه ينبعث في الأعصاب إلى سائر البدن ، ولما كان جوهر الدماغ شديد اللين اقتضت الحكمة أن يكون في غشاء رقيق وهي الأم لتحفظه وتكون وقاية له ثم خلق بين القحف والدماغ غشاء غليظا يلاقي القحف من داخل يكون كالبطانة لها ويكون هذا الغشاء وقاية للدماغ من الأشياء الغريبة ، ولما كان جوهر الدماغ لينا سريع الانفعال من أدنى سبب خلق له حصن صلب من العظم وهو القحف وجعل بعيداً منه ليدفع الآفات عنه ، وجعل خريطة للدماغ معلقة من القحف غير ملاقية له لأنها لو كانت ملاقية والقحف صلب يصادمه دائماً فينضغط عنه وكان دائم النكاية.
(حياة الحيوان / ج٢ / ص٢١٩)

٩ الرئة : وهو جسم متخلخل رخو كأنه زبد منعقد وذلك لكونه آلة الترويح عن القلب دعت الحاجة إلى الخفة والانبساط والانقباض ، ومعنى الترويح جذب هواء صافي يقع على القلب ويخرج هواء محترقاً أحرقته حرارة القلب ، ومدخل الهواء ومخرجه قصبة الرئة وخلقت مجرى واسعاً من عظم غضروفي على شكل حلق مربوطة بعضها ببعض ، وإنما خلق واسعاً لينفذ فيه من الهواء شيء كثير في زمان يسير ، وإنما خلق من حلق غضروفية ليكون مفتوحاً دائماً ولا يحتاج إلى آلة تفتحها لان الحاجة إلى التنفس ماسة دائماً.

وإنما خلقت قصبة الرئة محتاجة إلى أن تتسع في حال وتضيق في حال لاختلاف الحاجة عند شدة الصوت وضعفه ولذلك لم يخلق حلقاتها تامة وإلا لم تتمدد في العرض المذكور فخلق ثلاثة أرباعها غضروفية وتمم الباقي بالغشاء ، وجعل جانبها الغشائي إلى نحو المري ليتطاوع عند الازدراد ، وجانبها الغضروفي إلى الخارج لأنه أصلب فيكون أصبر على المصادم الخارجي ، ثم إن قصبة الرئة لما جاوزت الترقوة وانبسطت إلى فضاء الصدر انقسمت إلى قسمين يميناً ويساراً ثم ينقسم كل قسم منها إلى أقسام مختلفة على حسب أقسام الأوردة والشرايين في منافذ هذه القصبات ليدخل الهواء في الشرايين من الرئة عند انبساط القلب ويندفع فيها الدخان عند انقباضها. (حياة الحيوان / الدميري / ج٢ / ص٢٢٠).

The relationship of the brain[8] to the human body is like that of Mercury to the cosmos. The spiritual powers emanating from Mercury infuse the cosmos and endow sensation, perception and cognizance in all created things in every world, including the angels, humans, Jinn, satans and animals. A power emanates from the middle of the brain giving rise to sensations, perception, intelligence, thought, deliberation and all types of knowledge.

The relationship of the lungs[9] to the body is like that of the Moon to the cosmos. The spiritual powers that emanate from the rays of the Moon infuse the rest of the universe, sometimes in the elemental world and at other times in the celestial world. This is because half of the Moon is always light, and the other half is always dark. Sometimes its light side faces the elemental world at the beginning of the month and at other times it faces the celestial world at the end of the month.

---

8 The brain, which is the source of the soul-like spirit, is wrapped by two coverings. Nerves emerge from it to the rest of the body. Since the substance of the brain is delicate, wisdom necessitated that it be in a thin covering which is the "mother" that safeguards and protects it. Between it and the skull there is a thick covering that adheres to the skull and acts like a lining, protecting the brain from foreign objects. Since the brain is delicate and susceptible to injury even from the slightest event, it has a solid shield, the skull. It is detached from the skull so it is protected from harm and the it contents are suspended in the skull. It is not directly attached to it since the skull is solid and is subject to impact from time to time, which would put pressure on the brain and causing injury. *Ḥayāt al-ḥayawān*, 2:219.

9 The lungs are a rarefied, slack organ, resembling foam. Because it is the instrument of respiration in addition to the heart, it is necessary for it to be light in order to expand and contract. The meaning of respiration is to inhale clean air, send it to the heart and exhale "burnt" air, burnt by the heat of the heart. The entrance and exit of air is through the windpipe, composed of wide rings of cartilage. Its width allows for the respiration of ample air in a short amount of time. It has rings of cartilage that remain open that do not require any mechanism to keep it open for breathing is necessary at all times.

The windpipe was made to expand and contract according to need, such as when using a loud or soft voice. Its rings are not fully formed all the way around lest they constrict expansion, so three-fourths are formed of cartilage and the rest is a sheath. The sheath faces the esophagus to facilitate swallowing and the cartilagineous part faces the back since it is more resilient to jolts.

Furthermore, when the windpipe reaches the clavicle and opens into the chest it divides in two branches, right and left, then further into various branches to reach veins and arteries. Air from the lungs reaches the heart when it expands and repels vapors when it contracts. Damīrī, *Ḥayāt al-ḥayawān*, 2:220.

الأفلاك من آخر الشهر ، فهكذا ينبث من جرم الرئة قوة تجذب الهواء تارة من خارج الجسد ، وترسله إلى القلب ، ومن القلب تنفذه في العروق الضوارب إلى سائر أطراف الجسد ، وهو الذي يسمى النبض ، وبها تكون حياة الجسد ، وتارة ترد من ذلك الهواء من داخل وبها يكون التنفس والأصوات والكلام أجمع.[١٠]

١٠ رسائل إخوان الصفاء وخلان الوفاء / ج٢ / ص٤٧٧.

Similarly, the lungs inhale air from the outside of the body and send it to the heart, which then circulates it to the arteries into the remainder of the body; it is called the heartbeat and is the source of life. Conversely, air is exhaled from the inside and results in breathing, sound and speech."[10]

10 *Rasāʾil Ikhwān al-ṣafāʾ wa khillān al-wafāʾ*, 2:477.

الباب الرابع

التناسب بين الإنسان والشيطان

قال الشيخ النراقي (رحمه الله) : إن للشيطان[1] جندين : جند يطير وجند يسير ، والواهمة[2] جنده الطيار ، والشهوة جنده السيار[3] ، لان غالب ما خلقنا[4] منه هي النار التي خلق منها الشيطان ، فالمناسبة اقتضت تسلطه عليهما وتبعيتهما له.

ثم لما كانت النار[5] بذاتها مقتضية للحركة ، إذ لا تتصور نار مشتعلة لاتتحرك ، بل لا تزال تتحرك بطبعها ، فشأن كل من الشيطان والقوتين أن يتحرك ولا يسكن ،

---

١ الشيطان فِعلان : من شاطَ يَشيط ، وشاطَ الشيء شيطاً : احترق وعَجِل ، والإشاطة : الاهلاك. (لسان العرب / ج٧ / ج٢٥٧)

٢ القوة الواهمة : شأنها استنباط وجوه المكر والحيل ، والتوصل إلى الأغراض بالتلبيس والخدع ولها فائدة كما للقوى الثلاث وهي القوة العقلية الملكية والتي شأنها إدراك حقائق الأمور ، والتمييز بين الخيرات والشرور ، والأمر بالأفعال الجميلة ، والنهي عن الصفات الذميمة ، والقوة الشهوية البهيمة فائدتها بقاء البدن الذي هو آلة تحصيل كمال النفس ، فانه لا يصدر عنها إلا أفعال البهائم من عبودية الفرج والبطن ، والحرص على الجماع والأكل ، والقوة الغضبية السبعية تكسر الشهوية والشيطانية ، وتقهرهما عند انغمارهما في الخداع والشهوات ، وإصرارهما عليهما ، لأنهما لتمردهما لا تطيعان العاقلة بسهولة بخلاف الغضبية فانهما تطيعانها وتتأدبان بتأديبها بسهولة ، والقوة الوهمية فائدتها إدراك المعاني الجزئية ، واستنباط الحيل والدقائق التي يتوصل بها إلى المقاصد الصحيحة.

وقد يلتبس الأمر بين (الواهمة والخيال والمتخيلة) فهي ثلاث قوى متباينة ومباينة للقوى الثلاث (العاقلة ، والغضبية ، والشهوية). فشأن الواهمة إدراك المعاني الجزئية ، وشأن الخيال إدراك الصور ، وشأن المتخيلة التركيب والتفصيل بينهما. (جامع السعادات / ج١ / ص٣١)

٣ جامع السعادات / ج١ / ص١٢٥.

٤ ﴿خَلَقَ الإِنْسَانَ مِن صَلْصَالٍ كَالْفَخَّارِ ۞ وَخَلَقَ الْجَانَّ مِن مَّارِجٍ مِّن نَّارٍ﴾ [الرحمن :١٤-١٥]. (صلصال) طين يابس مطبوخ ، (الفخار) طين طبخ بالنار ، (مارج) لب النار الخالص من الدخان أو من نار مختلط. وقال تعالى : ﴿وَلَقَدْ خَلَقْنَا الإِنسَانَ مِن صَلْصَالٍ مِّنْ حَمَإٍ مَّسْنُونٍ ۞ وَالْجَآنَّ خَلَقْنَاهُ مِن قَبْلُ مِن نَّارِ السَّمُومِ﴾ [الحجر:٢٦-٢٧]

٥ النار : جرم بسيط طباعه أن يكون حاراً يابساً ، لا لون لها ، وأن النار الصرفة لا يدركها البصر ، وإنما التي يدركها البصر هو شعلة النار ، فأنا نرى الشمع إذا اشتعل كانت شعلته منفصلة

CHAPTER 4

The Correspondence Between Man and Satan

Shaykh Narāqī writes, "Satan[1] has two armies, an army that flies and an army that flows. The faculty of imagination[2] is the army that flies and the faculty of desire is the army that flows.[3] This is because the greater part of their composition is the same fire from which Satan has been created. These faculties are compelled to yield to his domination because of this correspondence.[4] Since fire[5] intrinsically moves, it is inconceiveable that a burning flame should

---

1 Lexically, *Shayṭān* is like *faʿlān*, which derives from the verb *shāṭā, yashīṭu*, meaning "to burn and hasten," and *ishāṭa* meaning "to perish." *Lisān al-ʿarab*, 7:257.

2 Sensory intuition (*al-wāhima*) contrives ways to deceive and plot, arriving at certain ends through deception and cunning. Yet, like the three other faculties, it is also beneficial.
The angelic, intellectual faculty perceives realities, differentiates between good and evil, enjoins beautiful deeds and renounces vile attributes.
The bestial faculty of desire maintains the body, which is an instrument for the perfection of the soul. It gives rise to animalistic impulses such as enslavement to the private parts and stomach, that is, indulgence in carnal pleasures and food.
The predatory faculty of anger breaks the faculties of desire and satanic imagination, subduing them when steeped in desires and deception or relentlessly hankering after them. These rebellious faculties do not readily obey the intellect, but succumb to the faculty of anger which disciplines them.
Sensory intuition conceptualizes the meaning of particulars to concoct stratagems and derive the means required to reach correct objectives.
The difference between the terms sensory intuition (*al-wāhima*), imagination (*al-khayāl*) and fantasy (*al-mutakhayyila*) may be unclear. Each of these is a distinct faculty, as distinct as the faculties of intellect, anger and desire are to each other. The function ofsensory intuition is to conceptualize the meanings of particulars, the function of the imagination is to perceive forms and the function of the fantasy is to synthesize and segregate between the two.

3 *Jāmiʿ al-saʿādāt*, 1:125.

4 "He created man from clay like the potter's and the Jinn from a smokeless fire" (55:14-15). *Ṣalṣāl* is dry, baked clay and *fakhkhār* is clay baked by fire. *Mārij* is the essence of fire that is unadulterated by smoke or impurities in fire. "We created man from moulded black mud, and before that, the Jinn from fire of a scorching wind" (15:26-27).

5 Fire is a simple element whose nature is hot and dry and does not have a color. Pure fire cannot be perceived by the eyes. What the eyes perceive is the flame of the fire. When we observe the flame of a candle we find that it appears detached from the

إلا أن الشيطان لما خُلق من النار الصرفة من دون امتزاج شيء آخر بها فهو دائم الحركة والتحريك للقوتين بالوسوسة[٦] والهيجان ، والقوتان لما امتزج بغالب مادتهما . أعني النار . شيء من الطين لم تكونا بمثابة ما خلق من صرف النار في الحركة ، إلا انهما استعدتا لقبول الحركة منه ، فلا يزال الشيطان[٧] ينفخ فيهما ويحركهما بالوسوسة والهيجان ويطير ويجول فيهما .

ثم الشهوة لكون النارية فيها أقل فسكونها ممكن ، فيحتمل أن يكف تسلط الشيطان عن الإنسان فيها ، فيسكن بالكلية عن الهيجان ، وأما الواهمة فلا يمكن أن يقطع تسلطه عنها ، فيمتنع قطع وسواسه عن الإنسان ، إذا لو أمكن قطعه

عن الفتيلة ولا شك أن الحرارة عند اتصال الفتيلة أقوى. وأيضاً إن كير الحدادين إذا بالغوا في نفخه صار هواء بحيث إذا دنا منه شيء يحترق ولا ضوء له ، والنار هي فوق العناصر في غاية القوة والخلوص فلذلك لا تدركه الأبصار ، والنار الحقيقة غير ملونة ، ومن عجيب خلقة الباري تعالى خروج هذا الجرم النوراني من الحديد والحجر الكثيفين أو من الشجر الأخضر الذي يخالف طبيعة النار أو من الحرارة والضياء اللتين يلازمانها ثم من غلبتها وسلطانها على الأجسام حتى على الصخرة الصماء فتجعلها تراباً وعلى الحديد فتذيبه. (حياة الحيوان الكبرى / الدميري / ج٢ / ص٦٧)

٦ الوسوسة : تقال لما يقع في النفس من الشر وما لا خير فيه ، يقابلها ما يقع في النفس من عمل الخير فهو (إلهام) ، وما يقع من الخوف (إيحاش) وما يقع من تقدير نيل الخير (أمل) ، وما يقع من التقدير الذي لا على الإنسان ولا له (خاطر). (معجم الفروق اللغوية / العسكري / ص٦٩)

٧ عن النبي ﷺ ، انه قال لأصحابه : « ألا أخبركم بشيء إن أنتم فعلتموه تباعد الشيطان عنكم كما تباعد المشرق عن المغرب ؟ قالوا : بلى ، قال الصوم يسود وجهه ، والصدقة تكسر ظهره ، والحب في الله ، والمؤازرة على العمل الصالح يقطع دابره ، والاستغفار يقطع وتينه. (البحار / ج٦٩ / ص٣٨٠)

من وصايا النبي ﷺ لابن مسعود ، يا ابن مسعود اتخذ الشيطان عدواً فان الله تعالى يقول : ﴿إِنَّ الشَّيْطَانَ لَكُمْ عَدُوٌّ فَاتَّخِذُوهُ عَدُوّاً﴾ [فاطر:٦] ويقول عن إبليس : ﴿ثُمَّ لآتِيَنَّهُم مِّن بَيْنِ أَيْدِيهِمْ وَمِنْ خَلْفِهِمْ وَعَنْ أَيْمَانِهِمْ وَعَن شَمَآئِلِهِمْ وَلاَ تَجِدُ أَكْثَرَهُمْ شَاكِرِينَ﴾[الأعراف:١٧]. ويقول : ﴿فَالْحَقُّ وَالْحَقَّ أَقُولُ ۞ لأَمْلأَنَّ جَهَنَّمَ مِنكَ وَمِمَّن تَبِعَكَ مِنْهُمْ أَجْمَعِينَ﴾ [ص:٨٤-٨٥] يا ابن مسعود لا تأكل الحرام ولا تلبس الحرام ولا تأخذ من الحرام ولا تعص الله لان الله تعالى يقول لإبليس : ﴿وَاسْتَفْزِزْ مَنِ اسْتَطَعْتَ مِنْهُمْ بِصَوْتِكَ وَأَجْلِبْ عَلَيْهِم بِخَيْلِكَ وَرَجِلِكَ وَشَارِكْهُمْ فِي الأَمْوَالِ وَالأَوْلادِ وَعِدْهُمْ وَمَا يَعِدُهُمُ الشَّيْطَانُ إِلاَّ غُرُوراً﴾ [الإسراء:٦٤]. (البحار / ج٧٧ / ص١٠٥)

be still; it will always move by nature. It is thus the nature of both Satan and the two faculties to always be moving. However, because Satan was created from pure fire without the admixture of anything else, he is constantly moving and stirs the two faculties through agitation and insinuation.[6] As for the two faculties, their substance is primarily composed of fire, yet admixed with earth, so their movement is not equivalent to something that was created out of pure fire, even if they have the capacity to emulate its movement. Thus, Satan constantly rouses and stirs each faculty through insinuation and agitation, and flies and flows in them.[7]

As the faculty of desire possesses a lesser degree of fire, it has the potential to remain still and hinder Satan's control over man, so that it may remain impervious to any agitation. However, it is not possible to sever Satan's influence over the faculty of imagination and thwart his insinuation in man. Had it been possible to completely sever his influence even for a moment,

---

wick. Undoubtedly, the heat of the fire at the wick is more intense. When air is added to the bellows of a blacksmith, it becomes so hot that if anything is lowered into it, it burns without producing any light. Fire is greater in strength and purity than all the other elements. Since true fire does not possess color it cannot be perceived by the eyes. It is remarkable that this luminous element created by God can be conjured from dense substances such as iron or stone, or from a green tree, whose nature opposes the nature of fire and its concomitants, heat and light. Finally, fire conquers and dominates material bodies, even turning an impervious stone into dust and melting iron. *Ḥayāt al-ḥayawān*, 2:67.

6 Insinuation (*waswasa*) is the evil that stirs in the soul, void of any goodness. In contrast, inspiration (*ilhām*) is that which occurs in the soul giving rise to virtuous deeds; desolation (*īḥāsh*) is a state that brings about fear; hope (*amal*) is the expectation of attaining goodness; and a passing thought (*khāṭir*) is a judgment that neither harms nor benefits a person. ʿAskarī, *Muʿjam furūq al-lughawī*, 69.

7 The Prophet said to his companions, "Shall I inform you of something that should you perform it, it will make Satan distant from you like the distance from the east to the west?" They said, "Yes, indeed." He said, "Fasting disgraces him, charity breaks his back, the love of God and supporting virtuous deeds cuts his root and repentance crops his foundation." *Biḥār al-anwār*, 69:380.

Among the advice given to Ibn Masʿūd is to take Satan as an enemy, as God says, "Satan is an enemy to you so take him as an enemy" (35:6). Iblīs says, "I will approach them from the front, from behind, from their right and from the left; You will not find many of them grateful" (7:17). God says, "This is the truth and the truth I speak, I will fill hellfire with you and all those that follow you" (38:84-85).The Prophet said, "O Masʿūd, do not eat the unlawful, nor dress the unlawful, nor take from the unlawful, and do not disobey God, for He says to Iblīs, 'Lead to destruction those whom you can amongst them, with your voice; make assaults on them with your cavalry and your infantry; mutually share with them wealth and children; and make promises to them. But Satan promises them nothing but illusion' (17:64)." *Biḥār al-anwār*, 77:105.

أيضاً بالمرة لصار اللعين منقاداً للإنسان مسخراً له ، وانقياده له هو سجوده له ، إذ روح السجود وحقيقته هو الانقياد والإطاعة ، ووضع الجبهة حالته وعلامته ، وكيف يتصور أن يسجد الملعون[٨] لأولاد آدم عليه السلام مع عدم سجوده لأبيهم واستكباره من أن يطمئن عن حركته ساجداً له معللاً بقوله : ﴿خَلَقْتَنِي مِن نَّار وَخَلَقْتَهُ مِن طِين﴾ [الأعراف :١٢] ، فلا يمكن أن يتواضع لهم بالكف عن الوسوسة ، بل هو من المنظرين[٩] لإغوائهم إلى يوم الدين .

فلا يتخلص منه أحد إلا من أصبح وهمومه هم واحد ، فيكون قلبه مشتغلاً بالله وحده ، فلا يجد الملعون مجالًا فيه ، ومثله[١٠] من المخلصين الداخلين في الاستثناء عن سلطنة هذا اللعين ، فلا تظن أنه يخلو عنه قلب فارغ بل هو سيال يجري من ابن آدم مجرى الدم ، وسيلانه مثل الهواء في القدح ، فإنك إن أردت أن تخلى القدح عن الهواء من غير أن تشغله بمثل الماء فقد طمعت في غير مطمع ، بل بقدر ما يدخل فيه الماء يخلو عن الهواء ، فكذلك القلب إذا كان مشغولاً بفكر مهم في الدين يمكن أن يخلو من جولان هذا اللعين ، وأما لو غفل عن الله ولو في لحظة ، فليس له في تلك اللحظة قرين إلا الشيطان كما قال سبحانه : ﴿وَمَن يَعْشُ عَن ذِكْرِ الرَّحْمنِ نُقَيِّضْ لَهُ شَيْطَاناً فَهُوَ لَهُ قَرِينٌ﴾ [الزخرف:٣٦] وقال رسول الله صلى الله عليه وآله : « إن الله يبغض الشاب الفارغ »[١١] لان الشاب إذا تعطل عن عمل مباح يشغل باطنه لابد أن يدخل في قلبه الشيطان ويعيش فيه ويبيض ويفرخ ، وهكذا يتوالد

---

٨ قال تعالى : ﴿وَإِذْ قُلْنَا لِلْمَلائِكَةِ اسْجُدُوا لآدَمَ فَسَجَدُوا إِلاَّ إِبْلِيسَ كَانَ مِنَ الْجِنِّ فَفَسَقَ عَنْ أَمْرِ رَبِّهِ أَفَتَتَّخِذُونَهُ وَذُرِّيَّتَهُ أَوْلِيَاء مِن دُونِي وَهُمْ لَكُمْ عَدُوٌّ بِئْسَ لِلظَّالِمِينَ بَدَلاً﴾ [الكهف:٥٠].

٩ قال تعالى : ﴿قَالَ رَبِّ فَأَنظِرْنِي إِلَى يَوْمِ يُبْعَثُونَ ۞ قَالَ فَإِنَّكَ مِنَ الْمُنظَرِينَ ۞ إِلَى يَومِ الْوَقْتِ الْمَعْلُومِ﴾ [الحجر:٣٦-٣٨].

١٠ قال تعالى : ﴿قَالَ رَبِّ بِمَآ أَغْوَيْتَنِي لأُزَيِّنَنَّ لَهُمْ فِي الأَرْضِ وَلأُغْوِيَنَّهُمْ أَجْمَعِينَ ۞ إِلَّا عِبَادَكَ مِنْهُمُ الْمُخْلَصِينَ ۞ قَالَ هَذَا صِرَاطٌ عَلَيَّ مُسْتَقِيمٌ ۞ إِنَّ عِبَادِي لَيْسَ لَكَ عَلَيْهِمْ سُلْطَانٌ إِلاَّ مَنِ اتَّبَعَكَ مِنَ الْغَاوِينَ﴾ [الحجر:٣٩-٤٢] .

١١ عن رسول الله صلى الله عليه وآله : « من تعلّم في شبابه كان بمنزلة الرّسم في الحجر ، ومن تعلم وهو كبير كان بمنزلة الكتاب على وجه الماء » (البحار / ج١ / ص٢٢٢ / ح٦).

وعن الإمام الصادق عليه السلام : « لَستُ أُحبُّ أن أرى الشاب منكم إلا غادياً في حالين : إما عالماً أو مُتعلماً ، فان لم يفعل فرَّط ، فان فرَّط ضيّع ، وإن ضيّع أثِم ، وإن أثِم سكن النار والذي بعث محمّداً بالحق ».

the Accursed (Satan) would become subservient and submissive to man. His obedience, then, would be tantamount to prostration before him, since the spirit of prostration is subservience and obedience, and lowering the forehead is simply its indication and state. How can it be imagined that the Accursed[8] will prostrate before the children of Adam and be still in the act of prostration when he arrogantly refused to do so before their father claiming, "You created me from fire and created him from clay" (7:12). He can never become humble before them and resist insinuation. He has been reprieved to lead them astray until the Day of Judgment.[9]

No one can elude him except the resolute, one whose heart is solely engaged with God so the Accursed finds no space to dwell. Similarly, the sincere ones are impervious to the dominion of the Accursed.[10] Let it not be imagined that an empty heart will be devoid of his influence, since he circulates in the children of Adam like blood and flows in him like air in an empty vessel. If you wish to empty a vessel of air without filling it with water or its like, it will be to no avail. The extent to which you fill it with water, air will be displaced; such is the case with the heart. If it is immersed in a lofty spiritual matter, it is possible then, that it will be free from the Accursed's movement. However, if one is heedless of God even for a moment, then for that very moment, his companion is Satan, as stated in the verse, "He who is blinded from the remembrance of the Merciful, we appoint for him a Satan who becomes his companion" (43:36). The Prophet has stated, "God dislikes a vacuous youth." This is because if a youth does not partake in lawful things that occupy his mind, Satan will certainly occupy his heart, take residence there, lay eggs and hatch in him.[11] Thus, Satan's offspring multiply faster than the offspring

---

8 God said, "When We said to the angels, 'Prostrate before Adam!' They all prostrated except Iblīs. He was of the Jinn, so he rebelled against the command of his Lord. Will you then take him and his progeny as protectors rather than Me? They are enemies to you! Evil is the recompense for the wrongdoers!" (18:50).

9 God said, "[Iblīs] said, 'My Lord, reprieve me till the day they are raised.' He replied, 'You have been given reprieve until the appointed Day'" (15:36-38).

10 God said, "[Iblīs] said: 'My Lord, because You have led me astray, I will seduce them on the earth, and I will mislead them all—except those among Your sincere servants.' [God] said: 'This is indeed the way that leads straight to Me. For you shall have no authority over my servants, except he who follows you and becomes deceived'" (15:39-42).

11 The Prophet said, "Whoever learns in his youth, it is like something etched in stone, and one who learns in his old-age it is like writing on the surface of water." *Biḥār al-anwār*, 1:222.

Imām al-Ṣādiq said, "I would like to see the youth coming and going only in two states, either learning or teaching. If they fail to do so then they are negligent; if they are negligent then they are in loss; if they are in loss, they have sinned; if they have

نسل الشيطان توالداً أسرع من توالد الحيوانات ، لأن الشيطان طبعه من النار ، والشهوة في نفس الشاب كالحلفاء اليابسة ، فإذا وجدها كثر تولده ، وتولدت النار من النار ولم تنقطع أصلاً.

فظهر أن وسواس الخناس لا يزال يجاذب قلب كل إنسان من جانب إلى جانب ، ولا علاج له إلا قطع[١٢] العلائق كلها ظاهراً وباطناً ، والفرار عن الأهل والمال والولد والجاه والرفقاء ، ثم الاعتزال إلى زاوية ، وجعل الهموم هماً واحداً هو الله. وهذا أيضاً غير كاف ما لم يكن له مجال في الفكر وسير في الباطن في ملكوت السماوات والأرض وعجائب صنع الله ، فان استيلاء ذلك على القلب واشتغاله به يدفع مجاذبة الشيطان ووسواسه ، وإن لم يكن له سير بالباطن فلا ينجيه إلا الأوراد المتواصلة المترتبة في كل لحظة من الصلوات والاذكار والأدعية والقراءة.

ويحتاج مع ذلك إلى تكليف القلب الحضور ، إذ الأوراد الظاهرة لا تستغرق القلب ، بل التفكر بالباطن هو الذي يستغرقه ، وإذا فعل كل ذلك لم يسلم له من الأوقات إلا بعضها ، إذ لا يخلو في بعضها عن حوادث تجدد وتشغله عن الفكر والذكر ، كمرض أو خوف أو إيذاء وطغيان ، ولو من مخالطة بعض لا يستغني عنه في الاستعانة في بعض أسباب المعيشة.

وأخيراً إذا علمت – ولو إجمالًا – المناسبة بين الإنسان والشيطان ، فاعلم أن المتفرس والشيخ المرشد يشخص أمراض النفس ووسوستها من أمراض الشيطان ووسوسته فيعطي الدواء للداء ، فتارة يعمد إلى سد الأبواب العظيمة للشيطان في القلب وهي الشهوة ، والغضب ، والحرص ، والحسد وغير ذلك من رؤوس ذمائم الصفات ورذائل الملكات ، وتارة كثرة الذكر بالقلب واللسان ، وعمارة القلب بأضدادهما من فضائل الأخلاق وشرائف الأوصاف ، والملازمة للورع والتقوى ، والمواظبة على عبادة ربه الأعلى وغيرها.

ثم اعلم أن السر في توقف قطع الوساوس بالكلية على التصفية والتخلية أولاً ثم المواظبة على ذكر الله فبعد حصول هذه الأمور للنفس تحصل لقوتها العاقلة ملكة الاستيلاء والاستعلاء على القوى الشهوية والغضبية والوهمية ، فلا تتأثر عنها وتؤثر فيها على وفق المصلحة ، فتتمكن من ضبط الواهمة والمتخيلة بحيث لو أرادت صرفهما

---

١٢ ليس المراد قطع العلائق بالمرة وعلى الدوام ، بل هي حالة علاجية يسعى إليها السالك.

of animals, for his nature is fire and the faculty of desire in a youth is like dried grass. Should it catch fire, it will spread incessantly adding fire to fire.

The insinuation of the Whisperer (Satan) relentlessly entices the heart of every human being from all sides. There is no cure for it except to sever all outward and inward attachments, including one's family, wealth, children, position and friends, then, seclusion in retreat making God one's solitary concern.[12] Even this is not sufficient without the opportunity for contemplation and wayfaring in the inward Dominion (*malakūt*) of the heavens, earth and wondrous creation of God. When this overtakes the heart, captivating it, Satan's enticement and insinuation is warded off. If there is no wayfaring of the inward, then only the continuous recitation of litanies, invocations, prayers and recitals can deliver him.

In addition, there must be presence of heart, because outward invocation by itself does immerse the heart, rather contemplation (*fikr*) of the inward (*bāṭin*)immerses it. Should he fulfill this in its entirety, then he will not yield to Satan except rarely, because there may be times that some external obstacle prevents him from his contemplation and invocation (*dhikr*), such as illness, fear, grievance, oppression or even association with those who assist him in securing his provision.

Finally, if you have come to know, even generally, the correspondences between man and Satan, then know that the clairvoyant and spiritual master (*shaykh*) differentiates between those illnesses and insinuations originating from the soul and those originating from Satan, and thereafter prescribe a remedy for each. At times, he may intend to shut the great doors of the heart on Satan, namely, desire, anger, greed, jealousy and other cardinal vices and wicked qualities. While at other times, he may enjoin their opposites, namely, increasing invocation with the heart and tongue, inculcating the heart with virtuous qualities and noble attributes, conforming to godliness, piety and devotion in worship of the Lord, the Most High, and so on.

Furthermore, know that the secret to severing all insinuation is purification and vacuity, then persisting in the remembrance of God. After the soul achieves these states, the faculty of intellect acquires the aptitude for governance and takes possession of the faculties of desire, anger and imagination. It is no longer influenced by them but it influences them in their favor. The intellect can restrain fantasy (*wāhima*) and imagination (*mutakhayyila*), and if it so

---

sinned they will remain in the fire—I swear by Him who has sent Muḥammad with the truth!"

12 Severing of relations does not mean severing them absolutely or indefinitely. Instead, it is a curative state for wayfarer.

عن الوساوس لأمكنها ذلك ، ولم تتمكن القوتان من الذهاب في أودية الخواطر بدون رأيها ، وإذا حصلت للنفس هذه الملكة وتوجهت إلى ضبطهما كلما أرادتا الخروج عن الانقياد والذهاب في أودية الوساوس وتكرر منها هذا الضبط ، حصل لهما ثبات الانقياد بحيث لم يحدث فيهما خاطر سوء مطلقاً ، بل لم يخطر فيهما إلا خواطر الخير من خزائن الغيب وحينئذ تستقر النفس على مقام الاطمئنان ، وتنسد عنها أبواب الشيطان وتنفتح فيها أبواب الملائكة ، ويصير مستقرها ومستودعها ، فتستضاء بشروق الأنوار القدسية من مشكاة الربوبية ، ويشملها خطاب : ﴿يَا أَيَّتُهَا النَّفْسُ الْمُطْمَئِنَّةُ ۞ ارْجِعِي إِلَى رَبِّكِ رَاضِيَةً مَّرْضِيَّةً﴾ [الفجر:٢٧-٢٨].

desires, employ them against insinuation, preventing them from plunging into the valley of thoughts without its approval. Thus, if the soul achieves this mastery and harnesses these powers, whenever they become unbridled and enter the valley of insinuation, it tightens the reigns and they return to obedience so that no evil thoughts occur in them. Only good thoughts enter from the treasury of the Unseen so the soul becomes established in the station of tranquility. The doors of Satan are shut and the doors of the angels are opened, becomming the soul's residence and repository. It then receives the lights of sanctity from the lamp-niche of Lordship, warranting the address, "O tranquil soul, return to your Lord, contented and earning your Lord's good pleasure" (89:27-28).

الباب الخامس

التناسب بين الأعضاء

إن أعضاء الأجسام الحية الطبيعية متناسبة في الشكل من حيث الطول والقصر والسمن والنحافة واللون وسائر الصفات. فالشجرة[1] المستطيلة كل شي فيها مستطيل من الساق والأغصان والورق والثمر وغيرها ، وهكذا الشجرة المستديرة أو أي شكل آخر. وعلى هذا فان كل جزء من أجزاء النبات يحكي خصوصيات النبات للمناسبة والسنخية بينها.

وكذا الأمر في أعضاء الحيوان فإنها متناسبة ومتسانخة الواحد منها يعبر عن طبعه وطبيعته ، ومثله في الإنسان ، فالطويل مثلاً يكون رأسه مستطيل ، وأطرافه مستطيله ، وكفاه مستطيلين وقدما مثل ذلك.

وربع القامة تميل أعضائه إلى التربيع ، والقصير إلى القصر ، فإدراك أي عضو وجزء من أعضاء وأجزاء الأجسام الحية يكشف عن صفات الأعضاء الأخرى ، وبالتالي تعرف صفاتها وأخلاقها ، وهي وظيفة أهل الفراسة وأصحابها.

وللتناسب بين الأعضاء قواعد وضوابط يسير عليها المختصون في علم الفراسة والطب وكذلك الفنانون والمصورون والنحاتون وغيرهم نذكر منها[2] :

---

١ الشجر : كل ما له ساق من النبات ، والأشجار العظام بمثابة الحيوانات العظام ، والنجوم بمثابة الحيوانات الصغار ، ومن عجيب صنع الباري خلق الأوراق على الأشجار زينة لها ووقاية لثمرها من نكاية الشمس والهواء ، ثم انه تعالى خلقها مرتفعة عن الثمار متفرقة بعض التفرق لا متكاثفة عليها ولا بعيدة عنها لتأخذ الثمار من النسيم تارة ، ومن الشمس أخرى ، فلو تكاثفت عليها حتى منعتها إصابة النسيم وشعاع الشمس لبقيت على فجاجتها غليظة الجلد قليلة المائية ، وإذا سقط منها بعض الورق أصابتها الشمس وأحرقتها ثم إذا فرغت الثمرة تناثرت الأوراق حتى لا تجذب مائية الشجر فتضعف قوتها كما ترى في الحيوان الأم تضعف من إرضاع أولادها ، وأعجب ما فيها ما ذكره الله تعالى . يسقى بماء واحد ، ونفضل بعضها على بعض في الأكل . (حياة الحيوان الكبرى / ج٢ / ص١٦٢).

٢ سوف يأتي تفصيل هذه المطالب في الجزء الثالث ، قسم الفراسة الحكمية.

CHAPTER 5

The Correspondence Between the Limbs

The limbs of a natural body are in proportion to each other with respect to length, girth, color and every other characteristic. For example, each part of a tall tree[1] is long, the trunk, the branches, the leaves and its fruit. Similarly, a round tree or any other shape is also in proportion. Each part of a plant exemplifies the whole plant because of the correspondence and homogeneity between each part.

Such is the case for the limbs of an animal which are proportional and homogeneous, each exemplifying its nature and constitution. In the human being, for example, the head of tall person is oblong, as well as the extremities, palms, feet and so on. A stout individual will have stout extremities and a short individual will have short extremities. Discerning any limb of the body reveals the characteristics of the other limbs, which allows one to know its qualities and attributes. This knowledge is important to the people of spiritual insight.

There are principles that govern the relationships between the limbs, which are well-known among the specialists of physiognomy[2] and medicine, as well as artists, painters and sculptors. Some of these principles are mentioned here:

---

1 A tree is any vegetation that has a trunk. Large trees are like large animals and the stars are like small animals. Among the wondrous designs of the Creator are the leaves of trees. They are an adornment and a protection for their fruits from the deleterious effects of the sun and wind. The Almighty fashioned them to be raised over fruits and slightly separated from them so that the leaves would not become too dense nor too distant and that the fruits would benefit from both the wind and the sun. If the leaves became too dense it would prevent the effects of the wind or the sun to reach them and they would remain unripe, dry and with thick skin. But if some of its leaves were to fall, the sun would burn the fruit. Without leaves and scanty fruit, the tree would not absorb adequate water and therefore weaken, just as in the animal kingdom the mother weakens when she nurses her young. What is more amazing is what God mentions—they are given but one water yet we have preferred some over others as food. *Ḥayāt al-ḥayawān*, 2:162.

2 This will be discussed in greater detail in the third volume of the book on analytical physiognomy (*al-firāsat al-ḥikmiyya*).

١ . التناسب بين الأطراف ، فإذا كانت الأيدي طويلة أو قصيرة تكون الأرجل مثلها ، وكذلك التناسب أصابع الرجل واليد وهكذا في سائر الأعضاء.

٢ . التناسب بين الرقبة والأكتاف ، فقصر الرقبة وثخامتها يتناسب مع عرض الأكتاف وثخامتها والعكس.

٣ . إن القامة ستة أضعاف طول القدم.

٤ . طول الوجه من أعلى الجبهة إلى اسفل الذقن ، كطول الكف من الرسخ إلى طرف الوسطى ، وكل منهما يساوي عُشر القامة.

٥ . الصدر ربع القامة.

٦ . إن من أعلى الصدر إلى الجبهة سبع القامة.

٧ . محيط الرسخ نصف محيط العنق.

٨ . إذا قسمت الوجه إلى ثلاثة أفسام متساوية ، انتهى القسم الأول منها عند التقاء الحاجبين ، والثاني في طرف الانف ، والثالث في أسفل الذقن.

٩ . القامة إذا قسمت إلى نصفين ، كانت السُّرة وسطاً بينهما ، فإذا توسد الإنسان على ظهره واسبل ذراعيه إلى جنبيه ، وجعل السّرة مركزاً ورسم دائرة ، فإنها تمس الرأس والقدمين على السواء ، وإذا بسط الرجل ذراعيه عرضاً على زاوية قائمة من جسمه كانت المسافة بين طرفي الأنامل طول القامة تماماً ، ولكن يندر أن يتفق ذلك التناسب بالضبط الكلي في جسم ، وذلك لميل الطبيعة إلى التنوع والتفرع تبعاً للمؤثرات الخارجية أو الوراثة أو لأحوال أخرى.

ومن أكثر المؤثرات في ذلك التفاوت اختصاص بعض الأعضاء بالعمل دون البعض الآخر ، وأكثر ما يكون ذلك في الرياضة البدنية ، فان الأعضاء التي تستعمل تنحو وتتقوى وتبقى سائر الأعضاء كما هي.

١٠ . إن الفرق بين العينين عين واحدة.

١١ . إن الأنف والأذنين على خط واحد.

١٢ . إن تكتل الجسم يتناسب مع كبر البطن طردياً.

١٣ . قوة البدن تتناسب مع قصر العنق وضخامتها.

١٤ . استدارة الفكين يتناسب مع استدارة الوجه.

١٥ . إحاطة الجسم بالشحم يتناسب مع صغر العينين ، وكأنهما جاحظتان.

١٦ . التناسب طردياً بين الرجلين والذراعين والرسخين ، والكفين ، والأصابع والأظافر ، طولاً وقصراً ، وشكلاً ، ولوناً وما إليها.

1. There is a correspondence between the limbs. If the arms are either long or short the legs will be proportional. Fingers, toes and other extremities will correspond accordingly.

2. There is a correspondence between the neck and the shoulders. A short and thick neck is in proportion to the width and thickness of the shoulders, and vice-versa.

3. The length of the body is six times the length of the foot.

4. The length of the face from the hairline to the lowest point of the chin is equal to the distance between the wrist crease to the tip of the middle finger; each is one-tenth the length of the body.

5. The chest is one-fourth the length of the body.

6. The top of the chest to the forehead is one-seventh the length of the body.

7. The circumference of the wrist is half of that of the neck.

8. If the face is divided into three equal sections, the first section ends at the meeting of the eyebrows, the second section at the tip of the nose, and the third section at the bottom of the chin.

9. If the length of the body is divided in half the navel is the midpoint. If a person outstretches his arms perpendicular to the torso, the distance from the fingertips is equal to the length of the body. It is rare for this to always be the case because of certain natural tendencies for difference that are due to various external factors, inherited traits or other conditions.

Most of the differences between the limbs result from a particular repetitive activity. These differences are more evident when one exercises. Limbs that are used more develop and become stronger while the other limbs remain as they are.

10. The distance between the eyes is an eye.

11. The ears and the nose are on the same horizontal plane.

12. The mass of the body is in proportion to the girth of the stomach.

13. The strength of the body corresponds to the shortness and thickness of the neck.

14. The roundness of the jaw corresponds to the roundness of the face.

15. The covering of the body with fat corresponds to the smallness of the eyes, as if they protrude.

16. There is a correspondence in the girth of the legs, arms, wrists, palms, fingers and nails with respect to their length, shape and color, as well as other qualities.

هذا وسوف نوضح ذلك مفصلاً عند الفراسة الحكمية ، ثم اعلم أن معرفة الأعضاء يقود إلى معرفة صفاتها والتناسب بين الأعضاء يقود إلى معرفة التناسب بين الصفات ، ومعرفة الموجودات وصفاتها يقود إلى معرفة الترابط بينها وبالتالي تشخيص أفراد العائلة الواحدة كالأنواع أو ما يكون قريب منها أي الأقرب فالأقرب.

ثم إن معرفة الأعضاء وصفاتها وتمييز كونها على الوضع الطبيعي أولاً ، وأثرها على الأعضاء الأخرى وأخلاق الإنسان ، ومقدار قوة ارتباطها أو ضعف ارتباطها بالموجودات وظيفة المتفرس الذي يشخص هذه المسائل وغيرها ، حتى يعين الدواء المناسب لها إن كان من أهل الهداية والتعليم.

We will elaborate on this more in our study of analytical physiognomy (*firāsa*). Know then, that knowledge of the limbs leads to knowledge of their characteristics, knowledge of the correspondences between the limbs leads to the knowledge of the correspondences between their qualities, and the knowledge of the entities and their qualities leads to knowledge of their interrelationships. This allows for the classification of members of a single family into a species, then those that are next of kin.

Thus, gaining knowledge of the limbs and their characteristics, discerning their natural state, their effect on the other limbs and human character, the strength or weakness of their connection with the entities is the work of the clairvoyant (*mutafarris*) who identifies these and other matters, so that if he is a guide and teacher, then he can prescribe a suitable remedy.

الباب السادس

التناسب بين الموجودات

اعلم أن التناسب والعلاقة كما أنها بين أعضاء وأجزاء الموجود الواحد كذلك بين الموجودات وأعضاءها ، فإذا نظرت إلى الكائنات رأيت لكل منها خصوصية يمتاز بها عن سواه ، فعالم النبات مثلاً بين أنواعه فرقاً تختلف باختلاف خصائصه ويقال مثل ذلك في الحيوان والإنسان والجماد ، ولكننا مع ذلك نرى أن المخلوقات تتشابه من وجوه كثيرة ، وعلى هذا التشابه قسموها إلى جماد ونبات وحيوان ، وذكروا لكل قسم خصائص يمتاز بها عن القسمين الآخرين ثم نظروا في هذه الأقسام فرأوا بين أجزائها تخالفاً يقضي بانقسامها إلى مجاميع ، فقسموا النبات إلى أنواع وهكذا الجماد والحيوان ، وقسموا كل نوع إلى ما تحته.

والتشابه قريب وثابت في الأجسام الجامدة ، ثم يبتعد ويتشوش في الأحياء ، ويزداد كلما ارتقى في سلم الحياة ، ومعنى ذلك أن أفراد النوع الواحد من المخلوقات يزيد الاختلاف بين ظواهرها بنسبة التفاوت في أعمالها ، فالجماد قليل العمل بسيط التركيب ، والاختلاف بين أفراده قليل .

والنبات وظائفه مركبة وأعماله أرقى فتنوعاته أكثر ، وأما الحيوان فانه أرقى من النبات ووظائفه أكثر ، والاختلاف بين أفراده أبعد وبعبارة أخرى إن التشابه مثلا بين بلورتين من بلورات الملح يكاد يكون تاماً.

وأما بين قمحتين أو شعيرتين أو تفاحتين فالتشابه أبعد ، وهو أبعد من ذلك بين فرسين أو نعجتين.

وأما في الإنسان فالاختلاف بين أفراده أبعد مما بين سائر أنواع الحيوان ، وهو أكثر في الأمم المترقية مما في الأمم البعيدة وأخيراً إذا اطلعت على شيء من قانون التشابه وناموس التناسب فاعلم :

أولاً : إن الأنواع المتشابهة شكلاً تتشابه عملاً وبالعكس فالتشابه بين بعض الناس وبعض الحيوانات شكلاً تتشابه عملاً وصفةً بحسب الطبيعة ، وإما المحيط والوراثة فلها أثر في تغيير الصفات والأفعال.

CHAPTER 6

The Correspondence Between Entities

Just as limbs of a single entity correspond to one another, there are correspondences between separate entities. If you observe creation you will see that entities each have distinct properties. Each species of plant has distinct characteristics that set it apart from another and this also applies to minerals, animals and human beings. Yet entities also share similarities in numerous aspects, the very basis for the classification as minerals, plants or animals. Differences among members of a single family also require further subdivision into species by descending order.

Similarities among inanimate objects are closely related but become more obscure and distant among living things, becoming increasingly so as they move up the hierarchy of life. What this means is that individuals of a single species increase in disparity in their outward characteristics in proportion to the diversity of their activities. Inanimate objects are simple in composition and have little movement; therefore, variation among them is slight.

Plants, however, have complex functions and more advanced activities, so variation among them is greater. Likewise, animals engage in more advanced activity than plants and their functions are more diverse; thus, variation among them is still greater. In contrast, there is almost complete similarity between salt crystals.

There is greater variance between two grains of wheat, barley or apples than two salt crystals, and still greater between two horses or two goats.

As for the human being, there is greater variance between its individuals than between all the species of animals. This is because man is the most advanced family of the developed creatures. Finally, having gained some insight into the principles of similarities and the laws of correspondences, then know that:

Firstly, species that resemble one another in form resemble one another in activity and vice-versa, and that resemblance between certain people or between certain animals is indicative of their similar activities and natural qualities. As for environmental and inherited qualities, they do have an effect in the transformation of traits and actions.

ثانياً : في التشابه في الجماد أكثر وضوحاً مما في النبات والأخير أوضح مما في الحيوان.

ثالثاً : إن ظواهر الأجسام تختلف باختلاف بواطنها ، فكلما تفرعت أعمال الجسم تعددت ظواهر وتعمقت بواطنه وتفرعت جذوره وما ذلك إلا لمناسبة الظاهر والباطن وبها يتفرس في الأشياء ويكشف خفاياها ، ويدرك مدى ارتباط الإنسان بها ، ودرجة الارتباط وكيفيته ، فإن آيات الله ومخلوقاته رسائله التي بها يهدي العباد إلى سبيله وصراطه المستقيم.

والله يقول الحق وهو يهدي السبيل.

Secondly, similarities between inanimate matter is more apparent than that of plants and animals.

Thirdly, bodies outwardly reflect their inward aspect. The more diverse the activities of a body, the more numerous its outward manifestations, the more profound its inward aspect and the more variegated its roots. This is due to the correspondence between the outward and inward, and the way in which one discerns the inward nature of things, unveils the hidden and perceives the type and degree of one's relation to them. The signs of God and His creatures are His communications through which the servants are guided on His way and the straight path.

God speaks the truth and guides the way.

الباب السابع

التناسب بين الصفات

لما كان ملاك سير النفس وتكاملها الفضيلة والرذيلة ، وأن الفضائل أربعة[1] والرذائل مثلها في بادئ النظر وهي أضدادها فالحكمة[2] ضدها الجهل[3] ، والشجاعة[4] ضدها الجبن[5] ، والعفة[6] ضدها الشره[7] والعدالة[8] ضدها الجور[9].

وعند التحقيق يظهر أن لكل فضيلة حداً معيناً ، والتجاوز عند الأفراط أو التفريط يؤدي إلى الرذيلة ، فالفضائل بمنزلة الأوساط ، والرذائل بمثابة الأطراف والوسط واحد

---

١ جامع السعادات / ج١ / ص٥٥.

٢ الحكمة : وهي معرفة حقائق الموجودات على ما هي عليه ، والموجودات إن لم يكن وجودها بقدرتنا واختيارنا ، فالعلم المتعلق بها هو الحكمة النظرية ، وان كان وجودها بقدرتنا واختيارنا فالعلم المتعلق بها هو الحكمة العملية.

٣ الجهل : وهو عدم معرفة الحقائق على ما هي عليه.

٤ الشجاعة : هي إطاعة القوة الغضبية للعاقلة في الإقدام على الأمور الهائلة وعدم اضطرابها بالخوض فيما يقتضيه رأيها حتى يكون فعلها ممدوحاً وصبرها محموداً.

٥ الجبن : وهو الحذر عما ينبغي الإقدام عليه.

٦ العفة : هي انقياد القوة الشهوية للعاقلة فيما تأمرها به وتنهاها عنه حتى تكتسب الحرية ، وتتخلص عن أسر عبودية الهوى.

٧ الشره : الانهماك في اللذات الشهوية على ما لا يحسن شرعاً وعقلاً.

٨ العدالة : هي انقياد العقل العملي للقوة العاقلة وتبعيته لها في جميع تصرفاته ، أو ضبطه الغضب والشهوة تحت إشارة العقل والشرع الذي يحكم العقل أيضاً بوجوب إطاعته ، أو سياسة قوتي الغضب والشهوة ، وحملها على مقتضى الحكمة ، وضبطهما في الاسترسال والانقباض على حسب مقتضاه ، وإلى هذا يرجع تعريف الغزالي :
« إنها حالة للنفس وقوة بها يسوس الغضب والشهوة ، ويحملهما على مقتضى الحكمة ، ويضبطهما في الاسترسال والانقباض على حسب مقتضاها ».
إذ المراد من الحالة والقوة هنا قوة الاستعلاء التي للعقل العملي لا نفس القوة العملية. والمقصود من العقل العملي هو مبدأ تحريك البدن في الأعمال الجزئية بالرَّوية. إذا كان العقل العملي مبدأ لتحريك البدن فهو قوة تحريك لا قوة إدراك ، وفي الحقيقة أن غرضهم من العقل العملي هو إدراك ما ينبغي أن يعمل.

٩ الجور : وهو التصرف في حقوق الناس وأموالهم بدون حق.

CHAPTER 7

The Correspondence Between Attributes

The criterion for the soul's movement and perfection are the virtues and vices. At first glance, there are four cardinal virtues and their contrary vices,[1] as wisdom[2] is contrary to ignorance,[3] bravery[4] is contrary to cowardice,[5] temperance[6] is contrary to covetousness[7] and justice[8] is contrary to oppression.[9]

Upon closer inspection, every virtue has a distinct boundary, any excess or deficiency thereof leads to vice. Virtue is akin to the midpoint of a circle and vices are on the periphery. The midpoint is a singular point that does not allow

---

1 *Jāmiʿ al-Saʿādāt*, 1:55.

2 Wisdom is to know realities of things as they truly are. If entities exist outside of our power and choice, then that knowledge relates to theoretical wisdom, and if their existence is within our power and choice, then that relates to practical wisdom.

3 Ignorance is the lack of knowledge of realities as they truly are.

4 Bravery is obedience of the faculty of anger to the intellect when confronted with a dangerous situation. It is to maintain composure when doing something that merits fear admiration and whose forbearance is praiseworthy.

5 Cowardice is fear of taking action when necessary.

6 Temperance is the submission of desire to the intellect's commands and prohibitions so that it is liberated from the bondage of vain desire.

7 Covetousness is absorption in pleasures of base desire to an extent unapproved by the intellect and divine code.

8 Justice is obedience of the practical intellect to the faculty of intellect, so that anger and desire is controlled under the aegis of the intellect and divine code to which the intellect must comply. In other words, it is to regulate the powers of anger and desire and bring them in conformity with wisdom, controlling their expansion and contraction accordingly.
Refer to al-Ghazālī's definition in the following: "[Justice] is a state of the soul and a power that regulates anger and desire, bringing them to comply with wisdom and controlling their expansion and contraction in that which is necessary." What is meant by state and power of the soul is the power to govern which belongs to the practical intellect, not the practical faculty. What is meant by the practical intellect is the origin of bodily movements for specific actions through the process of thinking. If the practical faculty is the origin of bodily movements, then it is the power of movement not the power of perception. However, the practical intellect is the awareness of that which must be done.

9 Oppression is wrongfully availing oneself of people's rights and wealth.

معين لا يقبل التعدد ، والأطراف غير متناهية عدداً فالفضيلة بمثابة مركز الدائرة ، والرذائل بمثابة سائر النقاط المفروضة من المركز إلى المحيط ، فان المركز نقطة معينه ، مع كونه أبعد النقاط من المحيط وسائر النقاط المفروضة من جوانبه غير متناهية ، مع أن كلا منها أقرب منه من طرف إليه.

وتكون الفضيلة في غاية البعد عن الرذيلة التي هي نهاية الرذائل ويكون كل كلا من الرذائل أقرب من الفضيلة إلى النهاية ، ومجرد الانحراف عن الفضيلة من أي طرف اتفق يوجب الوقوع في الرذيلة. والثبات على الفضيلة والاستقامة في طريقها بمنزلة الحركة على الخط المستقيم ، وارتكاب الرذيلة كالانحراف عنه ، ولا ريب في أن الخط المستقيم هو أقصر الخطوط الواصلة بين النقطتين ، وهو لا يكون إلا واحداً ، وأما الخطوط المنحنية بينهما فغير متناهية ، فالاستقامة في طريق الفضيلة وملازمتها في نهج الحق ، والانحراف عنه تكون له مناهج غير متناهية ، ولذلك غلبت دواعي الشر على بواعث الخير.

ويظهر أن وجدان الوسط الحقيقي صعب ، والثبات عليه بعد الوجدان أصعب لان الاستقامة على جادة الاعتدال في غاية الإشكال ، ولذلك لما أُمر الرسول الأكرم ﷺ بالاستقامة في قوله تعالى : ﴿فَاسْتَقِمْ كَمَا أُمِرْتَ﴾ [هود:١١٢] قال : شيبتني سورة هود ﵇ ، إذ وجدان الوسط الحقيقي فيما بين الأطراف الغير المتناهية المتقابلة مشكل ، والثبات عليه بعد الوجدان أشكل.

ثم الوسط إما حقيقي[١٠] أو إضافي[١١] ، فالتسمية بالوسط إنما هو بالنسبة إلى الأطراف التي هي أبعد من الحقيقي بالإضافة إليه ، وهذا كالاعتدالات النوعية والشخصية التي أثبتها الأطباء ، فان المراد منها الاعتدالات التي يمكن تحققها للأنواع والأشخاص ، وهو القدر الذي يليق بكل نوع أو شخص أن يكون عليه وان لم يكن اعتدالاً حقيقياً بمعنى تساوي الأجزاء البسيطة العنصرية وتكافؤها في القوة والأقربية إلى الحقيقي بالنسبة إلى سائر الأطراف سمي إضافياً.

---

١٠ الوسط الحقيقي : وهو ما تكون نسبته إلى الطرفين على السواء ، كالأربعة بالنسبة إلى الاثنين والستة.

١١ الوسط الإضافي : وهو أقرب ما يمكن تحققه للنوع أو الشخص إلى الحقيقي ويتحقق به كمالهما اللائق بحالهما وان لم يصل إليه.

for multiplicity, whereas, there are infinite peripheral points. In other words, the center of a circle is virtue and every other point on the circumference is vice. The center of the circle is the single furthest point from the circumference. While there are infinite points along the circumference, each adjacent point on the radius is a point closer to the center.

Nothing is further from (absolute) virtue than (absolute) vice, whereas, the distance of any vice adjacent to (absolute) virtue is infinitesimal. Even the slightest deviation to either side of virtue results in falling into vice. Thus, remaining steadfast on the path of virtue is tantamount to walking in a straight line, whereas vice is deviating from that line. Undoubtedly, the shortest distance between two points is a single straight line. However, there are an infinite amount of curved lines connecting two points. Adhering to the path of virtue and the way of truth is a straight path while deviation occurs in infinite ways. That is why summoners to evil are more plentiful than emissaries of good.

Finding the true center is difficult, but once found, remaining steadfast is harder still because the road to moderation is prohibitively arduous. Thus, when the Prophet was commanded to be steadfast in the verse, "Be steadfast as you have been commanded" (11:112), he said, "Surat Hūd has made my hair turn gray." If finding the true center between the infinite opposing sides is difficult, remaining steadfast once it is found is even more formidable.

The center is either a true center[10] or a relative center.[11] The latter is called a center in relation to the relative distance of its peripheral points from the true center. This is akin to the center found in individuals and types. The relative centers whose scope is appropriate for that type or individual are determined by physicians, even if in reality they are not true centers. Since the true center is defined as the equilibrium of all simple elements and the equanimity of all powers, it is, therefore, called a relative center due to its proximity to the true center.

---

10 The true center is one that is equidistant from its extremes, as the number four is in relation to the numbers two and six.

11 The relative center is the closest possible point that a person or type may reach befitting their state, even if the true center is not attained.

ثم الوسط المعتبر هنا هو الإضافي لتعذر وجدان الحقيقي والثبات عليه ، ولذا تختلف الفضيلة باختلاف الأشخاص والأحوال والأزمان ، فربما كانت مرتبة من الوسط الإضافي فضيلة بالنظر إلى شخص أو حال أو وقت ، ورذيلة بالنسبة إلى غيره.

إنه لا ريب في أن الوسط الحقيقي في الأخلاق لكونه في حكم نقطة غير منقسمة لا يمكن وجدانه ولا الثبات عليه ، ولذا ترى من هو متصف بفضيلة من الفضائل لا يمكن الحكم بكون تلك الفضيلة هي الوسط الحقيقي إلا انه لما كانت تلك الفضيلة قريبة إليه ولا يمكن وجود الأقرب منها إليه ، يحكم بكونها وسطاً إضافياً لأقربيتها إليه بالنسبة إلى سائر المراتب فالاعتدال الإضافي له عرض ، وسطه الاعتدال الحقيقي وطرفاه الأفراط أو التفريط وإذا خرج منهما دخل في الرذيلة.

والقانون اللازم بيانه هو أن الانحراف عن الوسط إما إلى طرف الإفراط أو إلى طرف التفريط ، فيكون بإزاء كل فضيلة جنسان من الرذيلة ، ولما كانت أجناس الفضائل أربعة فتكون أجناس الرذائل ثمانية هي :

بإزاء الحكمة « الجربزة[١٢] والبله »[١٣] ، بإزاء الشجاعة « التهور[١٤] والجبن »، بإزاء العفة « الشره والخمود »[١٥] ، بإزاء العدالة « الظلم والانظلام »[١٦].

قال الشيخ النراقي(رحمه الله) : والحق أن العدالة مع ملاحظة ما لا ينفك عنها من لوازمها ، لها طرف واحد يسمى جوراً وظلماً ، وهو يشمل جميع ذمائم الصفات ، ولا يختص بالتصرف في حقوق الناس وأموالهم بدون جهة شرعية ، لان العدالة عبارة عن ضبط العقل العملي جميع القوى تحت إشارة العقل النظري ، فهو جامع للكمالات بأسرها ، فالظلم الذي هو مقابله جامع للنقائص بأسرها ، إذ حقيقة الظلم وضع الشيء في غير موضعه ، وهو يتناول جميع ذمائم الصفات والأفعال فتمكين الظالم من ظلمه لما كان صفة ذميمة يكون ظلماً ، على أن من

---

١٢ الجربزة : في طرف الأفراط وهو استعمال الفكر في ما لا ينبغي أو في الزائد عما ينبغي.

١٣ البله : في طرف التفريط وهو تعطيل القوة الفكرية وعدم استعمالها في ما ينبغي أو في أقل منه.

١٤ التهور : في طرف الأفراط ، وهو الإقدام على ما ينبغي الحذر منه ، وأما الجبن ذكرناه سابقاً فراجع.

١٥ الخمود : في طرف التفريط ، وهو سكون النفس عن طلب ما هو ضروري للبدن ، وأما الشره فقد ذكرناه سابقاً.

١٦ الانظلام : في طرف التفريط ، وهو تمكين الظالم من الظلم عليه وانقياده له فيما يريده من الجبر والتعدي على سبيل المذلة ، وأما الظلم فقد ذكر.

The difficulty in finding and adhering to the real center leads to a relative center. This is why virtues differ in relation to individual, condition and time. In the context of a particular condition and time, the relative center may be a virtue for one individual but a vice for another.

There is no doubt that it is virtually impossible to find and uphold the true ethical center considering that it is an indivisible point. If it is said that someone has a given virtue, then it cannot be said that they possess the true ethical center of that virtue, but are simply close to it. If there is no possibility of becoming closer to the true center, then it is considered a relative center in view of the possible degrees of proximity. Thus, relative justice possesses breadth; the true center is its essence and the slightest excess or deficiency are on the periphery. One who departs from the center enters into vice.

As mentioned, straying from the center results in either excess or deficiency. Therefore, the absence of virtue results in two types of vice. Since the cardinal virtues are four, the resulting vices are eight:

The absence of wisdom results in either deceit[12] or stupidity,[13] the absence of bravery results in either recklessness[14] or cowardice, the absence of temperance results in either covetousness or indolence[15] and the absence of justice results in oppression or submission.[16]

Shaykh Narāqī writes, "The truth of the matter is that justice with all its necessary attributes, has only one opposing side which is called oppression and tyranny, and it comprises every negative attribute. It is not limited to transgressing the rights of people and their wealth. This is because justice occurs when the practical intellect harnesses of all the faculties under the theoretical intellect, which gathers all perfections. Oppression, on the other hand, gathers every defect since the reality of oppression is to place a thing where it does not belong. Oppression encompasses every negative attribute and action. When one oppresses another, the attribute of oppression is

12 Deceit is an excess condition; it is employing the intellect for something undesirable or using it inordinately for something that is desirable.

13 Stupidity is a deficient condition; it is the suspension of the faculty of intellect, not employing it in what is required, or even less.

14 Recklessness is an excess condition; it is to plunge into something that ought to be feared. Cowardice has been mentioned previously.

15 Indolence is a condition of deficiency; it is to be apathetic in fulfilling bodily needs. Covetousness has been mentioned previously.

16 Submission is a condition of deficiency which is to enable an oppressor against oneself and to obey him in his wish for domination, power and humiliating others. Oppression has been mentioned previously.

مكّن الظالم من الظلم عليه وانقاد له ذلة ، فقد ظلم نفسه ، والظلم على النفس أيضاً من أفسام الظلم.(١٧)

ثم لكل واحد من أجناس الرذائل والفضائل أنواع ولوازم من الأخلاق والأفعال ذكرها علماء الأخلاق ، وقد ذكروا للعدالة أيضاً أنواعاً وان تخصيص بعض الصفات بالاندراج تحتها مما لا وجه له ، إذ جميع الرذائل والفضائل لا يخرج عن التعلق بالقوى الثلاث ، وإن كان للقوة العملية مدخلية في الجميع من حيث التوسط.

ولمزيد الإحاطة نشير إجمالاً إلى أسماء الأجناس والأنواع واللوازم التي لكل جنس. أما جنسا الرذيلة للقوة العقلية فهما الجربزه(١٨) والجهل البسيط(١٩) ، وضدهما العلم والحكمة ، وأما الأنواع واللوازم المترتبة عليهما ، فمنها الجهل المركب(٢٠) ، ومنها الحيرة والشك(٢١) ، ومنها الشرك ، وضده التوحيد ، ومنها الوساوس(٢٢) ، وضدها الخواطر المحمودة التي من جملتها الفكر في بدائع صنع الله وعجائب مخلوقاته ، ومنها استنباط المكر والحيلة(٢٣).

وأما جنسا الرذائل للقوة الغضبية ، فهما التهور والجبن ، وضدهما الشجاعة ، وأما الأنواع واللوازم المترتبة عليهما ، فمنها الخوف(٢٤) ، ومنها صغر النفس(٢٥) ، ومنها دناءة الهمة(٢٦) ، ومنها عدم الغيرة والحمية(٢٧) ، ومنها العجلة(٢٨) ، ومنها

---

١٧ جامع السعادات / ج١ / ص٥٩ « بتصرف ».

١٨ الجربزة والسفسطة : وهي من طرف الأفراط.

١٩ الجهل البسيط : وهو من طرف التفريط.

٢٠ الجهل المركب : وهو من باب رداءة الكيفية.

٢١ الحيرة والشك : وهو من طرف الأفراط.

٢٢ الوساوس : أي الوساوس النفسانية والخواطر الشيطانية وهو من باب رداءة الكيفية.

٢٣ استنباط المكر والحيلة للوصول إلى مقتضيات الشهوة والغضب ، وهو من طرف الأفراط.

٢٤ الخوف : هيئة نفسانية مؤذية تحدث من توقع مكروه أو زوال مرغوب ، وهو مذموم إلا ما كان لأجل المعصية والخيانة ، أو من الله وعظمته.

٢٥ صغر النفس : أي ملكة العجز عن تحمل الواردات ، وهو من نتائج الجبن ، وضده كبر النفس أي ملكة التحمل لما يرد عليه كائنا ما كان.

٢٦ دناءة الهمة : وهو القصور عن طلب معالي الأمور ، وهو من لوازم ضعف النفس وصغرها وضده علو الهمة الذي هو من لوازم كبر النفس وشجاعتها.

٢٧ عدم الغيرة : أي الإهمال في محافظة ما يلزم حفظه ، وهو من نتائج صغر النفس وضعفها.

٢٨ العجلة : وهو المعنى الراتب (الدائم الثابت) في القلب الباعث للإقدام على أمر بأول خاطر من دون توقف فيه ، وهو من نتائج صغر النفس وضعفها ، وضده الإناءة والتأني.

substantiated in him, whereas one who accedes to being oppressed and becomes submissive, accepts humiliation and oppresses himself; oppressing oneself is also a type of oppression."[17]

Scholars of ethics have mentioned that for each type of vice and virtue there are various types of character traits and actions along with their subsidiaries. They have stated that there are also various types of justice, having specified certain attributes subsumed under it, since all vices and virtues are closely affiliated with one of the three faculties, even though the practical faculty intervenes in all of them.

For the sake of completeness, we will mention the types of vices along with their subsidiary qualities. The two vices pertaining to the faculty of intellect are deceit[18] and simple ignorance[19] and their contraries are knowledge and wisdom. Their subsidiary qualities are compound ignorance,[20] bewilderment and doubt;[21] polytheism whose contrary is divine unity; satanic insinuation[22] whose contrary is praiseworthy thoughts exemplified by reflecting on the marvels of God's design and the wonders of His creation; concocting deceit and guile.[23]

The two vices pertaining to the faculty of anger are recklessness and cowardice and their contrary is bravery. The types and subsidiary qualities arising from them are fear,[24] low self-esteem,[25] lowliness of aspiration,[26] lacking a sense of honor[27] and protectiveness, precipitance,[28] mistrusting God and the

---

17 *Jāmiʿ al-saʿādāt*, 1:59.

18 Deception and sophistry are excess conditions.

19 Simple ignorance is a deficient condition.

20 Compound ignorance is a vice measured qualitatively.

21 Bewilderment and doubt are excess conditions.

22 Insinuation is a satanic inclination originating from the lower self and a vice measured qualitatively.

23 Guile, an excess condition, is to devise stratagems to fulfil desire and anger.

24 Fear is a painful condition of the soul which occurs by expecting negative outcomes or the forfeiture of positive ones. Unless it involves committing sins or breaking trusts, or it is the fear of God and His greatness, it is blameworthy.

25 Low self-esteem is the inability of the self to bear anything that it confronts; it is a result of cowardice. Its opposite is self-confidence which is the ability of the self to withstand whatever comes its way.

26 Lowliness of aspiration is deficiency in seeking lofty pursuits which arises from weakness of the self and low self-esteem. Its opposite is high-minded aspiration which arises from self-confidence and bravery.

27 Lack of honor is to shirk the duty to protect that which is in your charge. It arises from low self-esteem and weakness.

28 Precipitance is to propel headlong into an action without forethought. It arises from low self-esteem and weakness and its opposite is deliberateness and purposefulness.

سوء الظن بالله[٢٩] تعالى وبالمؤمنين ، ومنها الغضب[٣٠] ، ومنها الانتقام[٣١] ومنها العنف[٣٢] ، ومنها سوء الخلق ومنها الحقد[٣٣] ، ومنها العداوة ، وضدها النصيحة أي إرادة الخير والصلاح ، ودفع الشر والفساد ، ومنها العجب[٣٤] ، وضده انكسار النفس واستحقارها ، ومنها الكبر[٣٥] ، وضده التواضع ، ومنها الافتخار[٣٦] ، ومنها البغي[٣٧]وضده التسليم ، ومنها تزكية النفس وضده الاعتراف بنقائصها ، ومنها العصبية[٣٨]ومنها كتمان الحق وضدها الإنصاف والاستقامة على الحق ، ومنها القساوة[٣٩] و ضدها الرحمة.

وأما جنسا الرذائل المتعلقة بالقوة الشهوية ، فهما الشرة والخمود وضدها العفة وأما الأنواع واللوازم المتعلقة بها ، فمنها حب الدنيا ، ومنها حب المال ، وضدهما الزهد ، ومنها الغنى ، وضده الفقر ، ومنها الحرص ، وضده القناعة ، ومنها الطمع وضده الاستغناء عن الناس ، ومنها البخل ، وضده السخاء ، ومنها طلب الحرام ، وضده الورع والتقوى بالمعنى الأخص ، ومنها الغدر والخيانة ، وضدهما الأمانة ، ومنها أنواع الفجور من الزنا واللواط وشرب الخمر والاشتغال بالملاهي وأمثالها ، ومنها الخوض في الباطل ، ومنها التكلم بما لا يعني والفضول ، وضدهما الترك والصمت أو التكلم بما يعني بقدر الضرورة.

وأما الرذائل والفضائل المتعلقة بالقوى الثلاث أو باثنين ، فمنها :الحسد وضده النصيحة ، ومنها الإيذاء والإهانة والاحتقار وضدها كف

---

٢٩ سوء الظن بالله والمؤمنين : من لوازم الجبن وضعف النفس ، وربما كان من باب رداءة الكيفية ، فضده حسن الظن بهما من آثار الشجاعة وكبر النفس.

٣٠ الغضب : حركة نفسانية يوجب حركة الروح من الداخل إلى الخارج للغلبة وهو من باب الأفراط ، وضده الحلم.

٣١ الانتقام : وهو من نتائج الغضب وضده العفو.

٣٢ العنف : وهو من نتائج الغضب وضده الرفق.

٣٣ الحقد : وهو العداوة الكامنة ، أي إرادة الشر وقصد زوال الخير ، وهو من ثمرات الغضب.

٣٤ العجب : وهو استعظام النفس.

٣٥ الكبر : وهو التعظيم الموجب لرؤية النفس فوق الغير ، وضده التواضع أن لا يرى لنفسه مزيه على الغير.

٣٦ الافتخار : وهو المباهاة بما يظنه كمالًا ، وهو من شعب الكبر.

٣٧ البغي : وهو عدم الانقياد لمن يجب أن ينقاد ، وهو من شعب الكبر.

٣٨ العصبية : وهي الحماية عن نفسه ، وعما ينتسب إليه بالباطل ، والخروج عن الحق.

٣٩ القساوة : وهو عدم التأثر عن مشاهدة تألم أبناء النوع.

believers,[29] anger,[30] vengefulness,[31] severity,[32] bad temperament, hatred,[33] enmity whose contrary is good counsel or good will; warding off evil and corruption; vanity[34] whose contrary is diffidence and self-effacement; arrogance[35] whose contrary is humility; pride,[36] rebellion[37] whose contrary is surrender; purification of the soul whose contrary is confession of defects; bigotry,[38] covering truth whose contrary is fairness and upholding truth; hard-heartedness[39] whose contrary is mercy.

The two vices pertaining to the faculty of desire are covetousness and indolence and their contrary is temperance. Their subsidiary qualities are love of the world, love of wealth whose contrary is asceticism; needlessness whose opposite is poverty; greed whose contrary is contentment; covetousness whose contrary is independence from people; stinginess whose contrary is generosity; seeking the unlawful whose contrary is godliness and piety in the specific sense; treachery and betrayal whose contrary is trustworthiness; sins such as fornication, sodomy, imbibing alcohol, preoccupation with vain amusements; delving into falsehood; speaking nonsense and in excess, whose contrary is silence and speaking according to need.

The vices that pertain to two or more faculties are as follows: Envy whose contrary is good counsel; causing harm, belittlement, and disdainfulness whose contraries are curtailing harm, respecting and honoring; frightening a believer and filling his heart with worry whose contrary is dispelling his fear and worry; neglecting to help the believer whose contrary is fulfilling

29 Having a negative opinion of God and the believers arises from cowardice and low self-esteem. It may be considered a qualitative vice. Its opposite is holding them in high esteem which arises from bravery and self-confidence.
30 Anger is a movement of the soul that brings the spirit from the inside outwardly in order to dominate. It is a condition of excess and its opposite is forbearance.
31 Vengefulness arises from anger and its opposite is forgiveness.
32 Severity arises from anger and its opposite is gentleness.
33 Hatred is inward hostility, ill will and the desire to deprive one of goodness. It is one of the fruits of anger.
34 Vanity is self-admiration.
35 Arrogance is the feeling of greatness, viewing oneself superior to others. Its opposite is humility which is not seeing the self as superior.
36 Pride is exultation in one's supposed perfection. It is a branch of arrogance.
37 Rebellion is refusing to obey rightful authority. It is a branch of arrogance.
38 Bigotry is self-preservation through false attribution and a departure from truth.
39 Hard-heartedness is apathy towards the suffering of one's own kind.

الأذى والإكرام والتعظيم ، ومنها إخافة المسلم وإدخال الكرب على قلبه ، وضدهما إزالة الخوف والكرب عنه ، ومنها ترك إعانة المسلمين وضده قضاء حوائجهم ، ومنها المداهنة في الأمر بالمعروف والنهي عن المنكر وضده السعي فيهما ، ومنها الهجرة والتباعد عن الإخوان وضده التآلف والتزاور ومنها قطع الرحم وضده الصلة ، ومنها عقوق الوالدين وضده البرّ إليهما ، ومنها تجسس العيوب وضده الستر ، ومنها إفشاء السر وضده الكتمان ، ومنها الإفساد بين الناس وضده الإصلاح بينهم ، ومنها الشماتة بمسلم ، ومنها المراء والجدال والخصومة وضدهما طيب الكلام ، ومنها السخرية والاستهزاء وضدهما المزاح ، ومنها الغيبة وضدها المدح ودفع الذم ، ومنها الكذب وضده الصدق ، ومنها حب الجاه والشهرة وضده حب الخمول ، ومنها النفاق وضده استواء السر والعلانية ، ومنها الغرور وضده الفطانة والعلم والزهد ، ومنها طول الأمل وضده قصره ، ومنها مطلق العصيان وضده الورع والتقوى بالمعنى الأعم ، ومنها الوقاحة وضده الحياء ، ومنها الإصرار على المعصية وضده التوبة ، ومنها الغفلة وضدها النية والإرادة ، ومنها عدم الرغبة وضده الشوق ومنها الكراهية وضده الحب ، ومنها الجفاء وضده الوفاء وهو تمام الحب ، ومنها البعد وضده الأنس ومن لوازمه حب الخلوة والعزلة ، ومنها السخط وضده الرضا ، وقريب منه التسليم ويسمى تفويضاً بل هو فوق الرضا ، ومنها الحزن وضده السرور ، ومنها ضعف الوثوق والاعتماد على الله ، ومنها الفسق وضده الطاعة والعبادة وتندرج تحته العبادات الموظفة في الشرع من الطهارة ، والصلاة ، والذكر ، وتلاوة القرآن ، والزكاة ، والخمس ، والصوم ، والحج ، والزيارات[٤٠].

إذا علمت هذا والتفصيل المذكور في كتب الأخلاق والسير والسلوك ، فاعلم أن المؤمن المتفرس والشيخ الهادي يدرك ذلك بنور الفراسة وسلامة البصيرة فيسعى بهداية الله ورعايته في معونة الطالب لاكتساب الفضائل على حسب الترتيب الذي

---

٤٠ أن كثيراً من الصفات لها جهات مختلفة كل منها يناسب قوة ، فالاختلاف في الإدخال لأجل اختلاف الاعتبار للجهات ، ثم بعض الصفات ربما كان ببعض الاعتبارات محموداً معدوداً من الفضائل وببعض الاعتبارات معدوداً من الرذائل وذلك كالمحبة والخوف والرجاء ، فان الحب إن كان متعلقاً بالدنيا ومتعلقاتها كان مذموماً معدوداً من الرذائل ، وإن كان متعلقاً بالله وأوليائه كان محموداً معدوداً من الفضائل ، وهكذا الخوف إن كان مما لا يخاف منه عقلاً كان من رذائل قوة الغضب ، وان كان من المعاصي أو من عظمة الله كان من فضائلها ، وكذا الرجاء إن لم يكن في موقعه كان من الرذائل وإلا من الفضائل ، وهكذا غيرها مما له الاعتبارات المختلفة.

his needs; feigning to enjoin the good and forbid the evil whose contrary is striving to accomplish them; withdrawing from and abandoning brethren whose contrary is mutual affection and exchanging visits with one another; severing ties of kinship whose opposite is establishing ties; disobedience to parents whose contrary is dutifulness; fault-finding whose contrary is concealing faults; divulging secrets whose contrary is concealing secrets; sowing dissension among people whose contrary is reconciling them; rejoicing at the misfortune of another believer; arguing, disputing and quarreling whose contrary is pleasant speech; sarcasm and derision whose contrary is joking; backbiting whose contrary is praise and repelling censure; lying whose contrary is truthfulness; love of position and recognition whose contrary is love of obscurity; hypocrisy whose contrary is uniformity of one's inward and outward; conceit whose contrary is astuteness, knowledge, renunciation; false hope whose opposite is realism; every kind of sinfulness whose opposite is godliness and piety in the general sense; shamelessness whose contrary is modesty; persisting in sinfulness whose contrary is repentance; negligence whose contrary is intention and will; lack of longing whose contrary is yearning; hatred whose contrary is love; estrangement whose opposite is loyalty, which is the entirety of love; isolation whose contrary is intimacy of which seclusion and solitude are concomitants; displeasure whose contrary is satisfaction, which is close to submission and is called entrustment, a state higher than satisfaction; sadness whose contrary is happiness; lack of trust and reliance on God; sinfulness whose opposite is obedience and worship which is subsumed under those acts stipulated by divine law such as purification, prayer, invocation, recitation of the Qur'ān, almsgiving, khums, fasting, pilgrimage and visitation of holy sites.[40]

If you have come to know this—the details of which are mentioned in books of ethics and wayfaring—know that the clairvoyant believer and the guiding master (*shaykh*) perceive these affairs through the light of clairvoyance (*firāsa*), the soundness of their inward vision under the auspices and

---

40 Many attributes have multiple aspects each corresponding to a particular faculty. Their different aspects require one to engage with each attribute individually. Some attributes are praiseworthy from certain perspectives and blameworthy from other perspectives, such as love, fear and hope. If love is tied to the world and its attachments, then it is blameworthy and considered a vice, but if it is directed towards God and His saints, then it is praiseworthy and a virtue. Likewise, if a person fears something that the intellect deems unworthy of fear, it is a vice of the faculty of anger, but if one fears committing sin or fears the greatness of God, then it is a virtue. Similarly, if a hope is unfounded, then it is considered a vice, otherwise it is a virtue. The same is true for other qualities that possess multiple aspects.

ينبغي أن لا يتعدى عنه وبيان ذلك : إن مبادئ الحركات المؤدية إلى الكمالات : إما طبيعية كحركة النطفة في الأطوار المختلفة إلى بلوغ كمال الحيوانية ، أو صناعية كحركة الخشب بتوسط الآلات إلى بلوغ كمال السريرية.

ثم الطبيعية وتحريكاتها لاستنادها إلى المبادئ العالية تكون متقدمة على الصناعية المستندة إلى الإنسان ، ولما كان كمال الثواني التشبه بالأوائل فينبغي أن تقتدي الصناعية المؤدية إلى كمالها بالطبيعية.

وإذا ثبت ذلك ما علم : إن تهذيب الأخلاق لما كان أمراً صناعياً لزم أن يقتفى في تحصيله من حيث الترتيب بأفعال الطبيعة في ترتيب حصولها ، فان أول ما يحصل في الطفل قوة طلب الغذاء ، وإذا زادت تلك القوة يبكي ويرفع صوته لأجل الغذاء ، وإذا قويت حواسه وتمكن من حفظ بعض الصور يطلب صورة الأم أو الظئر (المرضعة) وجميع ذلك متعلق بالقوة الشهوية ، ونهاية هذه القوة وكمالها أن يتم ما يتعلق بالشخص من الأمور الشهوية ، وينبعث منه الميل إلى استبقاء النوع فيحدث ميل النكاح والوقاح ، ثم تظهر فيه آثار القوة الغضبية حتى يدفع عن نفسه ما يؤذيه ولو بالاستعانة بغيره.

وغاية كمال هذه القوة حصول التمكن من حفظ الشخص والأقدام على حفظ النوع فيحدث فيه الميل إلى ما يحصل به التفوق من أصناف الرئاسات والكرامات ، ثم تظهر فيه آثار قوة التمييز وتتزايد إلى أن يتمكن من تعقل الكليات.

وهنا يتم ما يتعلق بالطبيعة من التدبير والتكميل ، ويكون ابتداء التكميل الصناعي ، فلو لم يحصل الاستكمال بالكسب والصناعة بقي على هذه الحالة ولم يبلغ إلى الكمال الحقيقي الذي خُلق الإنسان لأجله ، لأنه لم يخلق أحد مجبولا على الاتصاف بجميع الفضائل الخلقية إلا من أُيّد من عند الله بالنفس القدسية ، وان كان بعض الناس اكثر استعداداً لتحصيل بعض الكمالات من بعض آخر ، فلابد لجل الأنام في تكميل نفوسهم من الكسب والاستعلام فظهر مما ذكر : إن الطبيعة تولد أولا قوّة الشهوة ، ثم قوة الغضب ، ثم قوة التمييز ، فيجب أن يقتدى به في التكميل الصناعي ، فيهذب أولا الأولى ليكتسب العفة ، ثم الثانية ليتصف بالشجاعة ، ثم الثالثة ليتحلى بالحكمة فمن حصل بعض الفضائل على الترتيب الحكمي كان تحصيل الباقي له في غاية السهولة ، ومن حصل لا على الترتيب ، فلا يظن أن تحصيل الباقي متعذراً بل هو ممكن ، وإن كان أصعب بالنسبة إلى تحصيله بالترتيب.

guidance of God, striving to assist the seeker in acquiring virtues in the proper order in which they ought to be acquired.

To further elaborate, the principles of movement leading to perfections are as follows: Movement is either natural, such as the movement of the embryo through various stages until it reaches the completion of its animality, or it is synthetic, such as the movement of wood through various instruments to its final stage of becoming a bed.

Furthermore, natural movement which relies on higher principles is superior to synthetic movement which relies on the human being. Given that secondary perfections resemble primary ones, it is necessary that the synthetic emulates the natural.

Since moral edification is synthetic, it is necessary that it emulates natural movement with respect to the order in which it is acquired. The first thing that an infant acquires is the power to seek its nourishment. When that power increases it cries and raises its voice. Then, when its faculties grow in strength and it is able to remember faces, it seeks the face of its mother or nursemaid, which are all related to the faculty of desire. The culmination of this faculty and its perfection is related to a person's ultimate desires. What stems from it is also the desire to secure one's progeny, so the sexual desire arises along with immodesty.

Then, the influence of the faculty of anger enables it to defend itself from whatever pains it, even if it is with the assistance of another. The culmination of this faculty is the ability to protect oneself and the survival of the species, which also gives rise to the inclination for ascendency, leadership and honor. Thereafter, the ability to make distinctions arises enabling one to comprehend universals.

This concludes natural organization and perfection and the trajectory of synthetic perfection commences. If perfection through acquisition and synthesis does not develop further the human being remains stagnant and does not ascend to the real perfection for which he was created. This is because no individual has been created having been endowed with every human virtue except one who is endorsed by God through the Sanctified Soul, though some have more receptivity to acquire certain perfections over others. Therefore, it is a matter of great importance to perfect oneself through acquisition and study.

In summary, nature initially endows the faculty of desire, then the faculty of anger, then the power of discernment, from which synthetic perfection follows. By rectifying the first, one obtains temperance, by the second, bravery, and by the third, one is adorned with wisdom. One who acquires some virtues in a judicious order will be able to acquire the rest with facility. Whereas, one

ثم الفضيلة إن كانت حاصلة لزم السعي في حفظها وإبقائها ، وإن لم تكن حاصلة بل كان ضدها حاصلا وجب تحصيلها بإزالة الضد.

وهذا ما يهدي إليه طبيب النفوس برحمة الله الواهب المتعال.

والحمد لله ربّ العالمين.

who acquires them haphazardly, even though it is not impossible to acquire the rest, will face greater challenges.

Therefore, if a virtue is within grasp one must strive to preserve and maintain it, and if it is not, except through its contrary, one must arrive at the virtue by embracing its contrary.

This is what the spiritual physicians advise, by the mercy of God, the Generous, the Sublime.

All praises belong to God, Lord of the worlds.

الباب الثامن

التناسب بين الإنسان والحيوان

ان في الإنسان أربع قوى مجتمعة هي القوة العقلية الملكية[1] ، والقوة الوهمية الخيالية[2] ، والقوة الغضبية السبعية[3] ، والقوة الشهوية البهيمية[4] ، مثلُ اجتماعها كمثل اجتماع حكيم ، وشيطان ، وكلب ، وخنزير في مربط واحد ، فأيهما صار غالباً كان الحكم له ، ولم يظهر من الأفعال والصفات إلا ما تقتضيه جبلته ، فالحكيم هو القوة العقلية ، والشيطان هو القوة الوهمية ، والكلب هو القوة الغضبية فان الكلب ليس كلباً مذموماً للونه وصورته بل لروح معنى الكلبية أي الضراوة والتكلب على الناس ، فمن غلب فيه هذه القوة هو الكلب حقيقةً وإن أُطلق عليه اسم الإنسان مجازاً ، كما قال سيد الأوصياء عليه السلام (فالصورةُ صورة إنسان ، والقلب قلبُ حيوان)[5].

والخنزير هو القوة الشهوية ، والنفس لا تزال محل تنازع هذه القوى وتدافعها إلى أن يغلب أحدها ، فالغضبية تدعوه إلى الظلم والإيذاء ، والعداوة والبغضاء ، والبهيمية تدعوه إلى المنكر والفواحش ، والحرص على المآكل والمناكح ، والشيطانية تهيج غضب السبعية وشهوة البهيمية ، وتزيد فعلهما ، والعقل شأنه أن يدفع غيظ

---

١ شأنها إدراك حقائق الأمور ، والتمييز بين الخيرات والشرور ، والأمر بالأفعال الجميلة والنهي عن الذميمة.

٢ شأنها استنباط وجوه المكر والحيل ، والتوصل إلى الأغراض بالتلبيس والخدع.

٣ موجبة لصدور أفعال السباع من الغضب والبغضاء ، والتوثب على الناس بأنواع الأذى.

٤ لا يصدر عنها إلا أفعال البهائم من عبودية الفرج والبطن ، والحرص على الجماع والأكل. ولكل من هذه القوى فوائد ، فالفائدة في وجود القوة الشهوية بقاء البدن الذي هو آلة تحصيل كمال النفس ، وفي وجود الغضبية أن يكسر سور الشهوية والشيطانية ، ويقهرهما عند انغمارهما في الخداع والشهوات ، وإصرارهما عليهما لأنهما لتمردهما لا تطيعان العاقلة بسهولة ، بخلاف الغضبية فانهما تطيعانها وتتأدبان بتأديبها بسهولة ، والفائدة في القوة الوهمية إدراك المعاني الجزئية ، واستنباط الحيل والدقائق التي يتوصل بها إلى المقاصد.

٥ نهج البلاغة / ص١١٩ / صفات الفساق.

CHAPTER 8

The Correspondence Between Man and Animal

The human being possesses four collective faculties, the angelic faculty of intellect,[1] the imaginative faculty of fantasy,[2] the predatory faculty of anger[3] and the bestial faculty of desire.[4] Their relationship is like the coming together of a sage, devil, dog and pig in a single arena. Whichever faculty dominates governs the rest, displaying attributes prompted by its natural disposition. So the sage is the faculty of intellect, the satan is the faculty of imagination and the dog is the faculty of anger. In this example, the dog (*kalb*) is not disparaged because of its color or form but because of its spiritual reality, namely, the quality of rapaciousness and as defined in Arabic, "rushing upon people injuriously." Whomsoever is governed by this faculty is a dog in reality even if they are called "human", stated here by Imām ʿAlī, "His form is that of a human but his heart is that of an animal."[5]

The pig is the faculty of desire, so the soul never ceases struggling against it until one of them dominates. The faculty of anger summons oppression and harm, animosity and hatred. The bestial faculty summons indecency and immorality, and intemperance of food and sex. The satanic faculty incites and stimulates predatory anger and bestial desire. The intellect extinguishes animalistic rage by imposing desire upon it and breaks the fetters of desire

---

1 The intellect perceives realities, distinguishes between good and evil, enjoins beautiful deeds and shuns dishonorable ones.

2 Fantasy concocts deceit and subterfuges, achieving its ends through deception and guile.

3 Anger gives rise to predatory impulses such as rage, hatred and various forms of harm towards others.

4 Desire incites animal behavior such as subservience to the stomach and privates, that is, intemperance towards food and carnal pleasures.
There are benefits, however, to each of these powers. The benefit of desire is to sustain the body which is an instrument for the soul's perfection. The faculty of anger is used to break the fetters of desire and satanic (imagination). Anger overpowers them if they persist in carnal appetite and deceit, for these two faculties are rebellious, unwilling to submit to the intellect. In contrast, they obey the faculty of anger which rectifies them. The benefit of imagination is to perceive particular concepts (as opposed to universals) and to derive strategies to reach its ends.

5 *Nahj al-balāgha*, 119, On the attributes of the wicked.

السبعية بتسليط الشهوية عليها ، ويكسر سورة الشهوية بتسليط السبعية عليها ، ويرد كيد الشيطان ومكره بالكشف عن تلبيسه ببصيرته النافذة ، ونورانيته الباهرة ، فلو كانت القوى باسرها تحت إشارة العقل وقهرها وغلب عليها وقعت لانقيادها له المسالمة والممازجة بين الكل وصار الجميع كالواحد لان المؤثر والمدبر حينئذ ليس إلا قوة واحدة ، تستعمل كل منها في المواضع اللائقة والأوقات المناسبة ، فيصدر عن كل منها ما خُلق لأجل على ما ينبغي من القدر والوقت والكيفية ، فتصلح النفس وقواها قال تعالى : ﴿قَدْ أَفْلَحَ مَن زَكَّاهَا﴾ [الشمس:٩].

وإن لم يغلبها وعجز عن قهرها قهروه واستخدموه ، فلا يزال الكلب في العقر والإيذاء ، والخنزير في المنكر والفحشاء ، والشيطان في استنباط الحيل ، ووجوه المكر والخدع ، ليرضى الكلب ويشبع الخنزير ، فلا يزال في عبادة كلب عقور أو هو كلب عقور أو خنزير هلوع أو شيطان عنود فتدركه الهلاكة الأبدية ، والشقاوة السرمدية ، إن لم تغثه العناية الإلهية ، والرحمة الأزلية.

ولما عرفت أن القوى في الإنسان أربع ، فاعلم انه بإزاء كل واحدة منها لذة وألم[٦] ، فاللذات والآلام أيضاً أربعة أقسام : العقلية ، والخيالية ، والغضبية ، والبهيمية.

فاللذة العقلية كالانبساط والابتهاج الحاصل من معرفة الأشياء الكلية وإدراك الذوات المجردة النورية ، والآلام العقلية كالانقباض الحاصل من الجهل.

واللذة الخيالية ،كالفرح الحاصل من إدراك الصور والمعاني الجزئية الملائمة ، والألم الخيالي كإدراك غير الملائمة منها.

واللذة الغضبية كالانبساط الحاصل من الغلبة ونيل المناصب والرياسات ، وألمها كالانقباض الحاصل من المغلوبية والعزل والمرؤسية .

٦ اللذة : إدراك الملائم ، والألم : إدراك غير الملائم. فلكل من الغرائز المدركة لذة هو نيله مقتضى طبعه الذي خلق لأجله ، وألم هو إدراكه خلاف مقتضى طبعه. فغريزة العقل لما خلقت لمعرفة حقائق الأمور ، فلذتها في المعرفة والعلم ، وألمها في الجهل ، وغريزة الغضب لما خلقت للتشفي والانتقام فلذتها في الغلبة التي يقتضيها طبعها وألمها في عدمها ، وغريزة الشهوة لما خلقت لتحصيل الغذاء الذي به قوام البدن فلذتها في نيل الغذاء ، وألمها في عدم نيله. وهكذا الخيالية لذتها في إدراكها مقتضى الطبع وألمها إدراكها خلاف مقتضى الطبع.

through the domination of anger. Through its perceptive insight and effulgent light it repels the trickery of Satan by disclosing his wiles.

Thus, if all of the faculties surrender to the governance and guidance of the intellect, they will become integrated and appeased, fusing into a single power since their governor and administrator is one. Each is employed at the appropriate time and occasion, exhibiting precisely those qualities for which they have been created with respect to extent, time and manner. The soul and its faculties will then be rectified, as stated in the Qur'ān, "He who purifies it succeeds" (91:9).

Should the intellect fail to dominate the faculties, they overcome it and enlist it, so that the dog persists in harming and injuring, the pig persists in indecency and immorality, and the satan continues scheming, deceiving and cheating in order to appease the dog and satisfy the pig. Instead of serving the injurious dog the intellect becomes the injurious dog, or the anxious pig or the rebellious satan, and reaches everlasting perdition and eternal wretchedness—unless God intervenes in His infinite mercy.

Since there are four faculties in the human being, there exists a certain pleasure and pain[6] associated with each. Each of the pains and pleasures can be divided into four types: intellectual, imaginative, irascible and bestial. Intellectual pleasure lies in the expansion and delight felt from obtaining the knowledge of universals and perceiving luminous, immaterial essences. Its pain lies in the constriction felt due to ignorance.

The pleasure of the imagination lies in the joy of perceiving agreeable forms and particular meanings, and its pain lies in perceiving unpleasant ones.

The pleasure of anger lies in the expansion felt from domination and the acquisition of position and power, and its pain lies in the constriction felt from submission, isolation and being governed.

---

6 Pleasure is the perception of something agreeable and pain is the perception of something disagreeable. Each of the perceptive faculties possesses a pleasure that corresponds to the nature for which it was created. Pain is the perception of something in opposition to the exigencies of its nature. Since the intellect was created for perceiving realities, its pleasure lies in knowledge and understanding, and its pain lies in ignorance. Since the faculty of anger was created for retaliation, its pleasure lies domination, intrinsic to its nature, and its pain lies in its contrary. Since desire was created for obtaining nourishment, by which the body is sustained, its pleasure lies in food and its pain lies in hunger. Similarly, the pleasures of imagination are in perceiving things that are agreeable in nature and its pains are in the perception of the contrary.

واللذة البيهمية في الأكل والجماع وأمثالها ، وألمها في الجوع والعطش والحر والبرد وأشباهها ، وهذه اللذات والآلام تصل إلى النفس(٧) وهي الملتذة والمتألمة حقيقةً إلا أن كلا منها يصل إليها بواسطة القوة التي تتعلق بها ، وأقوى اللذات هي العقلية لكونها فعلية ذاتية غير زائلة باختلاف الأحوال ، وغيرها من اللذات الحسّية انفعاليّة عرضيّة منفعلة زائلة ، وهي في مبدأ الحال مرغوبة عند الطبيعة ، وتتزايد بتزايد القوة الحيوانية ، وتتضعف بضعفها إلى أن تنتفي بالمرة ، ويظهر قبحها عند العقل ، وأما العقلية فهي في البداية منتفية ، لأن إدراكها لا يحصل إلا للنفوس الزكية المتحلية بالأخلاق المرضية ، وبعد حصولها يظهر حسنها وشرفها ، وتتزايد بتزايد القوة العقلية ، إلى أن ينتهي إلى أقصى المراتب ، ولا يكون لها نقص ولا زوال.

والعجب ممن ظن انحصار اللذة في الحسية وجعلها غاية كمال الإنسان وسعادته القصوى ، والمتشرعون منهم قصّروا اللذات الآخرة على الجنة والحور والغلمان وأمثالها ، وآلامها على النار والعقارب والحيات وأشباهها ، وجعلوا الوصول إلى الأولى والخلاص عن الثانية غاية لزهدهم وعبادتهم ، وكأنهم لم يعلموا أن هذه عبادة الأُجراء والعبيد ، تركوا قليل المشتبهات ليصلوا إلى كثيرها ، فكيف يدل ذلك على الكمال الحقيقي والقرب الإلهي ، وهل الباكي خوفاً من النار وشوقاً إلى اللذات الجسميّة(٨) المطلوبة للنفس البهيمية يعد من أهل التقرب إلى الله سبحانه ، ويستحق التعظيم ويوصف بعلو الرتبة ، وكأنهم لم يدركوا الابتهاجات الروحانية ولا لذة المعرفة بالله وحبه وانسه ولم يسمعوا قول سيد الموحدين أمير المؤمنين عليه السلام « الهي ما عبدتك خوفاً من نارك ولا طمعاً في جنتك ، ولكن وجدتك أهلا للعبادة فعبدتك »(٩).

---

٧ النفس : جوهر ملكوتي يستخدم البدن في حاجاته ، وهي مجردة في الذات دون الفعل لافتقارها فعلا إلى الجسم وآلاته ، وهذا الجوهر حقيقة الإنسان وذاته ، والأعضاء والقوى آلاته التي يتوقف فعله عليها ، وله أسماء مختلفة بحسب اختلاف الاعتبارات ، فيسمى (روحاً) لتوقف حياة البدن عليه ، و(عقلا) لإدراكه المعقولات ، و(قلباً) لتقلبه في الخواطر ، وقد تستعمل هذه الألفاظ في معاني.

٨ إن كل لذة بدنية ونفسية إنما هي إشباع شهوة أو غريزة تتطلب الإشباع حتى طلب المعارف إنما هو لإشباع غريزة حب الاستطلاع ، إلا أن طلب العلم لا يصل إلى حد الإشباع أبداً ، ولذا قال صلى الله عليه وآله : « منهومان لا يشبعان طالب علم ، وطالب مال » وليست لكذلك الغريزة الجنسية وغريزة حب الأكل وأمثالها فإنها تصل إلى حد الإشباع فتكتفي.

٩ نهج البلاغة / خطبة ١٧٩.

Bestial pleasure lies in food and corporeal pleasures, and its pain lies in hunger, thirst, heat and cold, etc. These pleasures and pains reach the soul,[7] but in reality it is the soul itself that experiences them, even if they arrive through a particular faculty. The strongest of the pleasures are intellectual because they are intrinsically active and do not subside even in different states. The other sensory pleasures are passive, accidental, reactive and subsiding. Initially, they are advantageous in nature and are augmented as the animal powers strengthen but diminish when those powers weaken. They eventually cease altogether and appear repulsive to the intellect.

Intellectual pleasures are negligible in the beginning because its realities are perceived only by pure souls adorned with illustrious character. After attaining this state, the value and nobility of these realities appear which are augmented through the growth of the intellect, and after reaching its zenith, it precludes any deficiency or dissolution.

It is astonishing that one would limit pleasures to the sensory, making them the aim of human perfection and felicity. The devout limit pleasures of the hereafter to gardens, women and youths, etc., and pains to fire, scorpions, snakes, etc. Attaining the former and escaping the latter is the very purpose of their abstentions and worship, unaware that this is the worship of traders and slaves. They have relinquished their lesser desires for their greater desires. How is this an expression of real perfection and divine proximity? Can one who laments in fear of the fire or yearns for corporeal pleasures[8]—which is sought by the bestial soul—be considered among those close to God, deserved of exaltation and anointed this lofty station? It is as if they have never grasped spiritual bliss or the pleasure of knowing God, His love and intimacy, or they have never heard the statement of Amīr al-Mu'minīn, the foremost of monotheists, "My Lord, I have not worshipped You in fear of Your fire nor in eagerness of Your paradise, but I have found You worthy of worship and so I worshipped You."[9]

---

7 The soul is a spiritual substance that employs the body for its needs. It is immaterial in essence, but not in act, for it needs the body as an instrument for its activities. This substance is the reality and essence of man and his limbs and faculties are instruments for his actions. The soul has different names according to its various aspects. It is called spirit (*rūḥ*) because through it the body is alive; it is called intellect (*'aql*) since it perceives concepts; it is called heart (*qalb*) because it fluctuates due to the passing of thoughts. These terms are used in various ways.

8 Every pleasure the body and soul experiences is the satiation of a desire or the fulfilment of a natural impulse. Even knowledge is sought for the need to satisfy curiosity, but in reality the seeker of knowledge is never truly satiated. For that reason, the Prophet has said, "Two types of seekers are never satiated: the seeker of knowledge and the seeker of wealth." For, these are unlike the desires of carnal appetite and the love of food which become satiated when they reach their limit.

9 *Nahj al-balāgha,* Sermon 179.

وبالجملة : لا ريب أن الإنسان في اللّذة الغضبية والبهيمية يشارك الحيوانات[١٠] الكثيرة الأنواع والتي لكل نوع منها خاصيّة دون غيره ، والإنسان يشاركها كلها في خواصها ، ولكن لها خاصيتين تعمّانها كلها ، وهما طلبها المنافع وفرارها من المضار ، ولكن منها ما يطلب المنافع بالقهر والغلبة كالسباع ، ومنها ما يطلب المنافع بالبَصبصة كالكلب والسِّنَّور ، ومنها ما يطلبها بالحيلة كالثعلب والعنكبوت ، وكل ذلك يوجد في الإنسان ، فان الملوك والسلاطين يطلبون المنافع بالغلبة ، والمكَدّون بالسؤال والتواضع ، والصُّناع والتجار بالحيلة والرفق ، وكلها تهرب من المضار والعدو ، ولكن بعضها يدفع العدو عن نفسه بالقتال والقهر والغلبة كالسباع ، وبعضها بالفرار كالأرنب والظباء ، وبعضها يدفع بالسلاح والجواشن كالقنفذ والسُلحفاة ، وبعضها بالتحصن في الأرض كالفأر والهوام والحيات.

وهذه كلها توجد في الإنسان ، فانه يدفع عن نفسه العدو بالقهر والغلبة ، فإن خاف على نفسه لبس السلاح ، وإن لم يطقه نفَر منه ، فإن لم يقدر على الفرار تحصن بالحصون ، وربما يدفع الإنسان عدوه بالحيلة.

وأما مشاركة الإنسان في خواصّها ، فأعلم أن لكل نوع من أنواع الحيوانات خاصية هي مطبوعة عليها ، وكلها توجد في الإنسان وتناسبه ، فانه يكون شجاعاً كالأسد ، وجباناً كالأرنب ، وسخياً كالديك ، وبخيلا كالكلب ، وعفيفاً كالسمك ، وفخوراً كالغراب ، ووحشياً كالنمر ، وإنسياً كالحمام ، ومحتالا كالثعلب ، ومسالماً كالغنم ، وسريعاً كالغزال ، وبطيئاً كالدُّب ، وعزيزاً كالفيل ، وذليلا كالجمل ، ولصاً كالعقعق ، وزاهياً كالطاووس ، وهادياً كالقطا ، وضالا كالنعامة ، وماهراً كالنحل ، وشديداً كالتنين ، ومَهيباً كالعنكبوت ، وحليماً كالحمل ، وحقوداً كالحمار ، وكدوداً كالثور ، وشموساً كالبغل ، وأخرساً كالحوت ومنطقياً كالببغاء ، ومستحلا كالذئب ، ومباركاً كالطيطوي ، ومضراً كالفار ، وجهولا كالخنزير ، ومشوماً كالبوم ، ونفاعاً كالنحل وشرهاً كالبعوض الذي يمص الدم إلى أن ينشق ويموت أو إلى أن يعجز عن الطيران فيكون ذلك سبب هلاكه ، وفي التشدق[١١] في الكلام كالبقرة التي

---

١٠ أن البديهية حاكمة بأن هذه اللذات ليست لذات حقيقية ، بل هي دفع آلام حادثة للبدن ، فان ما يتخيل لذة عند الأكل والجماع إنما هو راحة من ألم الجوع ولذع المنى ، ولذا لا يلتذ الشبعان عند الأكل ، والراحة من الألم ليس كمالا ، وخيراً مطلقاً ، إذ الكمال الحقيقي والخير المطلق هو الأبدي.

١١ أي الذي يتشدق في الكلام ويفخم به لسانه ويلفه كما تلف البقرة الكلأ بلسانها لفاً.

In short, the human being undoubtedly shares the irascible and bestial pleasures with the multitude of animals,[10] each of which possesses particular characteristics. The human shares the characteristics of each animal which can be epitomized in two qualities, seeking gain and escaping harm. Some seek gain through force and domination like predators, while others through tail-wagging like the dog and cat, and some through deception like the fox and spider. All of that is present in the human being, for kings and rulers seek gain through domination and subjugation, making others beg via pleas and humility, whereas traders and merchants seek it through deception and amicability. Each avoids harm from its enemy; some take hostile measures through warfare, force and domination like predators; some flee their enemies like rabbits and gazelles; some defend themselves with weapons and armor like porcupines and turtles; and some through entrenching themselves in the earth like mice, insects, and snakes.

These qualities are also found in the human being. Man may defend himself through force and domination. In fear he may draw a weapon, but if he is unable to do so, he will flee. If he is unable to flee he will fortify himself or he may repel an enemy through subterfuge.

Every animal possesses specific qualities intrinsic to its type and the human shares a specific correspondence to each animal. Thus, the human being is brave like the lion, cowardly like the rabbit, generous like the rooster, stingy like the dog, chaste like the fish, haughty like the crow, wild like the tiger, sociable like the dove, cunning like the fox, gentle like the lamb, fast like the gazelle, slow like the bear, mighty like the elephant, servile like the camel, thieving like the magpie, resplendent like the peacock, poised like the cat, astray like the ostrich, skillful like the bee, severe like the dragon, dreadful like the spider, spiteful like the donkey, industrious like the bull, headstrong like the mule, mute like the whale, talkative like the parrot, usurping like the wolf, auspicious like the sandpiper, harmful like the rat, ignorant like the pig, haughty like the owl, beneficial like the bee, gluttonous like the mosquito—which sucks blood until it expands and dies or is unable to fly which is then the cause of its demise. He is boastful[11] like the cow, which ruminates grass

10 It is self-evident that these pleasures are not true pleasures, rather they repel the pain experienced by the body. What is imagined as a pleasure when eating or during intercourse is simply the removal of pain experienced during hunger or the burning of sexual desire. That is why one who is satiated does not feel pleasure when eating. As such, the comfort found in the removal of pain is not a perfection and a categorical virtue, rather true pleasure and real virtue is in that which is everlasting.

11 "*Tashadduq fi-l-kalām*" means to speak in an unrestrained manner or with affectations as if one is chewing.

تلف الكلأ بلسانها لفاً ، كما قال ﷺ : « إن الله يبغض البليغ من الرجال الذي يتخلل بلسانه كما تتخلل البقرة » .

وفي طول اللحى بلا دين كالتيوس . في فقدان الجهة والمقصد كالجراد ، فانه لا جهة له فيكون أبداً بعضه على بعض. وفي التلون كالحرباء ، فانه يتلون بلون الشجرة التي يكون عليها حتى يكاد يختلط لونه بلونها ، وفي شدة السمع والعدو كالحية فإنها تسرع إلى حجرها إذا راعها شيء ، قال ﷺ[١٢] : « إن الإيمان ليأرز إلى المدينة كما تأرز الحية إلى حجرها ».

وفي المشي رويداً وتقارب الخطو والإقبال والإدبار كالدجاج[١٣].

وفي صورة المكتسب الجاهل الذي أهلكه أهله وماله وتنعم ورثته بما شقى هو به كدودة القز فانه لا يزال ينسج على نفسه حتى لا يكون له مخلص فيقتل نفسه ويصير القز لغيره ، وفي معرفة الأوقات كالديك ، فانه يقسط أصواته عليها تقسيطاً لا يكاد يغادر من شيئاً سواء طال أو قصر وفي كثرة الحركة والاضطراب كالذباب[١٤] ، وفي العقوق كالضب[١٥] ، وفي الحمق كالضبع ، وفي النفور كالظبي ، وفي كثرة السفاد كالعصفور ، وفي الحرص كالنمل.

وفي العداوة ومنازعة من هو أكثر منه شراً كالعقرب ، وفي ضياع الأولاد والذرية كالنعامة التي تضيع بيضها وأفراخها وتشتغل ببيض غيرها.

وفي كثرة العيوب كالعنز ، وفي ضعف البناء كالعنكبوت ومنه قوله تعالى : ﴿مَثَلُ الَّذِينَ اتَّخَذُوا مِن دُونِ اللهِ أَوْلِيَاءَ كَمَثَلِ الْعَنكَبُوتِ اتَّخَذَتْ بَيْتاً وَإِنَّ أَوْهَنَ الْبُيُوتِ لَبَيْتُ الْعَنكَبُوتِ لَوْ كَانُوا يَعْلَمُونَ ۞ إِنَّ اللهَ يَعْلَمُ مَا يَدْعُونَ مِن دُونِهِ مِن شَيْءٍ وَهُوَ الْعَزِيزُ الْحَكِيمُ ۞ وَتِلْكَ الأَمْثَالُ نَضْرِبُهَا لِلنَّاسِ وَمَا يَعْقِلُهَا إِلاَّ الْعَالِمُونَ﴾ [العنكبوت: ٤١].

---

١٢ رواه مسلم والبخاري ، ومعنى (تأرز) أي تنظم وتجتمع بعضه إلى بعض فان المؤمن إنما يسوقه إلى المدينة إيمانه ومحبته للنبي ﷺ.

١٣ سميت الدجاجة دجاجة لإقبالها وإدبارها ، كما يقال دج القوم دجاً ودجيجاً إذا مشو مشياً رويداً في تقارب خطو أو أن يقبلوا ويدبروا.

١٤ سمي ذباباً لكثرة حركته واضطرابه ، وانه كلما ذب آب.

١٥ وفي العقوق أن الأنثى تأكل أولادها.

with its tongue, as stated in the hadith, "God despises the boastful person who is diffuse with his tongue like a grazing cow."

He is long-bearded but irreligious like the mountain goat, directionless and lacking in purpose like the locust, multicolored like the chameleon, for it assumes the color of the tree to the point of being indistinguishable from it, strong of hearing and swift like the snake which flees to a rock if something startles it, as stated by the Prophet, "Faith takes refuge (*ta'raz*) in Medina as a snake takes refuge in a rock."[12] If his gait is slow and he moves with his feet close together he is like the chicken.[13]

He is ignorant like the silk worm, like one whose family and wealth ruin him while his inheritors enjoy the fruits of his labor, in the same way that the silk worm spins a cocoon until it is unable to free itself, dying and leaving its silk for others. He is mindful of time like the rooster, for it crows precisely at an appointed time and rarely falters, excessive in movement and agitation like the fly,[14] barren like the lizard,[15] stupid like the hyena, fleeing like the gazelle, excessive in sexual intercourse like the sparrow and hoarding like the ant.

He is hateful and hostile like the scorpion, bereft of progeny like the ostrich, which loses its eggs and chicks and devotes itself to another's. He is blameworthy like the goat and a weak builder like the spider, as stated in the Qur'ān, "The parable of those who take protectors other than God is like that of the spider, who builds a house for itself; but truly the flimsiest of houses is the spider's house—if they but knew. Indeed, God knows of everything that they call upon besides Him, and He is Exalted, Wise. Such are the parables We set forth for mankind, but only those who have knowledge ponder them" (29:41-43).

---

12 Muslim and Bukhārī relate that the meaning of *ta'raz* is to bring together, that is, faith and love of the Prophet bring together the believers to Medina.

13 It is called *dajāja* because it comes and goes as it is said, "The people ambled, or they came and went."

14 It is called *zhubāb* because of its excessive movement and agitation. Whenever it is repelled (*zhabba*), it returns (*āba*).

15 It is considered barren because the female of a particular species of lizard eats its young.

وفي الحكاية والقباحة كالقرد ، فانه يحكي الإنسان في أفغاله وإذا رأى الإنسان تولع بفعل شيء أخذ يفعله مثله ، وفي سوء الخلق كالقمل قال ابن سيده في الحديث : « النساء غل قمل يقذفها الله في عنق من يشاء ثم لا يخرجها إلا هو ».

وفي الذي وعظته ضال وان تركته ضال كالكلب إن طردته لهث وإن تركته لهث كما قال تعالى : ﴿فَمَثَلُهُ كَمَثَلِ الْكَلْبِ إِن تَحْمِلْ عَلَيْهِ يَلْهَثْ أَوْ تَتْرُكْهُ يَلْهَث ذَّلِكَ مَثَلُ الْقَوْمِ الَّذِينَ كَذَّبُواْ بِآيَاتِنَا فَاقْصُصِ الْقَصَصَ لَعَلَّهُمْ يَتَفَكَّرُونَ﴾ [الأعراف:١٧٦].

وأخيراً بعد أن ذكرنا لك القوى الأربعة المودعة في الإنسان ومشاركته ومناسبته مع الحيوان في الغضبية والبهيمية ومشاركته في خواصها.

فانظر أين تضع نفسك ، فان كانت الغلبة لقوتك الشهوية حتى يكون اكثر همك إلى الشهوات الحيوانية كالأكل والشرب والجماع وسائر النزوات البهيمية كنت واحداً من البهائم. وإن كانت لقوتك الغضبية حتى يكون جلّ ميلك إلى المناصب والرياسات الردية ، وإيذاء الناس بالضرب والشتم وباقي الحركات السبعية نزلت منزلة السباع. وإن كانت لقوتك الشيطانية حتى يكون غالب سعيك في استنباط وجوه المكر والحيل للوصول إلى مقتضيات قوتي الشهوة والغضب بأنواع الخدع والتلبيسات الوهمية دخلت في حزب الأبالسة ، وإن كانت لقوتك العقلية حتى يكون جدّك مقصوراً على أخذ المعارف الإلهية واقتفاء الفضائل الخلقية عرجت إلى افق الملائكة القادسة.

وعلى أساس تلك الغلبة وخصوصياتها تكون حكومة الإنسان وتدار مملكته فيعرف من أي أنواع الإنسان هو هل من صنف الإنسان الناطق أم الإنسان الحيوان ؟ وهل الصورة صورة إنسان ، والقلب قلب إنسان أم الصورة صورة إنسان والقلب قلب حيوان ؟ ثم من أي الحيوانات هو ؟

فهذا ما يعرف لدى أهل البصيرة والمتنورة قلوبهم بنور الله المتفرسون في خلق الله كما قال ﷺ : « اتقوا فراسة المؤمن فانه ينظر بنور الله ».

فان أصحاب البصيرة والهداة المرشدين يتفرسون فيشخصون الداء ويرشدون للدواء من آية وذكر وعبادة ورياضة وغيرها.

والله يقول الحق وهو يهدي السبيل.

He is shameless and mimicking like the monkey, for it imitates humans when it sees an action being performed enthusiastically, and bad tempered like lice, as in the hadith, "God burdens whomever He wishes with the malice of lice that women can possess; there is no escape from it except through Him."

Man goes astray either when guided or left alone, like the dog that pants either when driven away or abandoned, as mentioned in the verse, "He is like the dog, which if provoked, lolls out his tongue, or if left alone, still lolls out his tongue. This exemplifies those who reject Our signs; So relate the story so that they may reflect" (7:176).

Finally, after explaining the four faculties of man, their interrelationships and correspondences to the predatory and bestial qualities of animals, see where you find yourself. If you are governed by desire and are preoccupied with satisfying corporeal appetites such as food, drink, carnal pleasures and every other animalistic urge, then you are among the beasts. If anger prevails within you and your primary objective is to acquire position and ignoble leadership, while abusing others physically or verbally and perpetrating various predatory acts, then you are among the predators. If the satanic faculty in you is dominant and you strive to concoct stratagems to fulfill the demands of desire and anger through various forms of deception and duplicity, then you are among the satans. However, if your intellect prevails and you aspire to acquire divine knowledge and pursue human virtues, then you will have ascended to the plane of sanctified angels.

The ascendency of the intellect and its effects percolates into the human being, governing and navigating his kingdom. Accordingly, he realizes the mode of his human existence, whether it is as a rational human or an animal human. Is the form a human form and a human heart or simply a human form but an animal heart? If the latter, then which type of animal? This is known to the people of spiritual insight among God's creatures whose vision has been illuminated by His light, as the Prophet states, "Be wary of the clairvoyance (*firāsa*) of the believer for he sees with the light of God."

Thus, those endowed with spiritual insight and spiritual guides deepen their gaze to diagnose illnesses and specify remedies through invocations, acts of worship and spiritual exercises.

God speaks the truth and guides the way.

الباب التاسع

التناسب بين الإنسان والنبات

اعلم أن النبات هي كل جسم يخرج من الأرض ويتغذى وينمو. فمنها ما هي أشجار[1] تغرس قضبانها أو عروقها ، ومنها ما هي زروع تبذر حبوبها أو بذورها أو قضبانها ، ومنها ما هي أجزاء تتكون من أجزاء الأركان إذا اختلطت وامتزجت كالكلأ والحشائش ، ومن النبات من ينبت على وجه الماء كالطُّحْلُب ، ومنه ما ينسج على الشجر والنبات كالكشوثي[2] واللبلاب ، ومنه ما ينبت على وجه الصُّخور كخضراء الدِّمَن[3] وغير ذلك.

فهذه الأجناس يتنوع كل واحد منها أنواع كثيرة من جهات عِدّة وصفات مختلفة قد جمعها الله سبحانه في مختصر العالم وزبدته فهو كالزُّبد من المخيض والدُّهن من السمسم، فما من شيء إلا والإنسان يناسبه من وجه ، فإنه كالأركان من حيث ما فيه من الحرارة والبرودة والرطوبة واليبوسة ، وكالمعادن من حيث ما هو جسم ، وكالنبات من حيث ما يتغذى ويتربى ، وكالبهيمة من حيث ما يحس ويتخيل ويتوهم ويلتذ ويتألم ، وكالشيطان من حيث ما يمكر ويحتال ويغوي ويضل ، وكالملائكة من حيث ما يعرف الله تعالى ويعبده ويخلفه ، وكاللوح المحفوظ من حيث قد جعله الله تعالى مجمع الحكم التي كتبها الله فيه على سبيل الاختصار ، فالإنسان من قوى أشياء مختلفة ومختلطة كما قال تعالى : ﴿إِنَّا خَلَقْنَا الإِنْسَانَ مِن نُّطْفَة أَمْشَاج﴾ [الإنسان:٢].

فمن هذا الوجه قالوا الإنسان عالم صغير ، فإن كان قد صرف همته إلى الجهة الطبيعية فيكون راضياً من أمر دنياه بالتغذي وتنقية الفضول ، وإن كان إلى الحيوانية فيتصف بصفاتها ويتميز بخصائصها ، وإن كان إلى المكر والحيلة فيكون شيطاناً

١ الشجر : كل نبت يقوم على ساقه منتصباً أصله ، مرتفعاً في الهواء ، ويدور عليه الحول لا يجف. وإما النجم فهو كل نبت لا يقوم أصله على ساقه مرتفعا في الهواء ، بل يمتد على وجه الأرض أو يتعلق بالشجر ، ويرتقي معه في الهواء ، كشجر الكَرْم والقَرْع ، والقُثاء والبطيخ وما شاكلها.

٢ الكشوثي : نبت يتعلق بالأغصان ولا عرق له في الأرض.

٣ خضراء الدِّمَن : ما نبت في الدمن من العشب ، وهي البقعة التي سوّدها أهلها وبالت فيها وبعرت مواشيهم.

CHAPTER 9

The Correspondence Between Man and Plant

A plant is any growing, vegetative body originating from the earth. Trees[1] have roots and branches that can be planted and crops have seeds, pits or branches that are disseminated. Grasses and herbs even when hybridized are composed of primitive elements. Certain plants grow on the surface of water such as water moss, others wrap around trees such as the dodder[2] and the ivy, and others grow on the surface of rocks, such as the verdure growing on manure.[3]

These species are further subdivided into numerous subspecies because of their variegated attributes and aspects. Just like the cream on milk or the oil from sesame, God has summarized each species in the quintessence of the world, the human being, who corresponds with everything in existence in a particular way.

Man is like the elements insofar as he possesses hot, cold, wet and dry; he is like the minerals since he possesses bodily form; like the plants as he grows and develops; like the beasts since he imagines, speculates, feels pleasure and pain; like the satans since he deceives, tempts and misguides; like the angels because he knows, worships and obeys God; and like the Guarded Tablet insofar as God has inscribed in him the essence of wisdom. Thus, man is composed of various and amalgamated powers, as God says, "We have created man from an amalgamated seed" (76:2).

From this perspective, it is said that man is the quintessence of the world, so if he exerts his will in the direction of nature, he will be satisfied with the affairs of this world, namely, eating and excreting. If he exerts his will in the direction of animality, he will be occupied by animal attributes and assume their characteristics. If he exerts his will in cheating and deceit, he will be among the rebellious satans. If he exerts his will in the direction of the angels,

---

1 A tree is any vegetation that stands upright by a trunk, possesses roots, grows upwardly in the air and does not dry annually. A vine is any vegetation that is not upheld by a trunk raised in the air, but extends on the surface of the earth or wraps around a tree and climbs it, like the grapevine, gourd, cucumber, watermelon and others.

2 The dodder is a type of vegetation that wraps around tree trunks and does not have roots in the earth.

3 It is the greenery that grows on dung, which is the piece of earth that has become sullied from urination and animal droppings.

مريداً ، وإن صرف همته إلى الجهة الملكية فيكون متوجهاً إلى العالم الأعلى ويرضى بالمنزل الأسفل فيكون مراداً من قوله عزّ وجلّ : ﴿وَفَضَّلْنَاهُمْ عَلَى كَثِيرٍ مِّمَّنْ خَلَقْنَا تَفْضِيلاً﴾ [الإسراء: ٧٠].

والإنسان يتكون أولا جماداً ميتاً كقوله تعالى : ﴿وَكُنتُمْ أَمْوَاتاً فَأَحْيَاكُمْ﴾ [البقرة:٢٨] وذلك حينما كان تراباً أو طيناً أو صلصالا ونحوها ، ثم يصير نباتاً نامياً كما قال تعالى : ﴿وَاللهُ أَنبَتَكُم مِّنَ الأَرْضِ نَبَاتاً﴾ [نوح:١٧].[٤]

فانه سبحانه يخلقنا من النطف وهي متولدة من الأغذية المتولدة من النبات المتولد من الأرض ، كما قال تعالى : ﴿أَكَفَرْتَ بِالَّذِي خَلَقَكَ مِن تُرَابٍ ثُمَّ مِن نُّطْفَةٍ ثُمَّ سَوَّاكَ رَجُلاً﴾ [الكهف:٣٧].

قال السيد الطباطبائي[٥] في تفسير قوله تعالى : ﴿وَاللهُ أَنبَتَكُم مِّنَ الأَرْضِ نَبَاتاً﴾ « أي أنبتكم إنبات النبات ، وذلك أن الإنسان تنتهي خلقته إلى عناصر أرضية تركبت تركيباً خاصاً به يغتذي وينمو ويولد المثل ، وهذه حقيقة النبات ، فالكلام مسوق سوق الحقيقة من غير تشبيه واستعارة ». فبالتغذية والنمو وتوليد المثل تناسب النفس الإنسانية الواحدة النفس النباتية[٦].

---

٤ قال الفخر الرازي ، أما قوله ﴿ أَنبَتَكُم مِّنَ الْأَرْضِ نَبَاتًا ﴾ ففيه مسألتان : ..المسألةالأولى : في هذه الآية وجهان : أحدهما : معنى قوله (أنبتكم من الأرض) أي انبت أباكم من الأرض كما قال : ﴿ إِنَّ مَثَلَ عِيسَى عِندَ اللهِ كَمَثَلِ آدَمَ خَلَقَهُ مِن تُرَابٍ ﴾ [آل عمران:٥٩]. والثاني : أنه تعالى أنبت الكل من الأرض لأنه تعالى إنما يخلقنا من النطف وهي متولدة من الأغذية المتولدة من النبات المتولد من الأرض.

المسألة الثانية : كان ينبغي أن يقال : أنبتكم إنباتاً إلا أنه لم يقل ذلك بل قال (أبنتكم نباتاً) ، وهذا الثاني أولى لان الإنبات صفة الله تعالى ، وصفة الله غير محسوسة لنا ، وهذا المقام مقام الاستدلال على كمال قدرة الله تعالى . (التفسير الكبير / ج٢٩-٣٠ ص١٢٥ الفخر الرازي).

٥ تفسير الميزان السيد الطباطبائي / ج٢٠ / ص٣٦.

٦ يعتقد ابن سينا أن النفس ذات واحدة لها قوى ثلاث :

القوة الأولى : نباتية ويسميها النفس النباتية وهي : كمال أول للجسم الطبيعي الآلي من حيث التوليد ، والتنمية ، والتغذية ، وهي على ثلاثة أقسام :

القسم الأول : الغاذية ، وهي التي تحيل جسماً آخر إلى مشاركة الجسم الذي هي فيه ، أي الغذاء الذي تحيله إلى دم أو ما أشبه ، يمتزج بالجسم ويصبح جزءاً منه.

orienting himself to the higher world, yet is content with its lowest station, he is described by the Qur'ān in the following, "We favored them above a multitude of what We have created" (17:70).

The human being is initially composed of inanimate matter, as stated in the Qur'ān, "You were without life and we brought you to life" (2:28), while he was still dust, wet clay then fired-clay. Then he became vegetative and growing, mentioned in the verse, "God produced you from the earth as vegetation" (71:17).[4]

God created us from sperm cells which are formed from the constituents of food originating from vegetation, as mentioned in the verse, "Do you disbelieve in Him Who created you of dust, then of a drop of seed, and then fashioned you a human?" (18:37).

Commenting on the verse, "God produced you from the earth as vegetation" (71:17), Sayyid Ṭabāṭabā'ī says, "He produced you like vegetation since man's creation commences with the earthly elements arranged such that he consumes, grows and reproduces his like; this is precisely the nature of plants. Therefore, the verse indicates something actual not metaphorical."[5] Nourishment, growth and reproduction corresponds with the vegetal aspect of the unitary human soul.[6]

---

4 Fakhr al-Rāzī writes that this verse addresses two issues. The first issue possesses two meanings: Firstly, that God produced your forefathers from the earth, as mentioned in the verse, "The example of 'Īsā with God is like that of Adam whom He created from dust" (3:59), and secondly, that God produced everyone from the earth because He created us from sperm, the product of food whose origin is the earth. The second issue is that the verse might have read, "God produced you in a manner that grows (*inbātan*)," but it reads, "God produced you *as* vegetation (*nabātan*)." The latter is superior because the former is a quality of God and is not perceptible by us, whereas vegetation is perceptible and visible and therefore is evidence for the perfection of His power. *al-Tafsīr al-kabīr*, 29-30:125.

5 *Tafsīr al-mīzān*, 20:36.

6 Ibn Sīnā holds that the soul is a unitary essence that possesses three faculties:
The first is the vegetative which is also called the vegetal soul. It is the first entelechy of an organic body that functions as an instrument, insofar as it enables nutrition, growth and reproduction; it has three divisions:

Nutrition: It is the ability to transform other substances to admix with the body, so that it transforms food into blood and similar substances which are then incorporated and become part of the body.

Growth: It is the body's ability to develop, mature and strengthen.

Reproduction: It is the ability to take a representative part of itself in potential and bring it into actuality through the agency of another body so as to produce something in its like. The culmination of the reproductive ability occurs through the creation of a child from the bodies of its parents as it were a part of them.

وبهذه المناسبة قد يظهر الإنسان في صفات النبات الحميدة والذميمة ، فيصير إما

القسم الثاني : المنمية : وهي التي تزيد في الجسم الذي هي فيه ، أي انها تساعد على نمو الجسد وتقويته.
القسم الثالث : المولدة : وهي التي تأخذ من الجسم الذي هي فيه ، جزءاً هو شبيه له بالقوة ، فتنفعل فيه ، بمساعة أجسام أخرى ، فيتولد منه ما يصير شبيهاً به ، أي أن التوالد يتم بفعل القوة المولدة ، التي تساعد على تكون الوليد من جسد أبويه وكأنه جزء منهما.
أما القوة الثانية : فهي الحيوانية ، ويسميها النفس الحيوانية ، وهي كمال أول للجسم الطبيعي الآلي من حيث إدراكه الجزئيات ، والتحرك بالإرادة ، ولها قوتان :
الأولى : محركة وهي قسمان : باعثة وفاعلة.
وللباعثة شعبتان ، الأولى : شهوانية ، والثانية : غضبية.
الثانية : مدركة ، وهي قسمان : الأولى : تدرك من الخارج ، والثانية تدرك من الداخل.
أما المدركة من الخارج ، فتدرك بواسطة الحواس الخمس ، وأما المدركة من الداخل ، فبعض قواها يدرك صور المحسوسات ، وبعضها يدرك معاني المحسوسات. يتم إدراك الصور باشتراك الحس الظاهر والنفس الباطنة ، فينقل الحس الظاهر إلى النفس الباطنة فتدركه ، مثل إدراك الحس الظاهر عند الشاة لهيئة الذئب وشكله ولونه ، وإدراك نفسها الباطنة للمضاد لها في الذئب ، هذا المضاد الذي يوجب خوفها وهربها منه. ومن القوى المدركة الباطنة :
١- قوة فنطاسيا (الحس المشترك) وهي التي تقبل الصور المنطبعة في الحواس الخمس ، ومركزها التجويف المقدم من الدماغ.
٢- المصورة أو الخيال : وهي التي تحفظ ما قبلته قوة الحسن المشترك من الحواس الخمس ، فيبقى فيها بعد غيبة المحسوسات ومركزها آخر التجويف المقدم من الدماغ.
٣- المتخيلة أو المفكرة : أي المتخيلة بالقياس إلى النفس الحيوانية ، والمفكرة بالقياس إلى النفس الإنسانية ، فهي تركب بعض ما في الخيال من بعض وتفصل بعضه عن بعض ، حسب الاختيار. مركزها التجويف الأوسط من الدماغ.
٤- القوة الوهمية : وهي التي تدرك المعاني غير المحسوسة الموجودة في المحسوسات كالقوة الحاكمة ان الطفل معطوف عليه. مركزها في نهاية التجويف الأوسط من الدماغ.
٥- القوة الحافظة أو الذاكرة : وهي التي تحفظ ما تدركه القوة الوهمية من المعاني ومركزها في التجويف المؤخر من الدماغ.
القوة الثالثة : هي الناطقة الإنسانية ، وهي قوتان عاملة وعالمة.
فالعاملة (العقل العملي) تحرك البدن نحو الأعمال التي فيها خير الإنسان ، والعالمة تدرك الكليات ، وتنظر إلى فوقها لتنفعل به وتستفيد منه ، وتقبل عنه أي التي تبحث عن الحق.
(دراسات في الفلسفة اليونانية والعربية / الجندي ص١٢٥).

It is through this correspondence that the human being exhibits the praiseworthy and blameworthy attributes of the plants. He is beneficial like

---

The second is the animal faculty which is also called the animal soul. It is the first actualization of an organic body that functions as an instrument, insofar as it perceives particulars and moves with intent; it further has two faculties: Locomotion and perception.

Locomotion: It is the power that allows for movement and activity. Movement has further two branches: The faculty of desire and the faculty of anger.

Perception: This faculty has two divisions: Outward perception and inward perception.

Outward perception: It occurs through the five senses.

Inward perception: Some of its faculties perceive sensory forms and some perceive sensory meanings. The culmination of the faculty of perception is in the integration of outward senses with the inward soul, inasmuch as the outward senses convey information for it to perceive. For example, a sheep perceives with its outward senses the shape, form and color of a wolf, and inwardly perceives hostility from the wolf. This hostility entails fear and the need to flee from it. The inward faculties of perception are the following:

Fantasy: Or *sensus communis* (*al-ḥiss al-mushtarak*), is the power that embraces the forms impressed on it by the five senses. Its locus is an area in the forebrain.

Imagination: The faculty of imagination is the repository of what the fantasy receives from the five senses. Thus, the content of sensory perceptions remain within it even after their disappearance. Its locus is another area of the forebrain.

Intellection: The faculty of intellection is called imagination in relation to the animal soul and rationality in relation to the human soul. It collates what is in the fantasy, separating some information according to its discretion. Its locus is the middle of the brain.

Speculation: The faculty of speculation perceives non-sensory meanings in perceptible things. For example, it is the faculty that determines that a particular child is lovable.

Memory: The faculty of memory stores the meanings that the faculty of speculation perceives. Its locus is an area in the back of the brain.

The third is the rational faculty of the human being. It further consists of two faculties, the practical intellect and the theoretical intellect:

Practical Intellect: It impels the body to perform beneficial actions.

Theoretical Intellect: It perceives universals and turns its gaze to that which is superior, communicating with it and benefiting from it. As a consequence, it accepts the truth that it seeks. *Dirāsāt fi-l falsafa al-yunāniyya wa-l-ʿarabiyya*, 125.

كالنخل(٧) أو الكرْم(٨) في النفع أو كالأترج الذي يطيب حمله ونَوره وعوده وورقه. أو كالكَشُوت(٩) في عدم الخير أو كالحنضل في خبث المذاق(١٠) ، أو عزيزاً كالتوت(١١) وسيداً كالرمان(١٢) ، وطيب الرائحة حسن الوجه كالسفرجل(١٣) ، وسالماً من كل داء وغائلة كالبطيخ(١٤) ، أو مريضاً مصفر الوجه كالليمون ، أو مباركاً كالزيتون

---

٧ النخل : شجرة مباركة ، قال ﷺ : « اكرموا عماتكم النخل » وإنما سماها عماتنا لأنها خلقت من فضلة طينة آدم عليه الصلاة والسلام ، وهي تشبه الإنسان من حيث استقامة قدها وطولها ، وامتياز ذكرها عن أنثاها ، واختصاصها باللقاح ، ولو قطع رأسها هلكت ولطلعها رائحة المني ولها غلاف كالمشيمة التي يكون الولد فيها ، والجمار الذي على رأسها لو أصابه آفة هلكت النخلة كهيئة مخ الإنسان إذا أصابه آفة ولو قطع منها غصن لا يرجع بدله كعضو الإنسان ، وعليها ليف كشعر الإنسان. (حياة الحيوان / ج٢ / ص١٧٧ / الدميري).

٨ الكَرْم : ورد في الحديث عن النبي ﷺ : « لا تُسمُّوا العِنب الكَرْم ، فإنما الكَرْم الرجل المسلم » قال الأزهري وتفسير هذا ، والله اعلم أن الكَرْم الحقيقي هو من صفة الله تعالى ، ثم من صفة من آمن به وأسلم لأمره ، فخففت العرب الكَرْم ، وهم يريدون كَرَمَ شجرة العنب ، لما ذُلِّل من قطوفه عند اليَنْع وكَثُر من خيره في كل حال ، وانه لا شوك فيه يؤذي القاطف ، فنهى النبي ﷺ عن تسميته بهذا الاسم لأنه يعتصر منه المسكر المنهي عن شربه ، وقال : الرجل المسلم أحق بهذه الصفة من هذه الشجرة.

وقال أبو بكر يسمى الكَرْم كَرْماً لان الخمر المتخذة منه تَحُثُّ على السخاء والكَرَم وتأمر بمكارم الأخلاق فأشتقوا له اسماً من الكَرَم للكرم الذي يتولد منه فكره النبي ﷺ أن يسمى أصل الخمر باسم مأخوذ من الكَرَم وجعل المؤمن أولى بهذا الاسم الحَسن وأنشد : والخمر مشتقة المعنى من الكَرَم. (لسان العرب / ج١٢ / ص٧٨).

٩ نبت يتعلق بأغصان الشجر من غير أن يضرب بعرق في الأرض (مجمع البحرين / ج٤ / ص٤٤).

١٠ نبت مر المذاق.

١١ شجرة من أعز الشجر ، لان دود القز لا يأكل إلا من شجره وورقه (حياة الحيوان / ج٢/ ص١٦٥).

١٢ عن النبي ﷺ قال : « الرمان سيد الفاكهة ، ومن اكل رمانة أغضب شيطانه أربعين صباحاً ». (مكارم الأخلاق الطبرسي / ص١٧١).

١٣ عن أمير المؤمنين ﷺ : « رائحة السفرجل ، رائحة الأنبياء » (مكارم الأخلاق / ص١٧٢).

١٤ قال أمير المؤمنين ﷺ : « البطيخ شحمة الأرض لا داء ولا غائلة فيه » ، وقال ﷺ : « فيه عشر خصال : طعام وشراب وفاكهة وريحان وأُدم وحلواء وأشنان. الأشنان ما تغسل به الأيدي والمراد أنه يغسل البطن. وخطمي وبقل ودواء » (مكارم الأخلاق / ص١٨٥).

the date-palm,[7] the grapevine,[8] or the citron, whose stalk, branch, blossom and leaf are pleasant. Or he is void of goodness like the dodder,[9] bad tasting like the colocynth,[10] noble like the mulberry,[11] supreme like the pomegranate,[12] pleasant smelling and delightful in form like the quince,[13] salubrious with respect to every illness and affliction like the melon,[14] sickly and yellow in color like the lemon, blessed like the olive and fig,[15] congruous inwardly and

---

7 The date-palm is a blessed tree, as mentioned by the Prophet, "Honor your paternal aunt, the date-palm." It was called our maternal aunt because it was created from the excess of Adam's clay. It resembles the human being in its standing upright and tall and in that its males differ from its females. It becomes pollinated and if its head is severed it dies. It gives off the smell of semen and has a cover like a placenta which becomes its child. If its core, which is at its head is afflicted by a disease, it perishes in a way similar to humans. In addition, if one of its branches is cut off, it does not grow back just as the limbs of a person do not grow back. It possesses fiber like the hair of humans. *Ḥayāt al-ḥayawān*, 2:77.

8 The grapevine is a blessed tree. The Prophet has said, "Do not name the grapevine *karam*, for *karam,* or generosity, in reality is the Muslim." Azharī explains that God knows that real generosity is a divine attribute, then an attribute of one who believes in Him and has submitted to His commandments. But the Arabs subdued this meaning and intended the grape tree because its bunches are lowered when ripened, its benefits are plentiful in all states and it does not have thorns which would vex its picker. The Prophet has forbidden calling it this name because wine, which is forbidden to drink, is squeezed from it. He further said, "The Muslim is more deserving of this name than this tree." Abū Bakr said that it is called *karm* because the wine which is derived from it encourages one to be generous and liberal and enjoins the most noble character traits.

Therefore, its name "*karm*" is derived from the word generosity (*karam*) but the Prophet detested that the word for the origin of wine should be derived from the word "generosity" and he made the believer more deserving of this goodly name. It is said, 'Wine is derivative in meaning from generosity.'" *Lisān al-ʿarab*, 12:8.

9 A certain plant that clings to the branches of trees having no root in the earth. *Majmaʿ al-baḥrayn*, 4:44.

10 Also known as bitter apple.

11 This is one of the greatest of trees since the silkworm only eats from its leaves. *Ḥayāt al-ḥayawān*, 2:165.

12 The Prophet states, "The pomegranate is the supreme fruit. If one eats the pomegranate Satan is angered for forty days." *Makārim al-akhlāq*, 171.

13 Imām ʿAlī states, "The scent of the quince is the scent of prophets." *Makārim al-akhlāq*, 172.

14 Imām ʿAlī states, "The melon is the pulp of the earth; it has neither illness nor affliction." He also said, "It has ten qualities: it is a food, a drink, a fruit, a fragrance, a skin, a sweetness, a washing (*ashnān*)–what is used to wash hands, and the meaning here is a wash for the stomach–a mallow, a legume and a medicine." *Makārim al-akhlāq*, 185.

15 These two blessed and famous fruits are mentioned in the Qurʿān in Surat al-Tīn, "By the fig and the olive" (95:1).

والتين[١٥] ، أو موافقاً ظاهر باطنة كالمشمش[١٦] ، أو منسجماً كالباذنجان[١٧] ، أو محتوياً على العلم ومنطوياً كالموز قال تعالى : ﴿وَطَلْحٍ مَّنضُودٍ﴾ [الواقعة:٢٩] [١٨] ، أو شريفاً كالنخل ، أو وضيعاً كخضراء الدِّمَن ، أو عالي المنزلة طيب اللسان كالمنّ كما قال تعالى[١٩] : ﴿وَظَلَّلْنَا عَلَيْكُمُ الْغَمَامَ وَأَنزَلْنَا عَلَيْكُمُ الْمَنَّ وَالسَّلْوَى كُلُواْ مِن طَيِّبَاتِ مَا رَزَقْنَاكُمْ وَمَا ظَلَمُونَا وَلَكِن كَانُواْ أَنفُسَهُمْ يَظْلِمُونَ﴾ [البقرة:٥٧] ، أو داني المنزلة كالبقل والقثاء والفوم والعدس والبصل كما قال تعالى[٢٠] : ﴿وَإِذْ قُلْتُمْ يَا مُوسَى لَن نَّصْبِرَ عَلَىَ طَعَامٍ وَاحِدٍ فَادْعُ لَنَا رَبَّكَ يُخْرِجْ لَنَا مِمَّا تُنبِتُ الأَرْضُ مِن بَقْلِهَا وَقِثَّآئِهَا وَفُومِهَا وَعَدَسِهَا وَبَصَلِهَا قَالَ أَتَسْتَبْدِلُونَ الَّذِي هُوَ أَدْنَى بِالَّذِي هُوَ خَيْرٌ اهْبِطُواْ مِصْراً فَإِنَّ لَكُم مَّا سَأَلْتُمْ وَضُرِبَتْ عَلَيْهِمُ الذِّلَّةُ وَالْمَسْكَنَةُ وَبَآؤُوْاْ بِغَضَبٍ مِّنَ اللَّهِ ذَلِكَ بِأَنَّهُمْ كَانُواْ يَكْفُرُونَ بِآيَاتِ اللَّهِ وَيَقْتُلُونَ النَّبِيِّينَ بِغَيْرِ الْحَقِّ ذَلِكَ بِمَا عَصَواْ وَّكَانُواْ يَعْتَدُونَ﴾ [البقرة:٦١].

---

١٥ فاكهتين مباركتين معروفتين ذكرهما الله تعالى في كتابه العزيز : ﴿ والتين والزيتون ﴾ [التين:١].

١٦ شجرة عجيبة شحم ثمرتها ولبها مأكولان طيبان ، خلاف غيرها فان المأكول إما شحمها أو لبها (حياة الحيوان / ج٢ / ص١٧٦).

١٧ قال أبو الحسن الثالث لبعض قهارمته (جمع قهرمان وهو أمين الدخل والخرج أو الوكيل) : استكثروا لنا من الباذنجان ، فانه حار في وقت الحرارة ، وبارد في وقت البرودة معتدل في الأوقات كلها ، جيد على كل حال (مكارم الأخلاق / ص١٨٣).

وقال رسول الله ﷺ : « كلوا الباذنجان ، فإنها شجرة رأيتها في جنة المأوى ، شهدت لله بالحق ولي بالنبوة ولعلي بالولاية ، فمن أكلها على أنها داء كانت داء ، ومن أكلها على أنها دواء كانت دواء » (مكارم الأخلاق / ص١٨٤).

١٨ (الطلح) ، الوحدة طلحة وهي شجرة الموز أو شجر هو من أحسن الأشجار منظراً.

١٩ قالوا في (المن) إنه المن الذي يعرفه الناس يسقط على الشجر ، وقالوا : إنه شيء كالصمغ كان يقع على الأشجار وطعمه كالشهد والعسل ، وقالوا : انه الخبز المرقق ، وقالوا : انه جميع النعم التي أتتهم مما منّ الله به عليهم ، مما لا تعب فيه ، ولا نصب ، وروي عن النبي ﷺ أنه قال : « الكمأة من المن وماؤها شفاء للعين » (مجمع البيان / ج١ / ص٢٢٤).

٢٠ (البقل) ما تنبته الأرض من الخضر ، و(القثاء) نوع من الخيار ، و(الفوم) الحنطة وقيل الثوم. واعلم أن لكل من هذه النباتات بالنسبة إلى السالك جهات وحيثيات تكون بها مفيدة ومضرة وهذا يرجع إلى حاله ومقامه.

outwardly like the apricot,[16] harmonious like the eggplant,[17] embracing of knowledge like the banana, as mentioned in the verse, "And clustered bananas" (56:29),[18] honorable like the date-palm, ignoble like verdure on manure, lofty in station and gracious in speech like the Manna, as mentioned in the verse, "We gave you the shade of clouds and sent down to you Manna and quails, saying: 'Eat of the good things We have provided for you.' To us they did no harm, but they harmed their own souls" (2:57).[19]

Or he is lowly like legumes, cucumbers, garlic, lentils and onions, as mentioned in the verses, "Remember you said: 'O Moses, we cannot endure one kind of food; so beseech your Lord for us to produce for us of what the earth grows,—its legumes, cucumbers, garlic, lentils and onions.' He said: 'Will you exchange the better for the worse? Go down to any town, and you shall find what you want!' They were covered with humiliation and misery; they drew on themselves the wrath of God. This is because they went on rejecting the signs of God and slaying His Messengers without just cause. This is because they rebelled and went on transgressing"(2:61).[20]

---

16 This is an interesting fruit whose pulp and core are both edible. Whereas, with other fruits, either the pulp is edible or its core. *Ḥayāt al-ḥayawān*, 2:76.

17 Abū-l-Ḥasan al-Thālith said, "Bring us more eggplant, for it is hot in the time of heat and cold in the time of cold and temperate in all times, wholesome in all states." *Makārim al-akhlāq*, 183.

The Prophet said, "Eat the eggplant for it is a tree that I saw in the paradise of *mằwā*. I witnessed that God is the Truth, I am the messenger and ʿAlī is the spiritual guardian (*walī*); one who eats it thinking it to be an infirmity, it is indeed an infirmity, and one who eats it thinking it to be a cure, it is truly a cure." *Makārim al-akhlāq*, 184.

18 This refers to the banana tree which is one of most delightful trees to look at.

19 It is said that *manna* is that which falls on trees, or it is said that it is the sap of trees that tastes like honey, or it is said that it is a loaf of bread. It is also said that it includes all the bounties that God bestowed upon them which caused no fatigue. The Prophet said, "The mushroom is among the *manna* and its extract is a cure for the eyes." *Majmaʿ al-bayān*, 2:224.

20 Legumes (*baql*) are green vegetation and *quththā'* is a type of cucumber. All of these plants are beneficial for the wayfarer from certain aspects and harmful to him from other aspects, which is on account of his particular state and station.

وعلى هذا نبّه الله تعالى بقوله : ﴿أَلَمْ تَرَ كَيْفَ ضَرَبَ اللَّهُ مَثَلاً كَلِمَةً طَيِّبَةً كَشَجَرة طَيِّبَة أَصْلُهَا ثَابِتٌ وَفَرْعُهَا فِي السَّمَاء ۞ تُؤْتِي أُكُلَهَا كُلَّ حِين بِإِذْنِ رَبِّهَا وَيَضْرِبُ اللَّهُ الأَمْثَالَ لِلنَّاسِ لَعَلَّهُمْ يَتَذَكَّرُونَ ۞ وَمَثلُ كَلِمَة خَبِيثَة كَشَجَرَة خَبِيثَة اجْتُثَّتْ مِن فَوْقِ الأَرْضِ مَا لَهَا مِن قَرَار ۞ يُثَبِّتُ اللَّهُ الَّذِينَ آمَنُواْ بِالْقَوْلِ الثَّابِتِ فِي الْحَيَاةِ الدُّنْيَا وَفِي الآخِرَةِ وَيُضِلُّ اللَّهُ الظَّالِمِينَ وَيَفْعَلُ اللَّهُ مَا يَشَاءُ﴾ [إبراهيم: ٢٤-٢٧].

ولما علمنا حصول المناسبة بين الإنسان والنبات ، فالواجب الاستفادة منه في الوقت المناسب والمكان المناسب والحال المناسب ، وهذا ما يتقيد به أهل الرياضة وطلاب الصحة البدنية والروحانية ، فيرشدهم إلى ذلك الطبيب الجسماني والطبيب الروحاني ، فالسالك مثلا إذا غلبت على حاله الصفات الحيوانية الشهوية والغضبية أمتنع عن الجنس الحيواني لفترة ما من لحوم وغيرها بما يوافق الدين والشريعة ومال إلى تناول النباتيات والتعامل مع جنس النبات في كل شؤونه على القدر المستطاع ، حتى إذا رقت النفس واستقرت عاد إلى ما كان عليه ، وعلى مثل ذلك يرشد المتفرسون والأطباء الروحانيون طلابهم ومرضاهم بحسب المناسبة الحاصلة بين الإنسان والنبات وما فيه من منافع ومضار لنفس السلاك وطلاب الحقيقة.« والله يقول الحق وهو يهدي السبيل ».

Accordingly, God has informed us by saying, "Do you not see how God sets forth a parable? A good word is like a good tree, its root firmly fixed, and its branches in the heavens. It produces fruit at all times, by its Lord's permission. So God sets forth parables for mankind, in order that they may receive admonition. The parable of an evil word is that of an evil tree: It is torn up by the root from the surface of the earth; it has no stability. God will establish in strength those who believe, with the word that stands firm, in this world and in the Hereafter; but God will leave to stray those who do wrong: God does what He wills" (14:24-27).

Since we know that there are correspondences between man and plants, it is therefore necessary to know how one should benefit from them at the appropriate time, place and situation. Practitioners of ascetic disciplines and students of physical and spiritual wellness are aware of those principles, receiving guidance from spiritual physicians and medical doctors. For instance, if the wayfarer's state is overcome by the attributes of animalistic desire and anger, he should abstain from animal products—meats and its derivatives—for a period of time, to the extent that is sanctioned by divine law. His diet should consist of plants, and as much as possible, interact with plant life in all of his affairs until his soul becomes rarified and stable. Then he should return to his normal way of life. In this manner, the people of inward vision and spiritual physicians guide their students and their patients according to the interrelationships between man and the plant world. They indicate that which is profitable and that which is harmful for the wayfarers and seekers of truth. God speaks the truth and guides the way.

الباب العاشر

التناسب بين الإنسان والبسائط والمركبات

إن الله سبحانه جمع في الإنسان قوى العالم وأُوجد بعد وجود الأشياء التي جمعت فيه كما قال تعالى : ﴿الَّذِي أَحْسَنَ كُلَّ شَيْءٍ خَلَقَهُ وَبَدَأَ خَلْقَ الإِنْسَانِ مِن طِينٍ﴾ [السجدة:٧] وقد جمع الله تعالى فيه قوى بسائط العالم و مركباته وروحانياته وجسمانياته ومبدعاته ومكوناته ، وهو من حيث أنه حصل بواسطة العالم وأوجد من أركانه وقواه هو العالم ، ومن حيث صغر شكله وجمع فيه قواه كالمختصر من العالم.

ثم ذكر الله سبحانه في كتابه العزيز العناصر التي خلق منها ، ونبّه على أنه جعله إنساناً في سبع درجات.

قال الراغب الأصفهاني : فقال سبحانه في مواضع خلقه من تراب إشارة إلى المبدأ الأول ، كما قال تعالى[1] : ﴿قَالَ لَهُ صَاحِبُهُ وَهُوَ يُحَاوِرُهُ أَكَفَرْتَ بِالَّذِي خَلَقَكَ مِن تُرَابٍ ثُمَّ مِن نُّطْفَةٍ ثُمَّ سَوَّاكَ رَجُلاً﴾ [الكهف:٣٧].

وفي آخر من طين إشارة إلى الجمع بين الماء والتراب ، كما قال تعالى : ﴿وَلَقَدْ خَلَقْنَا الإِنْسَانَ مِن سُلاَلَةٍ مِّن طِينٍ ۞ ثُمَّ جَعَلْنَاهُ نُطْفَةً فِي قَرَارٍ مَّكِينٍ﴾ [المؤمنون:١٢-١٣].

وفي آخر من حمأ مسنون ، إشارة إلى الطين المتغير بالهواء أدنى تغير ، كما قال تعالى : ﴿وَلَقَدْ خَلَقْنَا الإِنْسَانَ مِن صَلْصَالٍ مِّنْ حَمَإٍ مَّسْنُونٍ﴾ [الحجر:٢٦].

وفي آخر من طين لازب إشارة إلى الطين المستقر على حالة من الاعتدال يصلح لقبول الصور ، كما قال تعالى : ﴿إِنَّا خَلَقْنَاهُم مِّن طِينٍ لاَّزِبٍ﴾ [الصافات:١١].

---

١ وقال تعالى في سورة الحج / الآية ٥ « يا أيها الناس إن كنتم في ريب من البعث فإنّا خلقناكم من تراب... » وقال تعالى في سورة الروم / الآية٢٠« ومن آياته أن خلقكم من تراب ثم إذا انتم بشر تنتشرون ».كتاب تفضيل النشأتين وتحصيل السعادتين / ص٣٧ / الباب الثالث / الراغب الأصفهاني « بتصرف ».

CHAPTER 10

The Correspondence Between Man, the Elements and Compounds

God, the Almighty, gathered the powers of the world within man, who came to be after the existence of everything that is contained within him, as He says, "He who has perfected the creation of all things; He began the creation of man from clay" (32:7).

God converged in man the powers of the simple and compound elements, their spiritual and material properties, and their origins and constituents. Because he was engendered from the world and fashioned through its elements and their powers, he is the world itself, and because all of these powers are gathered in his small frame, he is considered the epitome of the world.

God mentions in His book the constituents from which man was created, indicating that he was formed in seven stages. Rāghib Iṣfahānī writes that when God mentions earth (*turāb*), it is in relation to his primordial genesis, as He says, "His companion said while disputing with him, 'Do you disbelieve in Him Who created you from dust, then of a drop of sperm, and then fashioned you a man?'" (18:37).[1]

In another verse, He mentions clay (*ṭīn*), which refers to the combination of water and earth, as He says, "We created man from the essence of clay. Then We made him a seed in a firmly fixed place" (23:12-13).

Then, He mentions molded mud (*hama'in masnūn*), which refers to clay slightly molded by wind, as He says, "We created man from clay (*ṣalṣāl*), a sound producing vessel, from mud molded into shape" (15:26).

Then, He mentions sticky clay (*ṭīn lāzib*) a reference to clay that solidifies in a state of equilibrium and is receptive to forms. "We created him from sticky clay" (37:11). Elsewhere, "Sound producing clay (*ṣalṣāl*) from molded mud (*hama 'in masnūn*)" (15:26) refers to the dryness and sound produced from it.

---

1 God says, "O mankind, if you are in doubt about the Resurrection, (consider) that we created you from dust..." (22:5). Elsewhere He says, "Among His signs is that He created you from dust; then behold, you are men scattered! (30:20) *Kitāb tafṣīl al-nash'atayn wa taḥṣīl al-sa'ādatayn*, 37.

وفي آخر ﴿مِن صَلْصَالٍ مِّنْ حَمَإٍ مَّسْنُونٍ﴾ [الحجر: ٢٦] إشارة إلى يبسه وسماع صلصلة منه.

وفي آخر من صلصال كالفخار وهو الذي قد أصلح بأثر من النار فصار كالخزف كما قال تعالى: ﴿خَلَقَ الإنْسانَ مِن صَلْصَال كَالْفَخَّارِ﴾ [الرحمن:١٤].

ثم نبّه الله تعالى على تكميل الإنسان بنفخ الروح فيه فقال سبحانه: ﴿إِنِّي خَالِقٌ بَشَراً مِن طِين ۞ فَإِذَا سَوَّيْتُهُ وَنَفَخْتُ فِيهِ مِن رُّوحِي فَقَعُوا لَهُ سَاجِدِينَ﴾ [ص:٧١-٧٢].

ثم دل على تكميل نفسه بالعلوم والآداب بقوله تعالى: ﴿وَعَلَّمَ آدَمَ الأَسْمَاء كُلَّهَا﴾ [البقرة:٣١].

ثم خلق بني آدم وعناصره التي أوجدها حالةً بعد حالة فنبّه على أنه جعلهم إنساناً في سبع درجات حيثما جعل آدم عليه السلام فقال تبارك وتعالى: ﴿وَلَقَدْ خَلَقْنَا الإنْسَانَ مِن سُلاَلَة مِّن طِين ۞ ثُمَّ جَعَلْنَاهُ نُطْفَةً فِي قَرَار مَّكِين ۞ ثُمَّ خَلَقْنَا النُّطْفَةَ عَلَقَةً فَخَلَقْنَا الْعَلَقَةَ مُضْغَةً فَخَلَقْنَا الْمُضْغَةَ عِظَاماً فَكَسَوْنَا الْعِظَامَ لَحْماً ثُمَّ أَنشَأْنَاهُ خَلْقاً آخَرَ فَتَبَارَكَ اللهُ أَحْسَنُ الْخَالِقِينَ﴾ [ص:٧١-٧٢]. وقوله تعالى: ﴿أَنشَأْنَاهُ خَلْقاً آخَرَ﴾ [المؤمنون:١٣] إشارة إلى ما جعل له من قوة العقل والفكر والنطق.

فذلك الإنسان من حيث ما اجتمع فيه قوى الموجودات صار وعاءَ معاني العالم ومظنّة صوره ومعادن آثاره ومجمع حقائقه وكأنه مركب من جمادات ونباتات وبهائم وسباع وشياطين وملائكة، وكما أنه يظهر بصفة وأخلاق الملائكة والشياطين والحيوانات والنباتات على ما تقدم للمناسبة وكونه مختصر العالم وخلاصته كذلك يظهر بصفة البسائط والجمادات فيجري مجراها في الكسل وقلة التحرك والانبعاث والصفات الدانية كما قال تعالى: ﴿ثُمَّ قَسَتْ قُلُوبُكُم مِّن بَعْدِ ذَلِكَ فَهِيَ كَالْحِجَارَةِ أَوْ أَشَدُّ قَسْوَةً﴾ [البقرة:٧٤] أو يتصف بصفاتها الفاضلة والحميدة، كما قال تعالى: ﴿فَكَشَفْنَا عَنكَ غِطَاءكَ فَبَصَرُكَ الْيَوْمَ حَدِيدٌ﴾ [ق:٢٢]، وكما قال تعالى: ﴿وَأَنزَلْنَا الْحَدِيدَ فِيهِ بَأْسٌ شَدِيدٌ وَمَنَافِعُ لِلنَّاسِ﴾ [الحديد:٢٥].

ولما كان الإنسان مركب من تراب وماء ونار وغيرها على ما ذكرناه سابقاً وأن البسائط هذه والمركبات ما تركب منها، وهي إما بارد يابس كالتراب أو بارد رطب كالماء، أو حارة يابسة كالنار، فإذا ناسبت أخلاق الإنسان أحد هذه الأنواع اتصفت بصفاتها وتخصصت بخصائص أفرادها.

Then, dry clay like the potter's (*ṣalṣāl ka-l-fakhār*) which is firm from the effect of firing in the making of a pot, "He created man from clay like the potter's" (55:14).

Then, God announced the completion of man's creation by breathing the spirit in him, as He says, "I am about to create a human from clay. When I have fashioned him and breathed into him of My spirit, fall down in prostration unto him" (38:71-72).

Thereafter, He indicates the soul's completion through knowledge and good character when He says, "He taught Adam the names, all of them." (2:31).

God then describes creating Adam's progeny through the elements in seven consecutive stages: "We created man from the essence of clay; then We made him a drop (of sperm) in a secure dwelling place; then of the drop We created a blood clot, then of the blood clot We created a lump of flesh, then of the lump of flesh We created bones and We clothed the bones with flesh; then We brought him into being as another creation. So blessed be God, the best of creators!" (23:12-14). His saying, "We brought him into being as another creation," means that He endowed him with the powers of intellect, thought and speech.

That human in whom the powers of creation converged is the repository for the meanings of the world, the locus of its forms, the storehouse of its signs and the aggregate of its truths. He is, as it were, a composite of the minerals, plants, beasts, predators, satans and angels. Just as he exhibits the attributes and the character traits of the angels, satans, animals and plants, he also exhibits the properties of inanimate matter—given that he is the summation of the universe.

This is observed when he exhibits laziness, inactivity or a base attribute, as mentioned in the Qur'ān, "Then your hearts became hardened, like a rock, and even more severe in hardness" (2:74), or when he is adorned with virtuous and praiseworthy attributes, "Now We have removed your veil, and your sight this Day is sharp" (50:22), and "We revealed iron, which possesses a mighty power, as well as many uses for mankind" (57:25).

The human being is a composition of earth, water, fire and other elements, as previously mentioned. Since these elements and their associated compounds are either cold and dry like earth, cold and wet like water, or hot and dry like fire, when human character correlates with one of these types, it can be characterized by the qualities of its constituents.

ثم اعلم أن المركبات على كثرة أنواعها مختلفة الطباع والشكل واللون والطعم والرائحة والثقل والخفة والمضرة والنفع وهذا ما يشاهد ويعرف في الجواهر المعدنية ، فمنها ما هو حجري صلب ، يذوب بالنار ويجمد إذا برد كالذهب والفضة والنحاس والأُسرب والرصاص والزجاج وما شاكلها.

هكذا أخلاق بعض الناس لا تتغير إلا بالشدة والغضب التي هي من جنس النار ، ثم تترك حتى تكون في القالب الذي أراده المعلم والمرشد ، كما أن الذهب والفضة وأمثالها لا يستفاد منها إلا بعد البرد.

ومنها ما هو صلب حجري لا يذوب إلا بالنار الشديدة كالياقوت والعقيق ، هكذا بعض الأخلاق متكلسة لا تذوب إلا بشدة الغضب وعزيمة القهر.

ومنها ترابي رخو لا يذوب ولكن ينفرك كالأملاح والزّجات والطّلق[٢] ، كذلك بعض الأخلاق باردة ، يابسة ، لينة ، لا تنفعها شدة النار ولكن ينفعها شيء من الشدة والغضب لما تتصف به من صفة الترابية.

ومنها مائية رطبة تفر من النار كالزئبق ، هكذا بعض المتعلمين يفرون من غضب المعلمين وغلظ أخلاقهم لما هم عليه من طبيعة المائية الرطبة الباردة المقهورة بالنار.

ومنها هوائي دُهني تأكله النار كالكباريت والزّرانيخ ، كذلك بعض النفوس البشرية ينمحي شخصها وشخصيتها ويندرس أثرها.

ثم اعلم أن لهذه الجواهر والمركبات خواص كثيرة وطباع مختلفة :

فمنها متضادة متنافرة ، ومنها متشاكلة متآلفة ، ولها تأثيرات بعضها في بعض إما جذباً أو إمساكاً أو دفعاً أو نفوراً ، ولها شعور خفي وحس لطيف كما للنبات والحيوان ، إما شوقاً ومحبة ، وإما بغضاً وعداوة هكذا قال الحكماء في كتب الأحجار ، أن طبيعةً تألف طبيعة ، وطبيعة تناسب طبيعة أخرى ، وطبيعة تلصق بطبيعة ، وطبيعة تأنس بطبيعة ، وطبيعة تقهر طبيعة ، وطبيعة تقوى على طبيعة ، وطبيعة تضعف على طبيعة ، وطبيعة تلهب طبيعة ، وطبيعة تحب طبيعة ، وطبيعة تطيب مع طبيعة ، وطبيعة تفسد مع طبيعة ، وطبيعة تبيض طبيعة ، وطبيعة تحمّر طبيعة ، وطبيعة تهرب مع طبيعة ، وطبيعة تبغض طبيعة ، وطبيعة تمازج طبيعة.

كذلك الإنسان الذي جمعت فيه البسائط وهذه الطبائع ، جمعت فيه صفاتها وانطبقت عليه أحكامها كل بحسبه.

---

٢ الطلق : دواء إذا طلي به منع حرق النار.

Know that the various types of compounds differ with respect to nature, shape, color, flavor, odor, weight, harm and benefit, as observed in the study of gemstones and minerals. Some are solid and stone-like, but melt with fire and solidify when cooled, such as gold, silver, copper, lead, glass, etc.

As such, some people's character traits are stubborn, changing only through austerity and severity, which have the qualities of fire. They are then left alone until they assume the particular shape that the teacher or spiritual guide desires, in the same way that gold and silver are utilized only after being cooled.

Then there are those whose nature is like hard stone, such as ruby or agate, which only melts in severe heat. As such, their character traits are recalcitrant and become pliable only through severity, austerity and domination.

There are those whose nature is like earth, because earth does not melt but crumbles, as in the case of salt, glass and talc.[2] Their nature is cold, dry and soft; intense fire does not benefit them but only a certain amount of severity and austerity that is appropriate to earth proves beneficial.

There are those whose nature is like water; they flee from fire like mercury. As such, certain pupils flee from the austerity and sternness of their teachers since their nature is watery, wet and cold and they become overwhelmed by fire.

There are those whose nature is like wind and oil, which are consumed by fire, such as sulfur and arsenic. As such, some personality types become extinguished and their traces effaced.

These minerals and compounds possess numerous properties and distinct natures. Some of them possess properties that are either contrary and repulsive or similar and attractive. Some affect others through attracting, suppressing, repelling or averting the effect of the other. They possess a subtle awareness and a hidden sense, similar to plants and animals, that include desire and love, hatred and animosity.

For this reason the sages have mentioned in the books of gemstones that a thing of particular nature is familiar to its like, corresponds to its like, adheres to its like, becomes intimate with its like, dominates its like, strengthens its like, weakens its like, enkindles its like, loves its like, purifies its like, corrupts its like, whitens its like, reddens its like, flees from its like, hates its like, and admixes with its like.

Just as these elements and their natures have been gathered in man, so too have their attributes and properties gathered in him, each individual accordingly.

2 Medicinally, talc prevents burns.

فأما الطبيعة التي تألف طبيعة أخرى ، فمثل الألماس ، فانه إذا قرب من الذهب ألتصق به وأمسكه ، ومثل طبيعة حجر المغناطيس في جذب الحديد فان المغناطيس يجذب الحجر إلى نفسه كما يفعل العاشق بالمعشوق ، والحبيب بالمحبوب ، وعلى هذا القياس ما من حجر من الأحجار المعدنية إلا وبين طبيعته وبين طبيعة شيء آخر ألفة واشتياق.

كما تنجذب القوة العاقلة في الإنسان إلى العلم والحكمة ولوازمها ، والقوة الواهمة إلى المكر والحيلة ولوازمها والقوة الغضبية إلى القهر والغلبة ولوازمها ، والقوة الشهوية إلى الشهوات والملذات ولوازمها على ما تقدم من ذكرها. ربنا الذي أعطى كل شيء خلقه ثم هدى ، خلقه وصوره وعرفه منافعه ومضاره وقواه وأعانه وحفظه ورعاه ودبره وساسه وهداه ، كما شاء وكيف شاء فتبارك الله أحسن الخالقين.

وأمّا الطبيعة التي تقهر طبيعة أخرى ، فمثل طبيعة السُّنباذج[٣] التي تأكل الأحجار عند الحك ، وتلينها وتجعلها مُلساً ، ومثل طبيعة الأُسرُب الوسخ الذي يفتت الماس القاهر لسائر الأحجار الصلبة ، وذلك أن الماس لا يقهره شيء من الأحجار وهو قاهر لها كلها ، فلو أنه تُرك على السَّندان وطرق بالمطرقة لدخل في أحدهما ولم ينكسر ، ومثل طبيعة الزئبق التيار[٤] الرطب القليل الصبر على حرارة النار ، إذا طليت به الأحجار المعدنية الصلبة مثل الذهب والنحاس والفضة ، أوهنها وأرخاها ، حتى يمكن أن تكسر بأسهل سعي وتُفتت قِطعاً قِطعاً ، ومثل الكبريت المنتن الرائحة ، المسوِّد للأحجار النيرة البراقة ، المذهب لألوانها وأصباغها ، يمكِّن النار منها حتى تحترق في أسرع مدة.

وكذلك في انكسار سور الشهوية والوهمية وانقهارهما تحت الغضبية فإنهما لتمردهما لا تطيعان العاقلة بسهولة بخلاف الغضبية تطيعانها وتتأدبان بتأديبها بسهولة.

وأما الطبيعة التي تزين طبيعة أخرى وتنورها فمثل النوشادر الذي يغوص في قهر الأحجار ويغسلها من الوسخ ، كذلك تزين العاقلة باقي القوى الثلاث وتنورها إذا أنقدن لها وأتمرن بأمرها. وأما الطبيعة التي تُعين على طبيعة أخرى فمثل البُورَق الذي يعين النار على سرعة سَبك هذه الأحجار المعدنية الترابية ، ومثل المينا[٥] والقِلى[٦] والمعينان على سبك الرمل وتصفيته ، حتى يكون زجاجاً شفافاً.

---

٣ السنباذج : حجر يجلو به الصيقل (السيوف).

٤ التيار : السريع الحركة والجري.

٥ المينا : جوهر الزجاج.

٦ القِلى : شيء يتخذ من حريق الحمض.

As for a nature which has an affinity to another, diamond, for example, attaches and adheres to gold when in proximity, or a magnetic stone attracts iron to itself in the way that a lover attracts its beloved. Accordingly, the nature of every mineral possesses a familiarity and attraction to the nature of another.

Comparably, the faculty of intellect in man is attracted to knowledge, wisdom and its corollaries, the faculty of imagination to guile, deception and its corollaries, the faculty of anger to power, domination and its associated attributes, and the faculty of desire to pleasures and its kin.

Our Lord has given everything its existence then guided it, created and fashioned everything, knew of their benefit and harm, strengthened, supported, protected, directed, supervised and guided all of it, as He willed, and in the manner that He so desired—so glory be to God, the best of creators!

As for things whose nature dominates another, grindstone,[3] for example, eats away at stone when chafed, softening it and making it smooth. Graphite weakens diamond, even though diamond overcomes every other hard stone. If diamond is placed in an anvil and struck with a hammer it will not break. The nature of mercury is wet,[4] fluid and intolerant of the heat of fire. Yet, if it coats solid minerals such as gold, copper or silver, they become very weak and break easily, shattering into pieces. Sulfur, which possesses a foul smell, blackens lustrous and shiny stones, removes their color and coating and makes them susceptible to combustion.

Likewise, one breaks and subjugates desire and imagination through the faculty of anger, since these faculties are obstinate and do not easily obey the intellect yet readily obey the faculty of anger and become trained by it.

The nature which adorns and illuminates another is exemplified by ammonia which cleans impurities. Similarly, the intellect adorns and illuminates the remaining three faculties if they obey it and are disciplined by it.

The nature which assists another is demonstrated by borax which assists fire in casting metal ore, and enamel[5] and alkali,[6] both of which assist in glazing pottery to make it clear like glass.

---

3 Grindstone is used for polishing swords.
4 "Wet" here means moving rapidly and flowing.
5 Enamel is a glassy substance.
6 Alkali reacts with acids to lowers the melt temperature of the glaze.

وهكذا القوة العاقلة التي تعين على اعتدال القوى الأخرى ، والغضبية التي تعين العاقلة على قهر الشهوية والوهمية.

وأما في الصفات والأخلاقيات فكالعلم الذي يعين على طرد الحيرة والشك والجهل المركب والوساوس وغيرها ، والشجاعة التي تعين على طرد الخوف وصغر النفس ، ودناءة الهمة والغيرة وغيرها ، والعفة التي تعين على دفع حب الدنيا والمال ، والنصيحة التي تعين على دفع الحسد والإيذاء والإهانة وأمثالها.

وعلى هذه الأمثلة والقياسات حكم سائر الصفات الإنسانية والأحجار المعدنية.

فلما كانت المناسبة حاصلة بين الإنسان والبسائط والمركبات وسائر الجمادات بحكم كونه مختصر العالم وزبدته ، لم يترك المشايخ والهداة المرشدون الطلبة والسالكين دون هدايتهم إليها وكيفية الاستفادة منها في عباداتهم وأذكارهم ورياضتهم لما فيها من منافع ومضار ، كما أوصى ونهى المشرعون وخلفائهم بذلك.

قال رسول الله ﷺ[٧] : « تختموا بخواتم العقيق ، فإنه لا يصيب أحدكم غم ما دام عليه ». وقال ﷺ[٨] : « التختم بالياقوت ينفي الفقر ، ومن تختم بالعقيق يوشك أن يقضى له بالحسنى ».

عن أبي عبد الله ، عن آبائه عليهم السلام قال[٩] : أمرنا رسول الله ﷺ بسبع ونهانا عن سبع : عن خاتم الذهب ، وعن الشرب في آنية الذهب ، وفي آنية الفضة ، وعن الجلوس على المياثر الحمر ، وعن الأرجوان ، وعن الحرير ، وعن الإستبرق ، وأمر بعيادة المريض ، واتباع الجنائز ، وإفشاء السلام ، ونصر المظلوم ، وإصابة الداعي ، وإبرار القسم ، وتسميت العاطس.

وعلى مثل ذلك يرتبط الإنسان بالبسائط والمركبات وسائر الجمادات إما بنفسه إن كان من أهل العلم أو عن طريق المرشد والمعلم المتفرس لا لبدعة ابتدعها أو هوى أو عمل بلا علم وغير ذلك بل ما يرشدون إليه قول بعلم وعمل مستند إلى نظر أو كشف أو ألقاء أو روية صادقة وما إليها وذلك بحكم المناسبة والفائدة والمضرة الحاصلة من البسائط والمركبات ، ومثل ذلك يجري في علم الطب فالدرّ مثلا ينفع في خفقان القلب من الخوف والجزع الذي يكون من المرّة السوداء لأنه يطرّي دم

---

٧ كتاب مكارم الأخلاق / الطبرسي / ص٨٧.

٨ كتاب مكارم الأخلاق / الطبرسي / ص٨٧.

٩ كتاب مكارم الأخلاق / الطبرسي / ص٨٧.

Similarly, the faculty of intellect assists in harmonizing the other faculties and the faculty of anger assists in subduing desire and imagination.

As for attributes and ethical qualities, knowledge assists in dispelling confusion, doubt, compound ignorance, insinuation, and so on. Bravery assists in dispelling fear, lack of self-esteem, meager aspiration and sense of honor, and so on. Temperance assists in removing love of the world and wealth, good counsel assists in dispelling jealousy, harm, humiliation and so on. Accordingly, all human attributes can be likened to minerals.

Since there is a correspondence between man, the simple and compound substances and all inanimate objects—given that man is the epitome and essence of the world—the spiritual masters and guides have taught their students how to benefit from these correspondences in their worship, invocations and spiritual exercises, with respect to their advantages and harm. This is in accordance with the advice of divine lawgivers and their successors.

The Prophet said, "Wear a ring of agate for none of you shall suffer grief as long as you wear it." He also said, "Wearing a ring of ruby prevents poverty and one who wears a ring of agate all but receives the best outcome."[7]

Imām Ṣādiq relates from his forefathers, "The Prophet commanded us with seven things and forbade us seven. He forbade us to wear a gold ring, drink from a gold or silver container and sit on a red, purple, silk, or brocade saddle cloth. He commanded us to visit the sick, attend funerals, offer salutations frequently, help the oppressed, respond to a request, fulfill a promise and bless one who sneezes."[8]

Thus, the human being corresponds with the simple and compound substances and all inanimate objects either through himself, if he is endowed with knowledge, or through a spiritual guide and clairvoyant teacher. This is not based on supposition, fancy or action without knowledge, since guidance and instruction from spiritual mentors are rooted in knowledge and deeds, based on visions, unveilings, gnosis and true dreams. These experiences reveal the governing properties of those correspondences and the benefit and harm found in simple and compound substances.

In medicine, for example, pearl alleviates constriction of the heart from the black bile that gives rise to fear and worry by moving the heart's blood. Pearl is used in remedies for the eye, it invigorates the nervous system and when crushed and applied externally, it treats leprosy, or if made into a decoction, it treats epilepsy.

---

7 *Makārim al-akhlāq*, 87.

8 *Makārim al-akhlāq*, 87.

القلب ، ويدخل في أدوية العين ويشد أعصابها وإن حُك وطلي به بياضُ البرص أذهبه ، وإن سُقي ذلك الماء من كان به صُرْعٌ أسكنه.

وأما اليواقيت من تختم بها سلم من الوباء والطاعون ، وسهل عليه قضاء حوائجه وأمور معيشته.

وأما الزمرد والزبرجد من اكثر النظر إليه ذهب عن بصره الكلال ومن تختم به سلم من الصدع.

وغير ذلك مذكور مفصلا في كتب الأحجار ومنافعها ومضارها نترك ذكرها خشية التطويل ونكتفي بالغرض الذي أردنا ذكره.

والحمد لله ربّ العالمين.

Whoever wears ruby is protected from epidemics and plagues and the affairs of his livelihood and needs are facilitated.

Gazing often at emerald and peridot removes myopia and safeguards one from headaches.

Other than these, there are many more benefits and harms described in the books of gemstones, which are outside the scope of these pages. What has been mentioned here suffices for our purpose.

All praise be to God, the Lord of the worlds.

الباب الحادي عشر

التناسب بين العمل والجزاء

قال الشيخ النراقي (رحمه الله) : كل نفس في بدء الخلقة خالية من الملكات بأسرها ، وإنما تتحقق كل ملكة بتكرر الأفاعيل والآثار الخاصة به ، فان كل قول أو فعل ما دام وجوده في عالم الأكوان الحسية لاحظ له من الثبات لأن الدنيا دار التجدد والزوال ، ولكنه يحصل منه أثر في النفس ، فإذا تكرر استحكم الأثر فصار ملكة راسخة مثاله الحرارة التي تحدث في الفحم فإنها ضعيفة أولا وإذا اشتدت تجمرت ثم استضاءت ثم صارت صورة نارية محرقة لما قارنها مضيئة لما قابلها ، وكذلك الأحوال النفسانية إذا تضاعفت قوتها صارت ملكات راسخة وصوراً باطنة تكون مبادئ للآثار المختصة بها ، فالنفوس الإنسانية في أوائل الفطرة[1] كصحائف خالية

---

١ الفِطرة : الخلقة والابتداء والاختراع.
ما فطر الله عليه الخلق من المعرفة به أو الخلقة التي يخلق عليها المولود في بطن أمه ، قال تعالى : ﴿ فِطْرَتَ اللهِ الَّتِي فَطَرَ النَّاسَ عَلَيْهَا ۚ لَا تَبْدِيلَ لِخَلْقِ اللهِ ﴾ [الروم:٣٠].
وقال تعالى : ﴿ الَّذِي فَطَرَنِي فَإِنَّهُ سَيَهْدِينِ ﴾ [الزخرف:٢٧] أي خلقني.
وقال تعالى : ﴿ وَمَا لِيَ لَا أَعْبُدُ الَّذِي فَطَرَنِي ﴾ [يس:٢٢].
وقيل : فُطِر كل إنسان على معرفته بأن الله رب كل شيء وخالقه ، وقد يقال كل مولود يولد على الفطرة التي فَطَر الله عليها بني آدم حين أخرجهم من صُلب آدم ، كما قال تعالى : ﴿ وَإِذْ أَخَذَ رَبُّكَ مِن بَنِي آدَمَ مِن ظُهُورِهِمْ ذُرِّيَّتَهُمْ وَأَشْهَدَهُمْ على أَنفُسِهِمْ أَلَسْتُ بِرَبِّكُمْ ۖ قَالُوا بَلَىٰ ﴾ [الأعراف:١٧٢].
وقال ﷺ : كل مولود يولد على الفطرة يعني الخِلقة التي فُطِر عليها في الرحم من سعادة أو شقاوة ، فإذا كان ولَدَاهُ يهوديان هَوّداه في حكم الدنيا ، أو نصرانيان نصّراه في الحكم ، أو مجوسيان مجّساه في الحكم ، وكان حكمه حكم أبوية حتى يعبِّر عنه لسانه ، فإن مات قبل بلوغه مات على ما سبق له من الفطرة التي فطر عليها ، فهذه فطره المولود ، وفطرة ثانية وهي الكلمة التي يصير بها العبد مسلماً ، وهي شهادة أن لا إله إلا الله وأن محمداً رسوله جاء بالحق من عنده فتلك الفِطرة للدين ، كما في حديث البَراء بن عازب أنه علم رجلا يقول إذا نام ، وقال : فإنك إن متّ من ليلتك مُتّ على الفِطرة.

CHAPTER 11

The Correspondence Between Action and Reward

Shaykh Narāqī writes, "Souls are devoid of traits at inception, but they are established in the soul through repetitive action along with their specific effects. As long as words and deeds exist in the sensory realm they have no share of permanence, for the world is the realm of renewal and extinction. However, their traces remain in the soul and through repetition, they become established as firm traits, like the effect heat has on coal. Coal is initially weak, but when heated, it becomes an ember. Then it emits light and takes the form of a burning fire which shines brightly. The same is true with the states of the soul. Initially, the powers of the soul are weak. As they grow stronger, their inward forms become the origins of specific effects. Human souls in their innate nature (*fiṭrā*)[1] are like pages devoid of insciption and image and

---

1 *Fiṭra* means creation, initiation and origination. It is God's predisposing creation with the innate knowledge of Himself or it is the nature with which He created them in their mother's wombs. God says, "The nature of God in which man has been originated; there is no modifying God's creation" (30:30); "I worship Him who originated me and He will certainly guide me" (43:27);"Why should I not worship the One who originated me" (36:22).

It is said that every person originates with the innate knowledge that God is Lord and Creator, or it is said that every child is born according to the innate nature upon which God originated the children of Adam when He produced them from his seed, as God says, "When your Lord brought forth the descendants of the Children of Adam from their loins bearing witness to themselves (saying) 'Am I not your Lord?' They said, 'Indeed!'" (7:172).

The Prophet said, "Every child is born according to innate nature," that is, the creation that originates in the womb either in felicity or wretchedness. If his parents are Jewish they make him Jewish in the life of this world, or if he is Christian they make him Christian, or if they are Magians, they make him Magian. He is governed by the religion of his parents until he is able to express himself. Thus, if he dies before he reaches puberty, he dies in accordance with innate nature upon which he was created. This is the inborn disposition.

Second nature is that by which a servant becomes a Muslim, and that is the statement, "There is no god but God and Muḥammad is His messenger, who brought the truth from Him'—that is the true nature of religion." It is mentioned in the narration of Barā'a b. 'Āzib that he knew a man who used to say before sleeping, "If you die this night you will have died according to your original nature."

من النقوش والصور تقبل كل خلق بسهولة ، وإذا استحكمت فيها الأخلاق تعسر قبولها لأضدادها ، ولذلك سهل تعليم الأطفال وتأديبهم وتنقيش نفسهم بكل صورة وصفه ويتعسر أو يتعذر تعليم الرجال البالغين وردهم عن الصفات الحاصلة لهم لاستحكامها ورسوخها.

ثم لا خلاف في أن هذه الملكات وأفعالها اللازمة لها إن كانت فاضلة كانت موجبة للالتذاذ والبهجة ومرافقة الملائكة والأخيار ، وان كانت ردية كانت مقتضية للألم والعذاب ومصاحبة الشياطين والأشرار ، وإنما الخلاف في كيفية إيجابها للثواب أو العذاب ، فمن قال إن الجزاء مغاير للعمل ، قال : إن كل ملكه وفعل يصير منشأ لترتب ثواب أو عقاب مغاير له بفعل الله سبحانه على التفصيل الوارد في الشريعة.

وقيل في معنى (فطرة الله... لا تبديل) أي لا تبديل لتلك الخلقة التي خلقهم عليها إما لجنة أو لنار حين أخرج من صُلب آدم كل ذرية هو خالِقُها إلى يوم القيامة ، فقال : هؤلاء للجنة وهؤلاء للنار ، فيقول كل مولود يولد على تلك الفِطرة ، ألا ترى غلام الخِضر عليه السلام ؟

قال رسول الله ﷺ : طبَعَه الله يوم طَبَعه كافراً وهو بين أبوين مؤمنين فأعلم الله الخضر عليه السلام بخلقته التي خلقه لها ، ولم يُعلم موسى عليه السلام.

وقوله ﷺ : فأبواهُ يهودانه ويُنصرانه أي يبين ما تحتاجون إليه في أحكامكم من المواريث وغيرها ، فإذا الأبوان مؤمنين فاحكموا لولدهما بحكم الأبوين في الصلاة والمواريث والأحكام ، وإن كانا كافرين فاحكموا لولدهما بحكم الكفر ، أنتم في المواريث والصلاة وأما خِلقته التي خُلق لها فلا عِلم لكم بذلك ، ألا ترى أن ابن عباس حين كتب إليه نَجْدَةُ في قتل صبيان المشركين ، كتب إليه : إن علمت من صبيانهم ما علم الخضر عليه السلام من الصبي الذي قتله فأقتلهم !

وكذا أطفال قوم نوح عليه السلام ، الذين دعا على آبائهم وعليهم بالغرق إنما استجاز الدعاء عليهم بذلك وهم أطفال ، لان الله عزّ وجلّ ، أعلمه انهم لا يؤمنون حيث قال له : ﴿ لَن يُؤْمِنَ مِن قَوْمِكَ إِلَّا مَن قَدْ آمَنَ ﴾ [هود:٣٦] فأعلمه أنهم فُطِروا على الكفر.

والفِطرة من الحالة كالجِلسة والرِّكبة ، والمعنى أنه يولد على نوع من الجِبِلَّة والطبع المنهي لقبول الدين فلو ترك عليها لاستمر على لزومها ولم يفارقها إلى غيرها وإنما يعدل عنه من يعدل لآفة من آفات البشر والتقليد ، ثم مثل بأولاد اليهود والنصارى في اتباعهم لآبائهم والميل إلى أديانهم عن مقتضى الفطرة السليمة. (لسان العرب / ج١٠ / ص٢٨٦).

easily accept every disposition. If certain traits become firmly established, it becomes increasingly difficult to accept their opposites. Thus, it is easy to teach and train children, sculpting their souls into any form and attribute, whereas it is difficult, to teach those adults and remove their acquired traits as they have become firmly rooted. If these traits and their accompanying actions are noble, then they are the source of felicity and joy, resulting in affinity with the angels and the virtuous. Yet, if these traits are base, then they result in pain, torment and affinity with the satans and the wicked. Difference of opinion in this matter pertains only to how these traits lead to bliss or perdition.

One who holds that recompense is separate from deed, states that every trait and deed is the origin of reward or punishment, which are ultimately in the hands of God, as described in the divine law.

It is said that the meaning of the verse, "The nature of God in which man has been originated; there is no modifying God's creation" (30:30), means that there is no change in creation, i.e., their being created for paradise or for hellfire. When God will have brought forth each lineage He will have created from the loins of Adam until the Day of Judgment, He will say, "Those are for paradise and those are for hellfire," and every child born with a given nature will say, "Do you not see the child of Khidr?"

The Prophet said, "God sealed the unbeliever the day He sealed him while he was still between his believing parents, and he informed Khidr about it but did not inform Moses."

The Prophet said, "Parents make their children Jews or Christians and instill them with the decrees, laws of inheritance, and so on. If the parents are believers they determine what is required with respect to prayers, laws and inheritance. If the parents are unbelievers they establish their child as an unbeliever. So, conduct your prayers and disburse your inheritance (as commanded), since you do not know how you have been created. Do you not see how Najdah replied to Ibn Abbas concerning the killing of the children of the unbelievers when he said, 'If you know about their children what Khidr knew about the child he killed, then kill them!'"

Likewise, Noah prayed to drown the parents and children of his nation. His prayer even included children because God knew that they were unbelievers when He said, "None among your nation will ever believe except for one who has already done so" (11:36). This is because they were originated in unbelief.

Fiṭra is akin to a state like sitting or riding. It means that if a person who is born with a particular type of disposition and nature that declines accepting religion and is left to his own devices, he will continue in that manner with all of its consequences. He will not depart from it and will be subject to the misfortunes that befall others. He will be resemble the children of the Jews and Christians insofar as they follow their forefathers and incline towards their religions at the expense of following sound original nature. *Lisān al-ʿArab*, 10:286.

من قال إن العمل نفس الجزاء ، قال : إن الهيئات النفسانية إذا اشتدت وصارت ملكة تصير متمثلة ومتصورة في عالم الباطن والملكوت بصورة يناسبها ، إذ كل شيء يظهر في كل عالم بصورة خاصة ، فإن العلم في عالم اليقظة أمر عرضي يدرك بالعقل أو الوهم ، وفي عالم النوم يظهر بصورة اللبن ، فالظاهر في العالمين شيء واحد وهو العلم ، لكنه تجلى في كل عالم بصورة ، والسرور يظهر في عالم النوم بصورة البكاء ، ومن يظهر انه قد يسرك في عالم ما يسوءك في عالم آخر.

فاللذات الجسمانية التي تسرك في هذا العالم تظهر في دار الجزاء بصورة تسوءك وتؤذيك ، وتركها وتحمل مشاق العبادات والطاعات والصبر على المصائب والبليات يسرك في عالم الآخرة مع كونها مؤذية في هذا العالم.

ثم القائل بهذا المذهب قد يطلق على هذه الصورة اسم الملك إن كانت من فضائل الأخلاق أو فواضل الأعمال ، واسم الشيطان إن كانت من أضدادها ، وقد يطلق على الأولى اسم الغلمان والحور وأمثالهما ، وعلى الثانية اسم الحيات والعقارب وأشباههما ، ولا فرق بين الإطلاقين في المعنى ، وإنما الاختلاف في الاسم.

وهذا المذهب يرجع إلى القول بتجسد الأعمال بصورة مأنوسة مفرّحة أو صورة موحشة معذبه ، وقد ورد بذلك أخبار كثيرة.

منها : ما روى أصحابنا عن قيس بن عاصم عن النبي ﷺ انه قال : « يا قيس إن مع العز ذلا ومع الحياة موت ومع الدنيا آخرة ، وإن لكل شيء رقيباً وعلى كل شيء حسيباً ، وإن لكل أجل كتاباً ، وانه لابد لك من قرين يدفن معك وهو حي وتدفن معه وأنت ميت ، فان كان كريماً أكرمك ، وإن كان لئيماً ألّمك ، ثم لا يحشر إلا معك ولا تحشر إلا معه ولا تسأل إلا عنه ، فلا تجعله إلا صالحاً ، فانه إن صلح أنست به وإن فسد لا تستوحش إلا منه وهو فعلك ».

ومنها : ما استفاض من قولهم عليهم السلام : « إن من فعل كذا خلق الله تعالى ملكاً يستغفر له إلى يوم القيامة ».

ومنها ما ورد : « إن الجنة قيعان وغرسها سبحان الله ».

ومنها ما روي : « إن الكافر خلق من ذنب المؤمن ».

ومنها قولهم : « المرء مرهون بعمله ».

ومنها قوله ﷺ : « الذي يشرب في آنية الذهب والفضة إنما يجري في بطنه نار جهنم » ويدل عليه قوله سبحانه : ﴿وَإِنَّ جَهَنَّمَ لَمُحِيطَةٌ بِالْكَافِرِينَ﴾ [العنكبوت: ٥٤].

However, one who holds that recompense is identical to deed, states that when forms in the soul intensify they become traits and resemble corresponding forms in the inward world of Dominion (*malakūt*), because all things are manifested in each world in a specific form. Knowledge is an accidental quality that the intellect and imagination perceives in wakefulness, but in the dream-world, it is represented by milk. Its outward form in both worlds is a singular thing, i.e., knowledge, but it manifests in each world in a particular form. Likewise, crying represents joy in the dream-world and someone who delights in one world harms you in another.

Corporeal pleasures that delight you in this world, harm and disturb you in the hereafter. Abandoning those pleasures, enduring the demands of worship and obedience, and maintaining resolve in the face of trials and tribulations, though painful in this world, will bring you delight in the hereafter.

The proponent of this school may call this form angelic, if it is a noble character trait or righteous deed, or satanic if it is the opposite. The former may also be called a paradisiacal youth or maiden, and the latter snakes and scorpions and their likes. There is no difference in meaning even if the terms vary. This school maintains the concept of the "embodiment of deeds" given that they are serene and joyous or vicious and painful. There are a number of narrations along these lines.

It has been narrated by Qays b. ʿĀṣim from the Prophet, "O Qays, honor and humiliation go together as do life and death and the world and the hereafter. For everything there is a guardian, for everything there is accountability and for every period there is a prescribed time. You will certainly have a companion buried with you and it will be alive; you will be buried with it but you will be dead. If you are noble it will honor you and if you are wretched it will pain you. Then, it will be resurrected with you alone and you will be resurrected solely with it. You will be asked about it so make it good, for if it is good then it will be your intimate companion and if it is evil, then you will not be antagonized except by it; these, indeed, are your deeds!"

Similarly, the same idea can be gleaned from the following statements, "Whoever performs such and such an act, God will create an angel who seeks forgiveness for him until the Day of Judgment," or, "Paradise has a bed and its crop is the invocation, 'Glory be to God,'" or, "The unbeliever was created from the sin of the believer," or, "A man is placed in the custody of his actions," or, "The fires of hell flow in the belly of one who drinks from a golden or silver vessel," which is affirmed by the verse, "Hellfire surrounds the unbelievers" (29:54).

وربما كان في قوله تعالى : ﴿وَلاَ تُجْزَوْنَ إِلاَّ مَا كُنتُمْ تَعْمَلُونَ﴾ [يس:٥٤] ، وقوله تعالى : ﴿إِنَّمَا تُجْزَوْنَ مَا كُنتُمْ تَعْمَلُونَ﴾ [الطور:١٦] إشارة إليه حيث قال عزّ وجلّ (ما كنتم) ولم يقل بما كنتم.

وقال فيثاغورس الحكيم : « ستعارض لك في أفعالك وأقوالك وأفكارك وسيظهر لك من كل حركة فكرية أو قولية أو عملية صورة روحانية ، فان كانت الحركة غضبية أو شهوية صارت مادة لشيطان يؤذيك في حياتك ويحجبك عن ملاقاة النور بعد وفاتك ، وان كانت الحركة عقلية صارت ملكاً تلتذ بمنادمته في دنياك وتهتدي به في أخراك إلى جوار الله وكرامته » انتهى.

وهذه الكلمات صريحة في أن مواد الأشخاص الأخروية هي التصورات الباطنية والنيات القلبية والملكات النفسية المتصورة بصور روحانية وجودها وجود إدراكي ، والإنسان إذا انقطع تعلقه عن هذه الدار وحان وقت مسافرته إلى دار القرار وخلص عن شواغل الدنيا الدنية وكشف عن بصره غشاوة الطبيعة ، فوقع بصره على وجه ذاته والتفت إلى صفحة باطنه وصحيفة نفسه ولوح قلبه وهو المراد بقوله سبحانه :

﴿وَإِذَا الصُّحُفُ نُشِرَتْ﴾ وقوله تعالى : ﴿فَكَشَفْنَا عَنكَ غِطَاءَكَ فَبَصَرُكَ الْيَوْمَ حَدِيدٌ﴾ [ق:٢٢] صار إدراكه فعلا وعمله عيناً وسره عياناً فيشاهد ثمرات أفكاره وأعماله ويرى نتائج أنظارة وأفعاله ويطلع على جزاء حسناته وسيئاته ، ويحضر عنده جميع حركاته وسكناته ، ويدرك حقيقة قوله سبحانه وتعالى : ﴿وَكُلَّ إِنسَانٍ أَلْزَمْنَاهُ طَائِرَهُ فِي عُنُقِهِ وَنُخْرِجُ لَهُ يَوْمَ الْقِيَامَةِ كِتَاباً يَلْقَاهُ مَنشُوراً ۞ اقْرَأْ كَتَابَكَ كَفَى بِنَفْسِكَ الْيَوْمَ عَلَيْكَ حَسِيباً﴾ [الإسراء:١٣-١٤] فمن كان في غفلة عن أحوال نفسه ، ومضيعاً لساعات يومه وأمسه يقول : ﴿مَالِ هَذَا الْكِتَابِ لاَ يُغَادِرُ صَغِيرَةً وَلاَ كَبِيرَةً إِلاَّ أَحْصَاهَا وَوَجَدُوا مَا عَمِلُوا حَاضِراً وَلاَ يَظْلِمُ رَبُّكَ أَحَداً﴾[الكهف:٤٩].

﴿يَوْمَ تَجِدُ كُلُّ نَفْسٍ مَّا عَمِلَتْ مِنْ خَيْرٍ مُّحْضَراً وَمَا عَمِلَتْ مِن سُوءٍ تَوَدُّ لَوْ أَنَّ بَيْنَهَا وَبَيْنَهُ أَمَداً بَعِيداً﴾ [آل عمران:٣٠].

وقد أيد هذا المذهب أعني صيرورة الملكات صوراً روحانية باقية أبد الدهر موجبة للبهجة والالتذاذ والتوحش والتألم ، بأنه لو لم تكن تلك الملكات والنيات باقية أبداً لم يكن للخلود في الجنة أو النار وجه صحيح ، إذ لو كان المقتضى للثواب أو العذاب نفس العمل والقول وهما زائلان لزم بقاء المسبب مع زوال السبب وهو باطل وكيف يجوز للحكيم أن يعذب عباده أبد الدهر لأجل المعصية في زمان قصير .

Perhaps the verses, "You will not be recompensed except for that which you used to do" (36:54), and, "You will only be recompensed for that which you used to do" (52:16), indicates the aforementioned point.

Pythagoras, the sage, said, "Your actions, speech, thoughts and every movement of the mind, word, or act will be presented before you and manifested in a spiritual form. If the movement is from the powers of anger or desire, it will become a satanic substance; it will distress you in your life and veil you from receiving the light after your death. If the movement is from the intellect, it will become angelic; you will be blissful in this world and it will guide you in your hereafter to God's proximity and His generosity."

It is obvious from these words that the substance of individuals in the hereafter are their inward forms, the heart's intentions, and the soul's traits, which possess a spiritual form and whose existence is something perceptible. When the human being severs his attachment to this world, his journey to the abode of permanence begins. He is liberated from worldly preoccupations, the curtain of nature is lifted and his inner vision falls on the essence of his being. He turns his attention to his inward face, the book of his soul, and the tablet of his heart, which is what the Qurʾān refers to here, "And when the scrolls are unrolled" (81:10), and "We have lifted your veil from you so this day your vision is sharp" (50:22).

His perception becomes reality, his deeds become actualized and his inner secret becomes eye-witnessed. He beholds the fruits of his thoughts and deeds, he sees the outcome of his observations and acts, his virtues and vices and recalls all of his movements and quietude. Then, he understands the reality of God's statement, "We have fastened every man's fate on his own neck: On the Day of Judgment We shall bring out for him a scroll, which he will see spread open. 'Read your own book: Sufficient is your soul this day as reckoning'" (17:13-14).

Whoever is negligent of the state of his own soul, and who has wasted his day and his yesteryear will say, "What kind of a book is this that it leaves out nothing small or great, but takes account thereof! They will find all that they did confronting them, and your Lord will not treat anyone with injustice" (18:49).

"On the Day when every soul will be confronted with all the good and all the evil it has done, it will wish there were a great distance between it and its evil" (3:30).

The view that traits develop into eternal spiritual forms which are the source of happiness, pleasure, pain and grief is supported by the following argument: Were it not the case that traits and intentions are permanent, it would not be justifiable to dwell eternally in paradise or hell. If the grounds for eternal reward or punishment were ephemeral actions and speech, a permanent

فإذاً منشأ الخلود هو الثبات في النيات والرسوخ في الملكات ، ومع ذلك فمن يعمل مثقال ذرة من الخير أو الشر يرى أثره في صحيفة نفسه أو في صحيفة أعلى وأرفع من ذاته أبداً كما قال سبحانه : ﴿فِي صُحُفٍ مُكَرَّمَةٍ ۝ مَرْفُوعَةٍ مُطَهَّرَةٍ ۝ بِأَيْدِي سَفَرَةٍ﴾ [عبس:١٣-١٥].

والسر فيه أن الأمر الذي يبقى مع النفس إلى حين مفارقتها من الدنيا ولم يرتفع عنها في دار التكليف يبقى معها أبداً ولا يرتفع عنها أصلا لعدم تجدد ما يوجب إزالته بعد مفارقته عن عالم التكليف.

ثم الظاهر إن هذا المذهب. عند من قال به من أهل الشرائع. بيان لكيفية الثواب والعقاب الروحانيين مع إذعانه بالجنة والنار الجسمانيين ، إذ لو كان مراده قصر اللذة والثواب والألم والعقاب والجنات والقصور والغلمان والحور والنار والجحيم والزقوم والضريع وساير ما ورد في الشريعة القادسة من أموز القيامة على ما ذكر فهو مخالف لضرورة الدين. انتهى.

فقد تبين إن بين العمل والجزاء لابد من مناسبة واقتضاء حال ولا يكون الجزاء من عطاء وحرمان أو ثواب وعقاب جزافياً لا يخضع لقانون ، فان ذلك مخالف لفعل الحكيم ، الخبير ، العالم ، الكامل في الصفات ومن هو عين الكمال ومنتهاه.

ولما كان الجزاء على أساس الملكات والصفات والتي منها تصدر الأفعال فلابد من حصول المناسبة بين الفعل والملكة والجزاء ، وان الجزاء الذي هو الجنة أو النار يناسب الملكات والأفعال فغداً انت في الجنة واليوم الجنة فيك.

وعلى أساس ذلك يدرك المتفرس الصفات والملكات المستحكمة والأحوال غير المستحكمة في نفس الغير ، فيرشده إلى الوقاية مما يلاقيه غداً يوم القيامة أو يثبته عليه بعبادة أو ذكر أو رياضة تزيد الملكات ثباتاً والصفات قوةً ورسوخاً بل لولا آية من كتاب الله العزيز : ﴿يَمْحُو اللَّهُ مَا يَشَاءُ وَيُثْبِتُ وَعِندَهُ أُمُّ الْكِتَابِ﴾ [الرعد:٣٩] لأخبر المؤمن المتفرس بنور الله ما يؤل إليه المصير. فانه ينظر بنور الله ويهتدي بتوفيق الله ويحكي بلسان الغيب الناطق عن الرب جعله الله تعالى وأمثاله هداية للبشر حتى يمكن تدارك ما فات ويصلح ما هو آت ، كما قال تعالى في كتابه العزيز : ﴿يَا حَسْرَتَى عَلَى مَا فَرَّطتُ فِي جَنبِ اللهِ﴾[الزمر:٥٦].

والله يقول الحق وهو يهدي السبيل.

effect would ensue from a temporary cause, which is untenable. How can the All-wise punish His servants eternally for a sin committed momentarily?

Remaining eternally in paradise or hell is on account of the permanence of intentions and the immutability of traits. One who performs an atom's weight of good or evil will see its consequence in the book of his soul, or in a loftier book as the verse states, "In honorable books, exalted and pure, written by the hands of scribes" (80:13-15).

The reason is that whatever remains in the soul after its departure from the world, having not been removed in this realm of responsibility, endures with the soul eternally and cannot be expunged. This is because there is no renewal for that which brings about its removal once it has left this world.

Furthermore, if this view—according to the exponents of the divine law—expresses the nature of spiritual reward and punishment as postulating only a physical paradise and hell, and all that is mentioned by the sanctified divine law, namely, pleasure, reward, pain, punishment, gardens, palaces, youth, maidens, fire, inferno (*jaḥīm*), the accursed tree (*zaqqūm*), bitter fruit (*ḍarīʿ*), then it contradicts the tenets of religion.

It is clear that there is an intrinsic relationship and correspondence between deeds and recompense insofar as bestowal, deprivation, reward or punishment, cannot be arbitrary and without justification, for this would contravene the workings of the Wise, the Aware, the Omnicient, the perfection of every attribute, who is perfection itself and its culmination.

Since recompense is based on traits and qualities that arise from deeds, there is a correspondence between deeds, traits and recompense. The recompense which is paradise or hellfire is analogous to one's traits and deeds. Thus, tomorrow you will be in paradise, but today paradise is within you!

On that basis, the clairvoyant perceives in a person's soul firmly rooted qualities and traits as well as states that are not, guiding him to safeguard from what he might encounter tomorrow, Judgment Day, or endorses him by recommending certain acts of worship, invocations or exercises that will increase the constancy of attributes and the strength and firmness of qualities. Were it not for the verse in the divine book, "God effaces what He wills and establishes what He wills and with Him is the Mother of the Book" (13:39), the clairvoyant believer endowed with the light of God could inform him of all that is in his destiny. This is because he sees with the light of God and is guided by His endorsement; he speaks with the tongue of the Unseen on behalf of the Lord. God has made him and his likes guides for humanity so that they may rectify what has lapsed and attain what is to come, as mentioned in the verse, "Woe is me, for I neglected my duty to God" (39:56).

God speaks the truth and guides the way.

الباب الثاني عشر

التناسب بين الإنسان والداء والدواء

قال أبو عبد الله عليه السلام : عرفان المرء نفسه أن يعرفها بأربع طبائع وأربع دعائم وأربع أركان . وطبائعه : الدم والمرة والريح والبلغم. ودعائمه الأربع : العقل ومن العقل الفطنة والفهم والحفظ والعلم . وأركانه : النور والنار والروح والماء.

فأبصر وسمع ، وعقل بالنور ، وأكل وشرب بالنار ، وجامع وتحرك بالروح ، ووجد طعم الذوق والطعم بالماء ، فهذا تأسيس صورته ، فإذا كان عالماً حافظاً ذكياً فطناً فهماً ، عرف فيما هو ومن أين تأتيه الأشياء ، ولأي شيء هو ههُنا إلى ما هو صائر بإخلاص الوحدانية ، والإقرار بالطاعة. وقد جرى فيه النفس ، وهي حارة وتجرية فيه وهي باردة ، فإذا حلّت به الحرارة أشر وبطر وارتاح وقتل وسرق وبهج واستبشر وفجر وزنا وأهتز وبذخ .

وإذا كانت باردة اهتم وحزن واستكان وذبل ونسي وأيس فهي العوارض التي يكون منها الأسقام فإنه سبيلها ولا يكون أول ذلك إلا لخطيئة عملها ، فيوافق ذلك مأكل أو مشرب في أحد ساعات لا تكن تلك الساعة موافقة لذلك المأكل والمشرب بحال الخطيئة فيستوجب الألم من ألوان الأسقام.

وقال : جوارح الإنسان وعروقه وأعضائه جنود الله مجندة عليه ، إذا أراد الله به سقماً سلطها عليه ، فأسقمه من حيث يريد به ذلك السقم.[١]

وذكر في التوراة صفة خلق آدم عليه السلام حين خلقه الله عزّ وجلّ وابتدعه ، قال الله تبارك وتعالى : إني خلقت آدم وركبت جسده من أربعة أشياء ، ثم جعلتها وراثة في ولده تنمي في أجسادهم ، وينمون عليها إلى يوم القيامة ، وركبت جسده حين خلقته من رطب ويابس ، وسخن وبارد ، وذلك إني خلقته من تراب وماء ، ثم جعلت فيه نفساً وروحاً ، فيبوسة كل جسد من قبل التراب ، ورطوبته من قبل الماء و حرارته من قبل النفس ، وبرودته من قبل الروح ، ثم خلقت في الجسد بعد هذا الخلق الأول أربعة أنواع :

---

١ علل الشرائع / ص١٣٣.

CHAPTER 12

The Correspondence Between Man, Illness and Cure

Imām Ja'far al-Ṣādiq said, "A man knowing his soul consists in knowing it in relation to the four natures, the four supports and the four pillars. The natures are blood, bile, wind and phlegm. The supports are intelligence, understanding, memory and knowledge, all of which originate from the Intellect. The pillars are light, fire, spirit and water.

Thus, he sees, hears, and thinks through light, eats and drinks through fire, procreates and moves through spirit. He finds the taste of food through water. This is the constitution of his form, so if he possesses knowledge, memory, intelligence, sagacity and understanding, he knows what he is engaged in, and whence things come to him, the reason why he is here, and what he is becoming, in a manner which accords with sincerity in divine unity and the admission of servitude. The soul moves in him and is hot, and moves in him and is cold. Thus, if he is overcome by heat, he becomes wicked, reckless, and satiated. He kills, steals, delights, rejoices, sins, fornicates, and becomes disconcerted and haughty.

If he is overcome by cold, he worries, grieves, submits, languishes, forgets and despairs. Illnesses originate from these disturbances, for they are its avenue and occur solely because of an error he has committed. When a person eats or drinks something at a time when those things should not be eaten or drunk, one suffers from a variety of ailments. A human being's limbs, veins and bones are God's conscripted army. If God wills illness for them, He overpowers them and afflicts them with an illness in the manner that He desires."[1]

The Torah describes God's engendering of Adam's creation: God said, "I created Adam and arranged his body from four things. Then I made his progeny increase in number, and they shall increase until the Day of Resurrection. When I created him I arranged his body with the wet, dry, hot and cold. That is because I created him out of clay and water, then I placed in him a soul and a spirit. So the dryness of every body corresponds to earth, its wetness corresponds to water, its heat corresponds to soul, and its coldness corresponds to spirit. After this initial creation, I then created in the body four humors.

---

1 *'Ilal al-Sharā'i*, 133.

وهن ملاك الجسد وقوامه بإذني لا يقوم الجسد إلا بهن ولا تقوم منهن واحدة إلا بالأخرى ، منها المرة السوداء والمرة الصفراء ، والدم والبلغم ، ثم أسكن بعض هذا الخلق في بعض ، فجعل مسكن اليبوسة في المرة السوداء ، ومسكن الرطوبة في المرة الصفراء ، ومسكن الحرارة في الدم ، ومسكن البرودة في البلغم ، فأيما جسد اعتدلت به هذه الأنواع الأربع التي جعلتها ملاكه وقوامه وكانت كل واحدة منهن أربعاً لا تزيد ولا تنقص ، كملت حصته واعتدل بنيانه ، فإن زاد منهن واحدة عليهن فقهرتهن ومالت بهن دخل على البدن السقم من ناحيتها بقدر ما زادت ، وإذا كانت ناقصة ثقل عنهن حتى تضعف عن طاقتهن وتعجز عن مقارنتهن .

وجعل عقله في دماغه ، وسرّه في طينته ، وغضبه في كبده ، وصرامته في قلبه ، ورغبته في رئته ، وضحكه في طحاله ، وفرحه في حزنه ، وكربه في وجهه ، وجعل فيه ثلاثمائة وستين مفصلا.[٢]

فالطبيب العالم بالداء والدواء يعلم من حيث يأتي السقم من قبل زيادة تكون في إحدى هذه الفطرة الأربع ، أو نقصان منها ، ويعلم الدواء الذي به يعالجهن فيزيد في الناقصة منهن ، أو ينقص من الزائد حتى يستقيم الجسد على فطرته ويعتدل الشيء بأقرانه ، ثم تصير هذه الأخلاق التي ركب عليها الجسد فطراً عليها تبني أخلاق بني آدم وبها توصف ، فمن التراب العزم ، ومن الماء اللين ، ومن الحرارة الحدة ومن البرودة الأناة ، فإن مالت به اليبوسة كان عزمه القسوة ، وإن مالت به الرطوبة كانت لينة مهانة ، وإن مالت به الحرارة كانت حدته طيشاً وسفهاً ، وإن مالت به البرودة كانت أناته ريباً وبلداً .

فإن اعتدلت أخلاقه وكن سواء ، واستقامت فطرته كان حازماً في أمره ليناً في عزمه حاداً في لينه ، متأنياً في حدته ، لا يغلبه خلق من أخلاقه ، ولا يميل به ، من أيها شاء استكثر ومن أيها شاء إستقل ومن أيها شاء عدل ويعلم كل خلق منها إذا علا عليه بأي شيء يمزجه ويقومه فأخلاقه كلها معتدلة كما يجب أن يكون.

فمن التراب قسوته وبخله وحصره وفظاظته وبرمه وشحه ويأسه وقنوطه وعزمه وأطراره ، ومن الماء كرمه ومعروفه وتوسعه وسهولته وتوسله وقربه وقبوله ورجاه واستبشاره ، فإذا خاف ذو العقل أن يغلب عليه أخلاق التراب ، ويميل به الزم كل

---

٢ علل الشرائع / ص١٣٤.

They are the foundation of the body and its edifice, by My permission, for the body does not subsist except through them and none of them subsists without the other. They are black bile, yellow bile, blood and phlegm. Then I made some of these reside in others, making the residence of dryness in black bile, the residence of wetness in yellow bile, the residence of heat in blood and the residence of coldness in phlegm.

In whichever body these four humors are harmonized, of which I have made its foundation and subsistence—they are no less nor greater than four—its share is complete and its edifice harmonized. But if one of them dominates the others, illness enters the body to the extent of that excess. If it is deficient, it becomes sluggish until its strength is weakened and is unable to correspond with its like.

God placed man's intellect in his brain, his mind in his flesh, his anger in his liver, his vigor in his heart, his yearning in his lungs, his laughter in his spleen, his happiness in his sorrow, his worry in his face, and He gave him three-hundred and sixty joints."[2]

A physician who knows about illness and cure is aware of the origins of an illness before the increase or deficiency of one of the four original natures. He knows wherein lies the cure so that he strengthens a deficiency or reduces an excess. In this way the body will be rectified according to its innate disposition and harmonized through its like.

These natures are the qualities of innate disposition which then become the character traits of man. Earth generates determination, water generates leniency, fire generates severity and cold generates patience. If dryness prevails his determination is severe, if wetness prevails his lenience is contemptible, if fire prevails his anger is reckless and foolish, if coldness prevails his patience is apprehensive and obtuse.

If, however, his character is harmonized, balanced and his disposition rectified, he is decisive in his affairs, lenient in his resolve, firm in his leniency, patient in his anger. No quality dominates another, nor does he incline to any quality over another. He can augment or diminish those qualities as he so desires and bring any one of them into balance. He knows the origin of every character trait such that if any excel in him in a given aspect, he integrates and sustains them. Thus, his character is completely in harmony, as it ought to be.

Earth gives rise to hardness, stinginess, constriction, crudeness, aversion, greed, despair, despondency, resolve and remoteness. Water gives rise to generosity, goodwill, expansion, mildness, entreaty, proximity, acceptance,

2 *ʿIlal al-Sharāʾiʿ*, 134.

خلق منها خلقاً من أخلاق الماء يمزجه بلينه ، ويلزم القسوة اللين ، والحصر التوسع ، والبخل العطاء ، والفظاظة الكرم ، والبرم التوسل ، والشح السماح ،واليأس الرجاء ، والقنوط الاستبشار ، والعزم القبول ، والأطرار القرب .

ثم من النفس حدته وخفته وشهوته ولهوه ولعبه وضحكه وسفهه وخداعه وعنفه وخوفه ، ومن الروح حلمه ووقاره وعفافه وحياؤه وبهاؤه وفهمه وكرمه وصدقه ورفقه وكبره .

وإذا خاف ذو العقل أن تغلب عليه أخلاق النفس وتميل به ، الزم كل خلق منها خلقاً من أخلاق الروح يقومه به يلزم الحدة الحلم والخفة الوقار ، والشهوة العفاف ، واللعب الحياء ، والضحك الفهم ، والسفه الكرم ، والخداع الصدق ، والعنف الرفق ، والخوف الصبر .

ثم بالنفس سمع ابن آدم وأبصر ، وأكل وشرب ، وقام وقعد ، وضحك وبكى ، وفرح وحزن ، وبالروح عرف الحق من الباطل ، والرشد من الغي ، والصواب من الخطأ ، وبه علم وتعلم وحكم وعقل ، واستحى وتكرم ، وتفقه وتفهم ، وتحذر وتقدم.

ثم يقرن إلى أخلاقه عشر خصال أخرى : الإيمان والحلم والعقل والعلم والعمل واللين والورع والصدق والصبر والرفق ، ففي هذه الأخلاق العشر جميع الدين كلّه .

ولكل خلق منها عدو ، فعدوا الإيمان الكفر ، وعدو الحلم الحمق ، وعدو العقل الغي ، وعدو العلم الجهل ، وعدو العمل الكسل ، وعدو اللين العجلة ، وعدو الورع الفجور ، وعدو الصدق الكذب ، وعدو الصبر الجزع ، وعدوا الرفق العنف.

فإذا وهن الإيمان تسلّط عليه الكفر وتعبّده وحال بينه وبين كل شيء يرجو منفعته ، وإذا صلب الإيمان وهن له الكفر وتعبَّده واستكان واعترف الإيمان .

وإذا ضعف الحلم علا الحمق وحاطه وذبذبه وألبسه الهوان بعد الكرامة ، فإذا استقام الحكم فضح الحمق وتبين عورته وأبدي سوءته وكشف ستره وأكثر مذمته .

فإذا استقام اللين تكرم من الخفة والعجلة واطردت الحدة وظهر الوقار والعفاف ، وعرفت السكينة ، وإذا ضعف الورع تسلط عليه الفجور وظهر الإثم وتبين العدوان وكثر الظلم ونزل الحمق وعمل بالباطل .

hope and happiness. If the possessor of intellect fears that the qualities of earth will subdue him, he tethers each of its qualities with those of water and mixes the former with the softness of water. Thus, he enjoins hardness with softness, constriction with expansion, stinginess with generosity, crudeness with nobility, aversion with acceptance, greed with munificence, despair with hope, despondency with happiness and remoteness with proximity.

The soul gives rise to severity, levity, desire, diversion, frivolity, laughter, foolishness, deceit, harshness, and fear. The spirit gives rise to forbearance, gravity, chasteness, modesty, radiance, understanding, magnanimity, truthfulness, friendship, and greatness.

If the possessor of intellect fears that the qualities of the soul will subdue him, he tethers each of its qualities with those of the spirit. Thus, he enjoins severity with forbearance, levity with gravity, desire with chasteness, frivolity with modesty, laughter with understanding, foolishness with nobility, deceit with truthfulness, harshness with friendship and fear with patience.

Through the soul, man hears and sees, eats and drinks, sits and stands, laughs and cries, rejoices and grieves. Through the spirit, he discerns truth from falsehood, right guidance from temptation, correctness from error, knows, learns, judges, reasons, feels shame, shows generosity, comprehends, realizes, takes precautions and moves forward.

In addition, there are ten other qualities associated with the spirit: Faith, understanding, intelligence, knowledge, action, gentleness, piety, truthfulness, patience and friendliness. These ten qualities epitomize the entirety of religion.

Since every creation possesses an adversary, the adversary of faith is unbelief, of understanding, stupidity; of intelligence, error; of knowledge, ignorance; of action, laziness; of gentleness, impetuousness; of piety, immorality; of truthfulness, falsehood; of patience, worr;, and of friendship, hostility.

If faith weakens, unbelief dominates him, subjugating him and creating a barrier between him and the things from which he hopes to benefit. When faith becomes strong, unbelief crumbles, submitting to him; thus, he becomes humble and acknowledges faith.

If understanding weakens, stupidity prevails, eclipsing him and making him vacillate; ignominy envelops him even after having possessed nobility. When wisdom arises, it exposes stupidity, revealing his defects; it divulges his iniquities and discloses his secrets, increasing him in self-reproach.

When gentleness is fostered, he shuns frivolity and impetuousness, and he refrains from severity; gravity and chasteness appear and he experiences serenity. If piety declines, immorality vanquishes him, sins appear, enmity becomes evident, oppression becomes abundant, folly and wrong action ensue.

وإذا ضعف الصدق كثر الكذب وفشت الفرية وجاء الإفك بكل وجه والبهتان ، وإذا حصل الصدق اختسأ الكذب وذل وصمت الإفك وأميتت الفرية وأُهين البهتان ودنا البر واقترب الخير وطرد الشره .

وإذا وهن الصبر وهن الدين وكثر الحزن وزهق الجزع وأميتت الحسنة وذهب الأجر وإذا صلب الصبر خلص الدين وذهب الحزن وأُخر الجزع وأحييت الحسنة وعظم الأجر وتبين الحزم وذهب الوهن .

وإذا ترك الرفق ظهر الغش وجاءت الفظاظة واشدت الغلظة وكثر الغشم وترك العدل وفشا المنكر وترك المعروف وظهر السفه ورفض الحلم وذهب العقل وترك العلم وفتر العمل ومات الدين وضعف الصبر وغلب الورع ووهن الصدق وبطل تعبّد أهل الإيمان.

فمن أخلاق العقل عشرة أخلاق صالحة : الحلم والعلم والرشد والعفاف والصيانة والحياء والرزانة والمداومة على الخير وكراهة الشر وطاعة الناصح ، فهذه عشرة أخلاق صالحة. ثم يتشعب من كل خلق منها عشرة خصال ، فالحلم يتشعب منه : حسن العواقب ، والمحمدة في الناس وتشرف المنزلة ، والسلب عن السفه ، وركوب الجميل ، وصحبة الإبرار ، والارتداع عن الضعة ، والارتفاع عن الخساسة ، وشهوة اللين ، والقرب من معالي الدرجات ، ويتشعب من العلم : الشرف وإن كان دنياً ، والعز وإن كان مهيناً ، والغنى وان كان فقيراً ، والقوة وإن كان ضعيفاً ، والنبل وإن كان حقيراً ، والقرب وإن كان قصياً ، والجود وإن كان بخيلا ، والحياء وإن كان صلفاً ، والمهابة وإن كان وضيعاً ، والسلامة وإن كان سقيماً. ويتشعب من الرشد : السداد ، والهدى ، والبر ، والتقوى ، والعبادة ، والقصد ، والاقتصاد ، والقناعة ، والكرم ، والصدق. ويتشعب من العفاف : الكفاية ، والاستكانة ، والمصادقة ، والمراقبة ، والصبر ، والنصر ، واليقين ، والرضا والراحة ، والتسليم.

ويتشعب من الصيانة : الكف ، والورع ، وحسن الثناء ، والتزكية ، والمروة ، والكرم ، والغبطة ، والسرور والمنالة والتفكير. ويتشعب من الحياء : اللين ، والرأفة ، والرحمة ، والمداومة ، والبشاشة ، والمطاوعة وذل النفس التقي ، والورع ، وحسن الخلق. ويتشعب من المداومة على الخير : الصلاح ، والاقتدار ، والعزم ، والإخبات ، والإنابة ، والسؤدد ، والأمن ، والرضا في الناس ، وحسن العاقبة.

If truthfulness weakens, falsehood increases, fabrications circulate and lies and slander appear from every side. When truthfulness arises, falsehood is expelled, lies are abolished and disgraced, fabrications perish and slander is scorned. Virtue and goodness draw near and wickedness is banished.

If patience weakens, religiosity erodes, sorrow increases, worry becomes tiresome, good deeds expire and reward is lost. When patience becomes firm, religiosity is refined, sorrow disappears, worry is deferred, good deeds are restored, reward is magnified, fortitude is visible and weakness vanishes.

If friendliness is relinquished, dishonesty arises, harshness emerges, rudeness intensifies, iniquity increases, justice is abandoned, wanton acts become rampant, goodwill is jettisoned, insolence appears, understanding is dismissed, intelligence departs, knowledge is lost, action becomes feeble, religion dies, patience wears thin, piety is vanquished, truthfulness is subverted, and service of the faithful is negated.

Among the characteristics of the intellect there are ten virtuous traits: Understanding, knowledge, right guidance, chasteness, preservation, modesty, gravity, constancy in good, repulsion of evil and complying with a sincere advisor; these are ten virtuous traits. Each of these traits gives rise to ten other traits.

Understanding fosters optimism, a good reputation and a noble position among people. It shuns foolishness, cultivates beautiful comportment and association with the virtuous, eschews humiliation, elevates one from base and resilient appetites and advances one towards lofty stations.

Knowledge cultivates dignity if one is lowly, distinction if contemptible, prosperity if poor, power if weak, nobility if base, intimacy if callous, generosity if stingy, modesty if conceited, respect if inferior and health if ill.

Rectitude cultivates correct action, guidance, virtue, piety, worship, aspiration, balance, contentment, generosity and truthfulness.

Chasteness cultivates sufficiency, humility, agreement, attentiveness, patience, assistance, conviction, satisfaction, serenity and submission.

Preservation cultivates abstention, godliness, distinction, purity, chivalry, generosity, joy, happiness, achievement and thoughtfulness.

Modesty cultivates leniency, clemency, mercy, endurance, cheerfulness, obedience and humility before a saintly person, godliness and nobility of character.

Persistence in good deeds cultivates righteousness, aptitude, fortitude, submissiveness, repentance, sovereignty, safety, satisfaction of the people and a good outcome.

ويتشعب من كراهة الشر : حسن الأمانة ، وترك الخيانة ، واجتناب السوء وتحصين الفرج ، وصدق اللسان ، والتواضع ، والتضرع لمن هو فوقه ، والإنصاف لمن هو دونه ، وحسن الجوار ومجانبة إخوان السوء. ويتشعب من الرزانة : التوقر ، والسكون ، والتأني ، والعلم ، والتمكين ، والحظوة ، والمحبة ، والفلح ، والزكاية ، والإنابة. ويتشعب من طاعة الناصح : زيادة العقل ، وكمال اللب ، ومحمدة الناس ، والامتعاض من اللوم ، والبعد من البطش ، واستصلاح الحال ، ومراقبة ما هو نازل ، والاستعداد للغد ، والاستقامة على المنهاج ، والمداومة على الرشاد. فهذه مائة خصلة من أخلاق العاقل.

وعن سماعة بن مهران قال : كنت عند أبي عبد الله عليه السلام وعنده نفر من مواليه فجرى ذكر العقل والجهل ، فقال أبو عبد الله عليه السلام :

أعرفوا العقل وجنده تهتدوا ، واعرفوا الجهل وجنده تهتدوا.

قال سماعة : قلت : جعلت فداك ، لا نعرف إلا ما عرفتنا ؟

فقال أبو عبد الله عليه السلام : إن الله تبارك وتعالى خلق العقل وهو أول خلق خلقه من الروحانيين عن يمين العرش من نوره ، فقال له : ادبر فأدبر ، ثم قال له : أقبل فأقبل ، فقال الله تبارك وتعالى له : خلقتك خلقاً عظيماً ، وكرمتك على جميع خلقي.

قال : ثم خلق الجهل من البحر الأجاج الظلماني ، فقال له : أدبر فأدبر ، ثم قال له : أقبل ، فلم يقبل ، فقال الله عزّ وجلّ : استكبرت فلعنت.

ثم جعل للعقل خمسة وسبعين جنداً ، فلما رأى الجهل ما أكرم الله به العقل وما أعطاه اضمر له العداوة ، فقال الجهل : يا رب هذا خلق مثلي خلقته فكرمته وقويته ، وأنا ضده فلا قوة لي به ، فأعطني من الجند مثل ما أعطيته ، فقال : نعم ، فإن عصيتني بعد ذلك أخرجتك وجندك من رحمتي ، قال : رضيت ، فأعطاه خمسة وسبعين جنداً.

فكان مما أعطاه الله عزّ وجلّ للعقل من الخمسة والسبعين الجند.(٣)

الخير وهو وزير العقل ، وجعل ضده الشر وهو وزير الجهل ، والإيمان وضده الكفر ، والتصديق وضده الجحود ، والرجاء وضده القنوط ، والعدل وضده الجور ، والرضا وضده السخط ، والشكر وضده الكفران ، والطمع وضده اليأس ، والتوكل

---

٣ علل الشرائع / ص١٣٨.

Loathing evil gives rise to trustworthiness, shunning disloyalty, relinquishing wickedness, safeguarding the privates, truthfulness of speech, humility, yielding to superiors, equity before subordinates, kindness to neighbors and avoidance of corrupt friends.

Self-possession cultivates gravity, tranquility, deliberateness, knowledge, stability, grace, love, success, integrity and remorse.

Complying with a sincere advisor fosters an increase in intelligence, perfection of one's innermost being, a good name in society, aversion to criticism, distance from oppression, amending affairs, vigilance of events, preparation for the future, adhering to one's way and persistence in rectitude. These are the hundred traits of the intelligent.

Samāʿa b. Mihrān relates that he was with Imām Jaʿfar al-Ṣādiq with other companions present when he began describing the Intellect and Ignorance. He said, "Know the Intellect and its soldiers—you will be guided. Know Ignorance and its soldiers—you will be guided." The listener said, "May I sacrifice myself for you! We do not know except what you have taught us." Then Abū ʿAbdallāh said, "God created the Intellect—the first creature He created among the spiritual beings (*rūḥāniyyūn*)—from the right side of His Throne from His light. He said to it, 'Turn away from Me,' so it turned away. Then He said, 'Turn towards Me,' so it turned towards Him. Then He said, 'I have created a great creature and ennobled him above all My creation.'

Then He created Ignorance from the briny, dark ocean. He said to it, 'Turn away from Me' so it turned away. Then He said, 'Turn towards Me,' but it did not turn. Then He said, 'Have you waxed proud?' So He cursed it.

Then God appointed for the Intellect seventy-five soldiers. When Ignorance saw how God had ennobled the Intellect and what He had given it, it conceived a hidden enmity toward it. Ignorance said, 'O Lord, this is a creature like me. You have created him, ennobled him and given him strength, while I am his opposite and I have no strength against him. Give me soldiers the like as You have given him.' So God said, 'Yes, but if you disobey Me after this, I will send you and your army away from My mercy.' Ignorance said, 'I am satisfied.' So God gave it seventy-five soldiers:

(He made) good the vizier of the Intellect and evil its rival, which is the vizier of Ignorance, then faith and its rival disbelief, attestation and its rival denial, hope and its rival despair, justice and its rival inequity, contentment and its rival resentment, gratitude and its rival ungratefulness, eagerness and its rival resignation, reliance and its rival greed, clemency and its rival cruelty, mercy and its rival anger hard-heartedness, knowledge and its rival ignorance, understanding and its rival stupidity, modesty and its rival shamelessness,

وضده الحرص ، والعلم وضده الجهل ، والفهم وضده الحمق ، والعفة وضدها التهتك ، والزهد وضده الرغبة ، والرفق وضده الخرق ، والرهبة وضدها الجرأة ، والتواضع وضده التكبر ، والتوءده وضدها التسرع ، والحلم وضده السفه ، والصمت وضده الهذر ، والاستسلام وضده الاستكبار ، والتسليم وضده التجبر ، والعفو وضده الحقد ، والرحمة وضدها القسوة ، واليقين وضده الشك ، والصبر وضده الجزع ، والصفح وضده الانتقام ، والغنى وضده الفقر ، والتذكر وضده السهو ، والحفظ وضده النسيان ، والتعطف وضده القطيعة ، والقنوع وضده الحرص ، والمواساة وضدها المنع ، والمودة وضدها العداوة ، والوفاء وضده الغدر ، والطاعة وضدها المعصية ، والخضوع وضده التطاول ، والسلامة وضدها البلاء ، والحب وضده البغض ، والصدق وضده الكذب ، والحق وضده الباطل ، والأمانة وضدها الخيانة ، والإخلاص وضده الشرك ، والشهامة وضدها البلادة ، والفطنة وضدها الغباوة ، والمعرفة وضدها الإنكار ، والمداراة وضدها المكاشفة ، وسلامة الغيب وضدها المماكرة ، والكتمان وضده الإفشاء ، والصلاة وضدها الإضاعة ، والصوم وضده الإفطار ، والجهاد وضده النكول ، والحج وضده نبذ الميثاق ، وصون الحديث وضده النميمة ، وبر الوالدين وضده العقوق ، والحقيقة وضدها الرياء ، والمعروف وضده المنكر ، والستر وضده التبرج ، والتقية وضدها الإذاعة ، والإنصاف وضده الحمية ، والنظافة وضدها القذارة ، والحياء وضده الخلع ، والقصد وضده العدوان ، والراحة وضدها التعب ، والسهولة وضدها الصعوبة ، والبركة وضدها المحق ، والعافية وضدها البلاء ، والقوام وضده المكاثرة ، والحكمة وضدها النقاوة ، والوقار وضده الخفة ، والسعادة وضدها الشقاوة ، والتوبة وضدها الإصرار ، والاستغفار وضده الاغترار ، والمحافظة وضدها التهاون ، والدعاء وضده الاستنكاف ، والنشاط وضده الكسل ، والفرح وضده الحزن ، والألفة وضدها الفرقة ، والسخاء وضدها البخل.

ولا تجتمع هذه الخصال كلّها من أجناد العقل إلاّ في نبي أو وصي أو مؤمن أمتحن الله قلبه للإيمان ، وأما سائر ذلك من موالينا ، فإن أحدهم لا يخلو من أن يكون فيه بعض هذه الجنود ، حتى يستكمل ويتقي من جنود الجهل ، فعند ذلك يكون في الدرجة العليا مع الأنبياء والأوصياء عليهم السلام ، وإنما يدرك الحق بمعرفة العقل وجنوده ، ومجانبة الجهل وجنوده ، وعصمنا الله وإياكم لطاعته ومرضاته.

renunciation and its rival craving, gentleness and its rival harshness, reverence and its rival impudence, humility and its rival pride, deliberation and its rival haste, discernment and its rival foolishness, silence and its rival idle talk, submission and its rival arrogance, surrender and its rival doubt, patience and its rival uneasiness, pardon and its rival vengeance, wealth and its rival poverty, remembrance and its rival deliberation, memory and its rival forgetfulness, vengeance reality, sympathy and its rival severing ties, contentment and its rival greed, altruism and its rival deprivation, friendship and its rival enmity, loyalty and its rival treachery, obedience and its rival disobedience, humility and its rival haughtiness, safety and its rival tribulation, love and its rival hatred, truthfulness and its rival lying, truth and its rival falsehood, trustworthiness and its rival deceit, sincerity and its rival corruption, acuity and its rival dullness, comprehension and its rival, idiocy, recognition and its rival rejection, graciousness and its rival exposing, security in absentia, collusion, confidentiality and its rival disclosure, prayer and its rival neglect, fasting and its rival breaking fast, jihad and its rival cowering, Hajj and its rival breaking the covenant, guarding one's tongue and its rival slandering, filial piety and its rival disobedience, reality and its rival ostentation, virtue and its rival vice, covering and its rival displaying, guarding and its rival advertising, fairness and its rival partiality, preparedness and its rival inequity, cleanliness and its rival filth, shame and its rival indecency, moderation and its rival excess, rest and its rival fatigue, ease and its rival difficulty, blessing and its rival obliteration (of reward), health and its rival trial, measure and its rival excess, wisdom and its rival caprice, dignity and its rival frivolity, happiness and its rival misery, repentance and its rival persistence (in sin), seeking forgiveness and its rival self-deception, mindfulness and its rival carelessness, supplication and its rival disdainfulness, liveliness and its rival indolence, joy and its rival sorrow, familiarity and its rival separateness, generosity and its rival stinginess."[3]

These qualities do not exist in a single person unless he is a prophet, saint or believer whose heart God has tested for faith. The rest of us possess some of these soldiers, strive to acquire them and refrain from obeying the soldiers of Ignorance. Thereafter, we will be able to attain the highest station along with the prophets and saints—peace be upon them all. Indeed, truth is discerned through the Intellect and its soldiers and by avoiding Ignorance and its soldiers—May God protect us and you from obeying and succumbing to Ignorance.

---

3 *ʿIlal al-Sharāʾiʿ*, 137.

وعلى أساس معرفة ما ذكرنا وأمثاله يشخص الطبيب الروحاني والمتفرس الإلهي المناسبة ويعرف الداء ثم يعين الدواء حتى يوصل السالك إلى الدرجة العليا مع الأنبياء والأوصياء عليهم السلام.

والحمد لله ربّ العالمين.

Based on all that has been said here, the spiritual physician or the divine clairvoyant is able to discern the correspondences, know illnesses then specify cures so that the wayfarer may reach the highest stations along with the prophets and saints—peace be upon them all.

Praise be to God, Lord of the worlds.

Bibliography

ʿAlī b. Abī Ṭālib. *Nahj al-balāgha.* Beirut: Mu'assasa al-Aʿlamī li-l Maṭbūʿāt, 1993.

Abū Dāwūd, Sulaymān b. al-Ashʿath al-Sijistānī. *Sunan Abī Dāwūd*, ed. S. al-Arnā'ūṭ et al. 6 vols. Beirut: Dār al-Risālah al-ʿĀlamiyyah, 2009.

Almajid, Akram. *al-Khalq al-jadīd*, trans. M. Ali, *The New Creation*. London: Sage Press, 2018.

Almajid, Akram. *Manāzil al-sā'irīn: bāb al-firāsa*, ed. Ḥ. al-Azraqī. Qum: Madyan, 2008.

Almajid, Akram. *Sharḥ muqaddimat al-Ājurrūmiyya wa iʿrābuhā.* Beirut: Dār al-Fayḥā' 2020.

Āmidī, ʿAbd al-Wāḥid. *Ghurar al-ḥikam wa durar al-kalim.* Tehran: Daftar-i Nashr-i Farhang-i Islāmī, 2000.

ʿĀmulī, Hurr al-. *Wasā'il al-shīʿa.* Beirut: Mu'assasa Āl al-Bayt li-Iḥyā'al-Turāth, 1993.

Āmulī, Sayyid Ḥaydar. *Tafsīr muḥīṭ al-aʿẓam wa-l-baḥr al-khiḍam fī taʾwīl kitāb Allah al-ʿazīz al-muḥkam*, ed. M. Tabrizi. Qum: Bīdār, 2001.

Āmulī, Sayyid Ḥaydar. *Asrār al-sharīʿa wa anwār al-ṭarīqa*, ed. M. Bīdārfar. Qum: Bīdār, 2003.

Angha, Nahid. *Stations of the Sufi Path.* Cambridge: Islamic Texts Society, 2010.

Anṣārī, ʿAbdallāh b. Muḥammad. *Manāzil al-sā'irīn*, ed. M. Bīdārfar. Qum: Bīdār, 1993.

ʿAyāshī, Muḥammad b. Masʿūd al-. *Tafsīr al-ʿAyāshī.* Beirut: Mu'assasa al-Aʿlamī li'l Maṭbūʿāt, 1991.

Baḥrānī, Abi-l-Ḥasan b. Muḥammad. *Tafsīr al-Burhān.* Beirut: Mu'assasa al-Aʿlamī li'l Maṭbūʿāt, 1999.

Bukhārī, Muḥammad al-. *Ṣaḥīḥ al-Bukhārī*, ed. M.D. al-Bughā. Damascus: Dār Ibn Kathīr, 1987.

Būnī, Aḥmad al-. *Shams maʿārif al-kubrā.* Qum: Dār al-Hujja, 2001.

Dumayrī, Kamāl al-Dīn. *Ḥayāt al-ḥayawān al-kubra.* Beirut: Dār Iḥyā' al-Turāth al-ʿArabī, 2001.

Durūdābādī, Ḥusayn Hamadānī. *Sharḥ al-asmā' al-ḥusna.* Qum: Bīdār, 2000.

Fanārī, Muḥammad b. Ḥamza. *Miṣbāḥ al-uns*, ed. M. Khwājavī. Tehran: Intishārāt Mawlā 1995.

Huwayzī, ʿAbd ʿAlī b. Jumʿa. *Tafsīr nūr al-thaqalayn.* Beirut: Mu'assasat al-Tārīkh al-ʿArabī, 2001.

Ḥillī, Ahmad ibn Faḥd. *ʿUddat al-dāʿī.* Qum: Mu'assasa al-Maʿārif al-Islāmī, 2000.

Hindī, al-Muttaqī. *Kanz al-ʿummāl.* Beirut: Dār al-Kutub al-ʿIlmīyya, 1997.

Ibn Māja, Muḥammad b. Yazid. *Sunan Ibn Mājah.* Beirut: Dār al-kutub al-ʿIlmiyyah, 2018.

Ibn Manẓūr, Jamāl al-Dīn Muḥammad. *Lisān al-'Arab*. Beirut: Dār Ṣādir, 1996.

Ibn Abi-l Ḥadīd. *Sharḥ Nahj al-balāgha li-Ibn Abi-l Ḥadīd*. Beirut: Mu'assasaal-Aʿlamī li'l Maṭbūʿāt, 1995.

Ibn al-ʿArabī, Muḥyī-l-Dīn. *Fuṣūṣ al-ḥikam*, ed. A. ʿAfīfī. Beirut: Dār al-Kutub al-ʿArabī, 1980.

Ibn al-ʿArabī, Muḥyī-l-Dīn. *al-Futūḥāt al-Makkiyya*, ed. O. Yahia, 4 vols. Beirut: Dar Ihyȧ Turath al-ʿArabī, 1997.

Ibn al-ʿArabī, Muḥyī-l-Dīn. *Kashf al-maʿnā ʿan sirr asmā' al-ḥusnā*. Qum: Maṭbūʿāt Dīnī, 2004.

Ibn ʿArabī, Muḥyī-l-Dīn. *al-Waṣāya*. Beirut: Dār al-Īman, 1997.

Ibn Sīnā, Abū ʿAlī al-Ḥusayn. *al-Ishārāt wa-l-tanbīhāt*, ed. S. Dunyā, 4 vols. Cairo: Dār al-Maʿārif, 1971.

Ibn Sīnā, Abū ʿAlī al-Ḥusayn. *Kitāb al-Najāt fī-l-ḥikma al-manṭiqiyya wa-l-ṭabīʿiyya wa-l -ilāhiyya*, ed. M. Fakhry. Beirut: Dār al-Āfāq al-Jadīda, 1985.

Ibn Sīnā, Abū ʿAlī al-Ḥusayn. *al-Shifā': al-ilāhīyāt*, trans. M. Marmura, The Metaphysics of the Healing. Provo: Brigham Young University Press, 2005.

Ikhwān al-Ṣafā'. *Rasā'il Ikhwān al-Ṣafā' wa khillān al-wafā'*. Beirut: Mu'assasat al-Aʿlamī li-l-Maṭbūʿāt, 2005.

Isfahānī, Rāghib. *al-Mufradāt fī gharīb al-Qur'*ān, ed. Ṣ. Dāwūdī. Damascus: Dār al-Qalam, 2011.

Jandī, Mu'ayyid al-Dīn. *Sharḥ fuṣūṣ al-ḥikam*, ed. J. Āshtiyānī. Qum: Bustān-i Ketāb, 2003.

Jāmī, ʿAbd al-Raḥmān. *al-Durrat al-fākhira fī taḥqīq madhhab al-ṣūfiyya wa-l-mutakallimīn wa-l-ḥukamā'*, eds. N. Heer and A. Bīhbahānī, Tehran 1980.

Jāmī, ʿAbd al-Raḥmān. *Lawā'iḥ*, trans. E.H. Whinfield and M.M. Kazwīnī, A Treatise of Sufism. London: Luzac, 1906.

Jāmī, ʿAbd al-Raḥmān. *Nafaḥāt al-Uns min Haḍarāt al-Quds*, ed. M. ʿĀbidī. Tehran: Intishārāt-i Iṭṭilāʿāt, 1991.

Jāmī, ʿAbd al-Raḥmān. *Naqd al-nuṣūṣ fī sharḥ naqsh al-fuṣūṣ*, eds. W. Chittick and J. Ashtiyānī. Tehran: Iranian Institute of Philosophy, 2001.

Jāmī, ʿAbd al-Raḥmān. *Sharh Fuṣūṣ al-ḥikam*. Beirut: Dār Kutub ʿIlmiyya, 2004.

Jīlī, ʿAbd al-Karīm. *al-Insān al-kāmil*. Beirut: Mu'assasat Tārīkh al-ʿArabī, 2000.

Jurjānī, ʿAlī b. Muḥammad. *Kitāb al-taʿrīfāt*. Beirut: Mu'assasat al-Aʿlamī li-l-Maṭbūʿāt, 2003.

Kāshānī, ʿAbd al-Razzāq. *Laṭā'if al-aʿlām fī ishārāt ahl al-ilhām*. Tehran: Mīrāth-i Maktūb, 2000.

Kāshānī, ʿAbd al-Razzāq. *Majmū-yi rasā'il wa muṣanifāt*, ed. M. Hādīzādā. Tehran: Mīrāth-i Maktūb, 2000.

Kāshānī, ʿAbd al-Razzāq. *Iṣṭilāḥāt al-ṣūfiyya*. Cairo: Dār al-Manār, 1992.

Kāshānī, ʿAbd al-Razzāq. *Sharḥ fuṣūṣ al-ḥikam*. Beirut: Dār Kutub ʿIlmiyya, 2007.

Kāshānī, ʿAbd al-Razzāq. *Sharḥ manāzil al-sāʾirīn*, ed. M. Bīdārfar. Qum: Bīdār, 1993.

Kāshānī, ʿAbd al-Razzāq. *Tafsīr Ibn al-ʿArabī*. Beirut: Dār Iḥyāʾ al-Turāth al-ʿArabī, 2001.

Kāshānī, Muḥsin Fayḍ. *al-Ḥaqāʾiq fī maḥāsin al-akhlāq*. Qum: Dār al-Kitāb al-Islāmī, 2002.

Kāshānī, Muḥsin Fayḍ. *Kalimāt al-maknūna*, ed. Ṣ. Ḥasanzāda. Qum: Maṭbūʿāt Dīnī: 2007.

Kāshānī, Muḥsin Fayḍ. *Maḥajjat al-bayḍāʾ*. Beirut: Dār al-Maḥajjat al-Bayḍāʾ, 2005.

Kāshānī, Muḥsin Fayḍ. *Tafsīr al-ṣāfī*, 5 vols. Tehran: Intishārāt al-Ṣadr, 1996.

Kāshānī, Muḥsin Fayḍ. *al-Usūl al-aṣīla*. Tehran: Sazimān-e Chāp-e Dānishgāh, 1971.

Kāshānī, Muḥsin Fayḍ. *Qurrat al-ʿuyūn fī-l-maʿārif wa-l-ḥikam*, ed. M. ʿAqīl. Tehran: Dār al-Kitāb al- Islāmī, 2002.

Kulaynī, Muḥammad b. Yaʿqūb. *al-Kāfī*, ed. ʿA. al-Ghaffārī, 8 vols. Tehran: Dār al-Kutub al-Islāmiyya, 1983.

Lane, E.W. *An Arabic-English Lexicon*. Repr. Cambridge: Islamic Texts Society, 1984.

Larre, Claude, and Rochat de la Vallée, Elisabeth. *Rooted in Spirit: The Heart of Chinese Medicine*. Barrytown: Station Hill Press, 1995.

Majlisī, Muḥammad Bāqir. *Biḥār al-anwār li-durar akhbār al-a ʾimmat al-aṭhār*. Beirut: Dār Iḥyāʾ al-Turāth al-ʿArabī, 1983.

Makkī, Abū Ṭālib. *Qūt al-qulūb fī muʿāmalat al-maḥbūb wa-waṣf ṭarīq al-mirīd ilā maqām al-tawḥīd*. Beirut: Dār Kutub ʿIlmiyya, 1997.

Muslim b. al-Ḥajjāj al-Qushayrī, Abū al-Ḥusayn. *Ṣaḥīḥ Muslim*, 19 vols. Beirut: Dār al-Maʿrifah, 1994.

Nābulusī, ʿAbd al-Ghanī. *Jawāhir al-nuṣūṣ fī ḥall kalimāt al-Fuṣūṣ*. Beirut: Dār al-Kutub al-ʿIlmiyya, 2008.

Naraqī, Muḥammad Mehdī. *Jāmiʿ al-Saʿādāt*. Beirut: Muʾassasa al-Aʿlamī liʾl Maṭbūʿāt, 1988.

Plato. Complete Works, eds. J. Cooper and D.S. Hutchinson. Indianapolis: Hackett Publishing Company, 1997.

Plotinus. *The Six Enneads*, trans. S. McKenna. Chicago: Encyclopaedia Britannica, 1952.

Qayṣarī, Sharaf al-Dīn Dāwūd. *Sharḥ fuṣūṣ al-ḥika*m, ed. Ḥ. Āmulī. Qum: Bustān-i Kitāb, 2002.

Qayṣarī, Sharaf al-Dīn Dāwūd. *Rasāʾil-i Qayṣarī*, ed. J. Āshtiyānī. Tehran: Muʾassasah-i Pizhūhishī-i Ḥikmat va Falsafah-i Īrān, 2003.

Qayṣarī, Dāwūd b. Maḥmūd, and Mukhtar H. Ali. *The Horizons of Being: The Metaphysics of Ibn al-ʿArabī in the Muqaddimat al-Qayṣarī*. Leiden: Brill, 2020.

Qummī, ʿAlī b. Ibrāhīm al-. *Tafsīr al-Qummī*. Beirut: Muʾassasa al-Aʿlamī liʾl Matbūʿāt, 1991.

Qummī, Muḥammad b. Bābawayh al-. *al-Tawḥīd*. Qum: Mu'assasa Nashr al-Islāmī, 1978.

Qummī, Muḥammad b. Bābawayh al-. *'Ilal al-sharā'i*. Beirut: Dar al-Hujja, 2001.

Qummī, Muḥammad b. Bābawayh al-. *al-Khiṣāl*. Qum: Mu'assasa Nashr al-Islāmī, 2004.

Qūnawī, Ṣadr al-Dīn. *I'jāz al-bayān fī ta'wīl umm al-Qur'ān*, ed. J. Āshtiyānī. Qum: Bustān-i Kitāb, 2002.

Qūnawī, Ṣadr al-Dīn. *al-Fukūk fī mustanadāt ḥikam al-Fuṣūṣ*, ed. M. Khwājavī. Tehran: Intishārāt Mawlā. 1992.

Qūnawī, Ṣadr al-Dīn. *Miftāḥ al-ghayb*, ed. M. Khwājavī. Tehran: Intishārāt Mawlā, 1995.

Qūnawī, Ṣadr al-Dīn. *al-Nafaḥāt al-ilāhiyyah*, ed. M. Khwājavī. Tehran: Intishārāt Mawlā, 2005.

Qūnawī, Ṣadr al-Dīn. *Risālat al-nuṣūṣ fī taḥqīq al-ṭawr al-makhṣūṣ*, ed. J. Āshtiyānī, Beirut: Dār al-Kutub al-'Ilmiyya, 2008.

Qūnawī, Ṣadr al-Dīn. *Sharḥ al-asmā' al-ḥusnā*, ed. Q. Ṭehrānī. Beirut: Dār wa Makatabat al-Hilāl, 2008.

Qushayrī, 'Abd al-Karīm. *al-Risāla al-Qushayriyya fī 'ilm al-taṣawwuf*, ed. M. Zurayq, Beirut: Dār al-Kutub al-'Ilmiyya, 2001, trans. B. Von Schlegell, *Principles of Sufism*. Berkeley: Mizan Press, 1992.

Rāzī, Fakhr al-Dīn al-. *al-Tafsīr al-kabīr*. Istanbul: Dār al-Ṭiba'at al-'Āmira, 1307-08/1889-91.

Sabzawārī, Mullā Hādī. *Sharḥ al-asmā' al-ḥusnā*, ed. N. Ḥabībī. Tehran: Intishārāt-I Dānishgāh-i Tihrān Tehran, 1996.

Sabzawārī, Mullā Hādī. *Sharḥ al-manẓūma*, ed. Ḥ. Āmulī. Qum: Nashr-i Nāb, 1995.

Sha'rānī, 'Abd al-Wahhāb. *al-Yawāqīt wa-l-jawāhir and al-Kibrīt al-aḥmar fī bayān 'ulūm al-Shaykh al-Akbar*. Beirut: Dār al-Kutub al 'Ilmiyya, 2010.

Ṭabāṭabā'ī, Muḥammad Ḥusayn. *al-Mīzān fī tafsīr al-Qur'ān*. Beirut: Mu'assasa al-'Alamī li-l-Maṭbū'āt, 1997.

Ṭabrisī, Mirza Nūrī. *Mustadrak al-wasī'il*. Beirut: Mu'assasa Āl al-Bayt li Iḥyā' al-Turāth, 1991.

Ṭabrisī, Faḍl al-. *Majma' al-bayān*. Beirut: Mu'assasa al-A'lamī li'l-Maṭbū'āt, 1995.

Ṭabrisī, Faḍl al-. *Makārim al-akhlāq*. Beirut: Mu'assasa al-A'lamī li'l-Maṭbū'āt, 1994.

Tilmisānī, 'Afīf al-Dīn. *Sharḥ Manāzil al-sā'irīn*, ed. M. Bīdārfar. Qum: Bīdār, 1992.

Ṭurayḥī, Fakhr al-Din. *Majma' al-baḥrayn*. Beirut, Maktabat al-Hilāl, 1985.

Index of Qur'ānic Verses

General Index

ل

لا تُسمُّوا العنب الكَرْم ، ١٣٢
لَستُ أحب أن أرى الشاب منكم ، ٨٢
له معقبات ما بين يديه ، ٤٨

م

من توضأ مثل وضوئي ، ٤٢
المرء مرهون بعمله ، ١٥٤
من تعلّم في شبابه كان بمنزلة الرَّسم ، ٨٢
من عرف نفسه فقد عرف ربه ، ٣٤
من قارف ذنباً فارقه عقل ، ٤٢
منهومان لا يشبعان طالب علم ، ١١٨
من يزرع خيراً يوشك ، ٤٦

ه

هم أعلم خلقك ، ٣٦

و

والذي نفس محمّد بيده ، ١٨
والذي نفسي بيده ، ٣٦
ومنهم أمناء على وحيه ، ٥٠
و وشج بينها ، ٥٤

ي

يا ابن مسعود أتخذ الشيطان عدوا ، ٨٠
يا ابن مسعود لا تأكل الحرام ، ٨٠

ص

فالصورةُ صورة إنسان ، والقلب قلبُ حيوان ، ١١٤

ط

طَبَعَه اللهُ يومَ طبَعَه ، ١٥٢

ع

عرفان المرء نفسه ، ١٦٠

غ

غارس شجرة الخير ، ٤٦

ف

فأبواه يهودانه ويُنصرانه ، ١٥٢
فعل الخيرة ذخيرة باقية وثمرة زاكية ، ٤٦

ق

قال إبليس خمسة أشياء ليس لي فيهن حيلة ، ٤٦
قال جبرئيل عليه السلام يا رسول الله إنا ، ٤٤

ك

كل مولود يولد على الفطرة ، ١٥٠
كلوا الباذنجان ، ١٣٤
الكمأة من المن ، ١٣٤

ب

ت

ج

خ

ذ

ر

ش

فهرس الأحاديث والروايات

ا

سورة الفجر - ٨٩

سورة البلد - ٩٠

سورة الشمس - ٩١

سورة الشرح - ٩٤

سورة العلق - ٩٦

سورة الحديد ـ ٥٧

سورة التحريم ـ ٦٦

سورة نوح ـ ٧١

سورة المُدّثر ـ ٧٤

سورة الإنسان ـ ٧٦

سورة عبس ـ ٨٠

سورة التكوير ـ ٨١

سورة المطففين ـ ٨٣

سورة الأحقاف ـ ٤٦

سورة محمّد ـ ٤٧

سورة ق ـ ٥٠

سورة الطُّور ـ ٥٢

سورة النجم ـ ٥٣

سورة الرحمن ـ ٥٥

سورة الواقعة ـ ٥٦

سورة يس - ٣٦

سورة الصافَّات - ٣٧

سورة ص - ٣٨

سورة الزُّمَر - ٣٩

سورة فُصّلت - ٤١

سورة الزّخُرف - ٤٣

سورة المؤمنون - ٢٣

سورة النمل - ٢٧

سورة العنكبوت - ٢٩

سورة الرُّوم - ٣٠

سورة السجدة - ٣٢

سورة الأحزاب - ٣٣

سورة فاطر - ٣٥

سورة النحل ـ ١٦

سورة الإسراء ـ ١٧

سورة الكهف ـ ١٨

سورة طه ـ ٢٠

سورة الأنبياء ـ ٢١

سورة الحج ـ ٢٢

فهرس الآيات

سورة البقرة ـ ٢

سورة آل عمران ـ ٣

سورة الأنعام ـ ٦

سورة الأعراف ـ ٧

ه

و

ي

ك

ل

م

غ

ف

ق

خ

د

ذ

فهرس الموضوعات

ا

ب

www.ingramcontent.com/pod-product-compliance
Lightning Source LLC
Chambersburg PA
CBHW030511100426
42813CB00002B/425
* 9 7 8 0 9 8 3 7 5 1 7 6 2 *